Alla Sacharow

CLASSIC RUSSIAN CUISINE

Photographs by BRUNO HAUSCH

Translated by
Ursula Zilinsky and Courtney Searls-Ridge

ARCADE PUBLISHING • NEW YORK

To my husband, Igor, and my daughter, Sonja

Special thanks to all who have enthusiastically added
to the success of this book:

Dorothee and Hartwig-Ulrich von Both
Baroness Elisabeth von Cramer-Klett
Josef and Anne Riedmiller
Helga Roechling
Tomara and Leonid Winokurow

The accompanying text was written by Erni Gehrig
who also edited the recipes.

FIRST ENGLISH-LANGUAGE EDITION

Library of Congress Cataloging-in-Publication Data

Sacharow, Alla.
[Russische Küche. English]
Classic Russian cuisine / Alla Sacharow; photographs by Bruno Hausch;
translated by Ursula Zilinsky and Courtney Searls-Ridge.
1st English-language ed.
p.   cm.
Translation of: Russische Küche.
Includes index.
ISBN 1-55970-174-9
1. Cookery, Russian.   2. Soviet Union—Social life and customs.   I. Title.
TX723.3.S2313 1993
641.5947—dc20   92-322

Published in the United States by Arcade Publishing, Inc., New York
Distributed by Little, Brown and Company

10   9   8   7   6   5   4   3   2   1

PRINTED IN GERMANY

Contents

Publisher's Note

Because of the repressive events of the last seventy-five years in the former Soviet Union, we tend to forget that Russian cuisine was one of the richest and most varied in the world. Accounts of food shortages, together with images of long lines of people waiting for the most basic foodstuffs, should not blind us to the fact that, in earlier times, Russians ate heartily and indeed richly. Alla Sacharow has done a great service by reminding us how important this cuisine was—and is. It seems fitting to approach the recipes in this elegant book of cuisine from greater Russia as one would the paintings in a museum, paying homage to an art and enjoying what once was in its full historical context.

The reader may be surprised at the often extraordinary list of rich ingredients—large quantities of eggs, butter, heavy cream, chicken or goose fat. Keep in mind that the Russian gastronomy recreated here emanates from centuries of glorious eating ceremonies predating our concerns with weight and cholesterol. What was once the norm has in many instances become today's taboo. In bringing these remarkable Russian recipes to North America, we were tempted to adapt all 550 to today's western dietary demands. But in order to preserve their integrity as well as authenticity, we opted to leave them as they were. Those who have dietary concerns should feel free to substitute low- or nonfat and no-cholesterol ingredients. For example, light cream or even skim milk or nonfat yogurt could be used when the recipe calls for heavy cream. Margarine may be substituted for butter. Or the original rich, cholesterol-laden ingredients could simply be used in more modest quantities.

Some of the author's ingredients may be difficult to obtain. Certain fish, for example, are limited to specific geographic areas. Substituting another type of fish is acceptable, so long as it approximates the flesh consistency of the fish called for in the recipe. For descriptions of other ingredients that might pose difficulties, as well as suggestions on where to find the more unusual ones, refer to the following list:

Almond milk: Available in health food stores and used in the preparation of pastry or sauces.

Bitter almonds: Rare in the United States. Substitute with regular almonds and disregard the "bitter" aspect.

Black radish: A long tuberlike radish with black exterior. Unlike the little red radish, its peel must be discarded before use. May be obtained in specialty grocers.

Crayfish: Though popular in Russia, crayfish are not always available everywhere here, except maybe in New Orleans. Recommended substitutions are crabmeat, shrimp, or a combination of the two.

Gooseberries: A green berry with fuzzy outer skin, the gooseberry has a delicious and tart taste. Available in specialty produce stores.

Groats: Grain exclusive of hull; a term also used to refer to cooked cereal. Available in health food stores.

Kvass: A popular nonalcoholic beverage made from various grains, fruits, and vegetables and used as an ingredient in a number of cold dishes and sauces. Beginning on page 263 there are several recipes for kvass.

Millet: A cereal available in health food stores.

Nettles: Mostly unavailable in American stores. (Can be picked in open fields.) Substitute with bitter greens.

Orange blossom water: Available in most health food stores.

Potato flour: Available in health food stores. If unavailable, substitute with cornstarch.

Quark: A Russian dairy product, close in consistency to American farmer cheese, ricotta cheese, or cottage cheese. Quark is available in specialty stores. Substitute with the American equivalent if not available.

Rowanberries: Difficult to find outside Russia. Blackberries or raspberries are acceptable substitutes.

Soup greens: A combination of herbs such as parsley, thyme, and dill, and root vegetables such as turnips, rutabagas, carrots, parsley roots, celery roots, and leeks in any proportion, depending on availability. Soup greens are mostly used in soups and broths and impart a wonderful flavor. "A bunch" of soup greens means about 1–2 pounds.

Wheat berries: A cereal available in health food stores.

A final note: Whenever baking or oven roasting, be sure to preheat the oven for 15 minutes.

Foreword

Deeply attached to Russia, her homeland, which she was forced to leave, Alla Sacharow remains faithful to her cultural and religious roots. Exile was a source of great pain, but also inspiration, for her. Perhaps it is this separation that has fueled her passion for sustaining the rich traditions of Russian cuisine that her mother and grandmother so reverently passed on to her.

Russian gastronomic ceremonies are regarded as all important. Much care and time are given to celebrating traditional feasts such as Easter, Lent, and many more. Days of preparation during the Orthodox Easter season culminate in a meal that is a gastronomic encyclopedia beyond the comprehension of anyone who has not experienced it firsthand.

Alla has prepared every recipe in this book from start to finish, not in her own apartment with familiar equipment, but in a test kitchen. The 550 recipes offered here are only the tip of the iceberg. She has translated thousands more. Ask her if she knows how to prepare them all and she will answer, nonplussed, "but of course."

Personally, I think it is a pity that some of the more exotic and colorful recipes, such as horse stomach Tartar or stuffed pork intestines (known colloquially as, of all things, "Nanny"), fell victim to the selection process. But today, who would bother to cook anything that unique when it is so much easier to reach for the daily ubiquitous hamburger—the same the world over?

In the past, traditional Russian cuisine made use of every part of the animals slaughtered for food. Everything from head to tail was eaten, and recipes abound for every single part of the animal.

The long fasting seasons of the Orthodox church have led to a separate vegetarian cuisine.

Embracing as it does groats, barley, buckwheat, nettles, sour cream, sauerkraut, pickled cucumbers, pickled tomatoes, and white cabbage, these recipes are likely to be rediscovered in light of the present vegetarian trend and health food boom.

Russian cuisine as a whole is one of the highest cultural achievements of the Slavic people, though of course there are vast regional differences.

I believe Alla when she tells me that there are not many classical Russian recipes for pork, lamb, or veal—"calves are for petting," she tells me. Beef, venison, fish, and poultry (including duck and goose) predominate.

And she emphasizes one other important point: Russians never serve only a main course. A classic Russian meal without several appetizers is unthinkable. This is as true for the very rich as for the poorest of the poor. This tradition, however, has practically disappeared in Russia. This is mostly due to the country's prevalent scarcity of food these past decades but also reflects a general change of life-style. In Russia, as in other parts of the world, canned goods and boxes of prepared food are relegating our cookbooks to pretty picture books of the past.

This volume is probably more carefully prepared and accurately written than any cookbook in print in Russia at this time. Were it to be published in Russia today, it might become a classic there, an irony not without precedent. Russian cuisine influenced the French throughout the nineteenth century and vice versa.

Daniel Spoerri

Introduction

My compatriots say that one is wiser after a good meal, and they use this maxim to make eating well a rule of life. In fact, Russians have always enjoyed eating and drinking. This is not something that will change. We take our time—time to cook and time to enjoy. We are gregarious, hospitable, and aware of our traditions. Our cuisine enhances all of these qualities. It offers tremendous variety, because greater Russia, spread over two continents, is multinational, and each ethnic group has its own specialties.

I became acquainted with many aspects of the culinary culture of my country—in my youth in southern Russia, during my university years in Leningrad (St. Petersburg), and later through extensive travel. And I learned that even during lean times it was possible to set a generous table and celebrate splendid feasts.

In 1978 my family and I were suddenly torn from our culture and traditions. We were forced to emigrate and were given very little time to decide which of our beloved possessions we would take with us on this journey into the unknown, into our new life.

The decision was a difficult one. I wanted to have something tangible to connect me to my Russian homeland. I remembered a book I had been given as a young girl about the cuisine of old Russia. Since I had always been an enthusiastic cook, I suddenly realized that no matter where I lived this book would bring to me a piece of my homeland. Miraculously, this work by Ignatiew about the basics of Russian cooking had not been lost in the terrible postrevolutionary years.

To add to its traditional, plain dishes, I collected numerous recipes shared by my mother, relatives, and friends. Finally, I also discovered here in the West several interesting Russian cookbooks that were unknown in the then Soviet Union. My collection of recipes is, therefore, rather extensive. That is why I decided to write a book about classic Russian cuisine—because I had this vast resource and because I noticed that my friends and guests had no concept of the variety of traditional Russian cooking. Most westerners know only about Russian caviar, vodka, borscht, and pirogi. The Russian language as well as cuisine has long been subjected to foreign influence. With this book I want to present unadulterated Russian cooking. To that end, I have been careful to select only those recipes I know for a fact did not derive from foreign cultures.

Alla Sacharow

Appetizers
and Snacks

ZAKUSKI

Russian cuisine has a long tradition of hot and cold hors d'oeuvres. Already in the tenth century dried or salted fish, meat or poultry in aspic, marinated mushrooms, vegetable preserves, and salted lemons were served before the main meal.

Over the centuries Russian housewives—always keen to provide a special treat for their guests—have cultivated this fine tradition and developed a multitude of imaginative recipes. Nevertheless, the most important hors d'oeuvre, without which no meal is complete, was and still is bread: round, fresh, and aromatic. Guests are received with bread and salt on an embroidered napkin and offered the best places at the table. Only after the bread has been ceremoniously cut and passed around are the many different hors d'oeuvres served—meat, fish, and vegetables, not to mention the famed and extremely popular *pirozhki* with its filling that varies from region to region. This is served with vodka or other hard drinks such as *pertsovko* or *sveroboi*. And spicy home-made mustard is served to aid digestibility.

On feast or mourning days traditional dishes are served, but in general no limits are set on creativity concerning the selection and composition of hors d'oeuvres. Traditionally, they are always carefully decorated and beautifully presented; they are there not merely to stimulate the appetite but to banish ill humor and daily cares.

My recommendation of caution is, however tempting and irresistible the beautiful spread of traditional Russian hors d'oeuvres seems to be, it represents but the beginning of any Russian meal.

Russian Salad
RUSSKY SALAT
Serves 4–6

1 black radish
2 carrots
2 apples
1 parsley root
½ medium white cabbage
2 tablespoons oil
1 tablespoon vinegar
salt, pepper
sugar
parsley, chopped
dill, chopped

Peel and grate the radish, carrots, apples, and parsley root. Shred the cabbage in very thin strips. Mix well with oil, vinegar, and salt, pepper, and sugar to taste. Marinate briefly. Sprinkle with chopped herbs.

Black Radish Salad
SALAT IZ CHORNOY REDKI
Serves 4–6

2–3 black radishes
salt
3 tablespoons oil
1–2 tablespoons vinegar
1 slice rye bread
1 slice white bread
1 medium onion
1 tablespoon goose or chicken fat
parsley

Peel and grate the radishes. Sprinkle with salt and let steep for 15 minutes. Add oil and vinegar to taste. Toss well. Dice bread, sprinkle with salt, and dry in 350°F oven for 20 minutes.

Chop onion and brown in goose or chicken fat.

Transfer salad to a bowl. Surround with diced bread, top with browned onions, and garnish with parsley.

◁ Cathedral of the Annunciation in Moscow

Black Radish Salad ▷

Cabbage Salad

KAPUSTNY SALAT

Serves 4

½ medium white cabbage
salt
4 apples
3 tablespoons mayonnaise
juice of 1 lemon
1 tablespoon sugar
1 teaspoon cinnamon
1 cup grated cheese
1 boiled carrot, sliced
1 tablespoon chopped walnuts
parsley leaves
dill, snipped

Remove core from cabbage and discard tough outer leaves. Rinse and slice into thin strips. Sprinkle cabbage with salt, toss, and set aside. Peel, core, and slice apples into strips. Mix with cabbage.

Blend mayonnaise with lemon juice, salt, sugar, and cinnamon. Pour over salad, sprinkle with grated cheese, and garnish with carrot, nuts, parsley leaves, and dill.

Moscow Salad

MOSKOVSKY SALAT ILI "OLIVIE"

Serves 8–10

3 oven-ready grouse (or 1 large chicken)
2 tablespoons unflavored gelatin
5 boiled medium potatoes
1 pound fresh cucumbers
½ cup olives, pitted
½ cup cornichons
2–3 truffles (optional)
¼ pound cooked crayfish meat
lettuce leaves
1 cup sauce Provençale (see basic recipe, page 155)
½ bunch dill, snipped
½ bunch parsley, chopped

Roast the grouse or chicken and let cool. Bone and dice meat.

To prepare aspic: In a kettle, cover bones with water. Bring to a boil and simmer, covered, for an hour, adding water as necessary. Discard bones. In a saucepan, sprinkle gelatin with water. Add 1 cup broth. Stir and bring to a boil. Remove from heat, cool, and refrigerate until the aspic is firm (about 1 hour).

Dice potatoes, cucumbers, olives, and cornichons. Cut truffles into thin slices. Chop crayfish.

Line a bowl with lettuce and fill with alternating layers of the diced meat and vegetables. Dress each layer with sauce Provençale and garnish with herbs, crayfish, and truffles.

Remove firm, chilled aspic and slice into thin strips. Decorate the salad in a gridlike pattern.

This salad is also excellent with chopped, hard-boiled eggs, diced apples or carrots, or thinly sliced scallions.

Sauerkraut Salad

SALAT IZ KISLOY KAPUSTY

Serves 4

1 pound sauerkraut
2 apples, grated
2 medium onions, grated
1 tablespoon grated horseradish
⅓ cup mayonnaise

Wash sauerkraut under running water. Squeeze dry. Toss with apples, onions, horseradish, and mayonnaise.

Bean Salad with Walnuts

SALAT IZ FASOLI S OREKHAMI

Serves 2–3

1½ cups dried red beans
1 cup shelled walnuts
2–3 cloves garlic
½ bunch cilantro
salt
2 small onions, finely chopped
3 tablespoons wine vinegar

Soak beans overnight and simmer in salty water about 1 hour until tender. (Do not overcook.) Strain.

Mash half of the walnuts with garlic, half of the cilantro, and salt to taste. Add this mixture and onions to the beans and stir. Add vinegar. Garnish with remaining walnuts and cilantro leaves.

Marinated Cabbage Georgian-Style

KAPUSTA MARINOVANNAYA
PO GRUZINSKY

Serves 6

---

2 pounds white cabbage
3 medium beets, cooked, peeled, and diced
4 stalks celery, diced
6–8 cloves garlic, peeled
3 chili peppers, seeded and diced
tarragon leaves
basil leaves, chopped
mint leaves
dill, chopped
olive oil

MARINADE

1¼ cups vinegar
2 cups water
10 peppercorns
2 bay leaves
1 tablespoon salt
2 tablespoons sugar

Marinated Cabbage Georgian-Style

Remove core from cabbage and discard outer leaves. Rinse and cut into 6–8 pieces.

In an earthenware pot, layer cabbage with beets, celery, garlic, chili peppers, and herbs. Salt each layer.

To prepare marinade: Boil all ingredients for 2–3 minutes, cool slightly, and pour over the vegetables. Cover with a cloth, weigh down with a heavy plate or a couple of cans, and marinate for 2–3 days in a cool place. (Do not refrigerate.) Remove cabbage, beets, and celery from the marinade, dress with olive oil, and serve.

Russian Vinaigrette
RUSSKY VENIGRET
Serves 4–6

---

2 pounds perch, sturgeon, salmon, trout, or
   whitefish, boned
3–4 medium beets
dash of vinegar
oil
3–4 medium potatoes
1 fresh cucumber (1 pickled cucumber may be
   substituted)
2 cups sauce Provençale (see basic recipe, page
   155)
¼ pound marinated mushrooms
½ cup olives
1 truffle
1 bunch parsley, chopped
1 cup aspic (see basic recipes, pages 14 and 26)

Bake fish 15 minutes in a 375°F oven, cool, and cut into bite-sized pieces.

Bring beets to a boil covered with water and a dash of vinegar for 30 minutes, peel, and cool. Dice beets and cover with oil to keep them from coloring the other ingredients. Boil potatoes 15 minutes or until tender, drain, peel, and cool.

Slice cucumber (or pickled cucumber) and potatoes and cut into circles, diamonds, or stars. Chop the vegetable trimmings (cucumber,

◁ *Russian Vinaigrette (bottom)*
Moscow Salad (left)
Bean Salad with Walnuts (right)

17

potatoes, and mushroom stems) and mix with a small amount of sauce Provençale. Transfer mixture to the middle of a bowl, surround with fish, vegetable slices, mushrooms, and olives. Dress with sauce Provençale and garnish with parsley and slices of truffle. Cut cooled aspic into thin strips and decorate salad with a gridlike pattern. Chill well.

This salad can also be garnished with crayfish, or a variation can be prepared using any one of the following ingredients:

1–2 salted herring (or boiled or roasted meat)
4–5 boiled potatoes, sliced
1–2 cooked beets, sliced
1 boiled carrot, sliced
1 cup braised green peas
¼ pound sauerkraut
1 apple, peeled and sliced
½ cup marinated mushrooms
½ bunch scallions, chopped
sauce consisting of 2–3 tablespoons oil, 1–2 tablespoons vinegar, 1 teaspoon mustard, and salt and sugar to taste

Beet Salad

SALAT IZ KRASNOY SVYOKLY
Serves 4

4 medium onions, chopped
1 tablespoon oil
2 tablespoons grated fresh horseradish or 1 tablespoon prepared
2 cups beets, cooked, peeled, and diced
salt
⅓ cup mayonnaise
1 tablespoon vinegar
1 teaspoon mustard
½ cup green peas, cooked
parsley, chopped

Sauté chopped onions in oil until light brown. Cool and mix with horseradish and beets. Add salt to taste. Blend mayonnaise with vinegar and mustard and toss with salad. Garnish with green peas and parsley.

Slavic Salad

SLAVYANSKY SALAT
Serves 6

½ pound white cabbage
½ cup red bell pepper
½ cup celeriac, peeled
½ cup parsley root, peeled
½ cup rutabaga, peeled
½ cup thinly sliced apples
½ cup thinly sliced fresh cucumber
3–4 tablespoons cranberry jelly
3–4 tablespoons lemon juice
scant ½ cup heavy cream, whipped
½ pound watermelon or honeydew melon

Slice cabbage, bell pepper, celeriac, parsley root, and rutabaga into thin strips. Blanch in boiling water for 5–10 minutes. Drain and mix well with apples and cucumber. Mix cranberry jelly and lemon juice and stir until smooth. Pour over salad and toss. Fold in whipped cream. Toss salad well once more. Garnish with slices of melon.

Mushroom Aspic

ZALIVNOYE IZ GRIBOV
Serves 4

1 bunch parsley
1 bunch dill
1 bunch watercress
¼ cup dried wild mushrooms
salt
½ pound fresh mushrooms
2–3 cloves garlic, mashed
6 tablespoons unflavored gelatin
¼ pound marinated mushrooms
lemon slices
carrot slices

Reserve a few sprigs of parsley, dill, and watercress. Soak dried mushrooms 20 minutes, rinse thoroughly, and simmer in fresh water with remaining parsley, dill, watercress, and a little salt

Mushroom Aspic ▷

for 2 minutes until soft. Strain and reserve cooking liquid. Chop the mushrooms.

Blanch fresh mushrooms briefly in boiling, lightly salted water. Drain and slice thinly. Reserve broth.

Season 2–4 cups of mushroom broth strongly with garlic and salt. Prepare aspic according to instructions on gelatin package, using mushroom broth for liquid.

Rinse a glass bowl with cold water and coat thinly with aspic. Let set. Add marinated mushrooms, lemon slices, and carrot slices in a decorative design. Cover with more aspic and let it set again. Cover with a layer of fresh mushrooms and parsley sprigs. Pour aspic over it. Allow to set and finally top with dried mushrooms and remaining aspic. Chill for several hours or overnight in refrigerator.

To serve, immerse bowl briefly in hot water and invert the aspic on a platter. Garnish with parsley, watercress, and dill.

Russian Deviled Eggs

FARSHIROVANNIYE YAITSA

Serves 4

---

4 eggs
1 apple, peeled and cored
1 small onion, chopped
1 herring fillet
1 tablespoon mayonnaise
1 teaspoon butter
parsley, chopped
capers
1 red bell pepper

Hard-boil eggs, plunge into cold water, peel, and cut in half lengthwise. Remove the yolks with a spoon and puree in a food processor with apple, onion, herring, mayonnaise, and butter. Fill egg halves with puree and garnish with parsley, capers, and strips of bell pepper.

◁ Baked Deviled Eggs

Baked Deviled Eggs

YAITSA FARSHIROVANNIYE ZAPECHONIYE

Serves 4

---

4 eggs, hard-boiled
1 tablespoon butter
2 tablespoons heavy cream
1 tablespoon of any of the following, chopped: mushrooms, tiny shrimp, anchovies, herbs, Parmesan, truffles, etc.
salt, pepper
grated cheese

Cut eggs in half lengthwise. Remove yolks and mix with butter and cream to soften. Stir in either the mushroom, shrimp, anchovies, herbs, Parmesan, or truffles. Season to taste. Spoon mixture into egg halves and put the egg halves back together to form a whole egg.

Place in an ovenproof pan, cover with a sauce (e.g., béchamel or tomato; see recipes on pages 147 and 150), and sprinkle with grated cheese.

Bake 15 minutes in a 375°F preheated oven until lightly browned.

These eggs may also be fried in deep fat and served with fried parsley and a piquant sauce.

Eggplant Caviar

BAKLAZHANNAYA IKRA

Serves 4

---

3 medium eggplants	salt
2 medium onions, minced	cayenne
2½ tablespoons oil	parsley, chopped
1 tablespoon tomato paste	scallions, chopped
3–4 cloves garlic, mashed	

Bake eggplants in a 350°F oven for approximately 30 minutes. Peel under cold water and discard peelings. Chop.

Sauté onions in oil until light brown. Add tomato paste, stir, and cook 2–3 minutes. Remove from heat. Add eggplant, garlic, salt, and cayenne. Mix well. Serve with parsley and scallions.

Mushroom Caviar

GRIBNAYA IKRA
Serves 4

---

³⁄₄ pound fresh mushrooms (or ¹⁄₂ pound
    marinated mushrooms or 1 cup dried
    mushrooms, reconstituted)
2 tablespoons oil
1 medium onion, minced
salt, pepper
vinegar or lemon juice
scallions, sliced

Slice mushrooms paper-thin and cook in 1 tablespoon oil and their own juice until all the liquid
has evaporated.

Sauté onions in oil until light brown, cool, and
add to mushrooms. Season with salt, pepper, and
vinegar or lemon juice.

Sprinkle with scallions.

Fish Aspic

ZALIVNOYE IZ SUDAKA I SHCHUKI
Serves 4

1¹⁄₄ pounds perch or similar fish
1 medium onion, minced
3 tablespoons butter
2 slices white bread
1 bunch parsley, chopped
1 bunch dill, chopped
¹⁄₂ cup milk
¹⁄₃ cup bouillon
¹⁄₂ cup heavy cream
salt, pepper
1¹⁄₂ teaspoons nutmeg
2 cups aspic (see basic recipes, pages 14 and 26)
carrot slices and lemon slices for garnish

Fillet fish and cut into small pieces. Sauté onion
and fish in 1 tablespoon butter.

Reserve several sprigs of parsley and dill. Soak
bread in milk and squeeze dry. Mix well with remaining butter, fish, bouillon, cream, herbs, and
spices. (If necessary, puree in a food processor.)

Rinse a mold with cold water and coat with a
thin layer of aspic. Decorate with carrot and
lemon slices and herbs. Cover with another layer
of aspic and allow to set. Fill with fish puree and
top with remaining aspic. Refrigerate until set.

Unmold by immersing mold for a few seconds
in warm water and inverting onto a serving plate.

Marinated Sardines

MARINOVANNIYE SARDINY
Serves 4

---

1 pound fresh sardines
salt
flour
1 egg, beaten
bread crumbs
oil

Dress sardines and soak for 10 minutes in salted
water. Rinse and dry thoroughly and add salt.
Coat with flour, dip into egg, and coat with bread
crumbs. Fry in oil until golden brown. Cool.

MARINADE

4 medium onions, chopped
1 carrot, chopped
1 parsley root, peeled and chopped
1 stalk celery, chopped
4 tablespoons oil
4 tablespoons tomato paste
1 cup fish stock
salt, pepper
sugar
bay leaf
2–3 tablespoons vinegar or lemon juice
parsley, chopped
dill, snipped

To prepare the marinade, sauté vegetables in oil
with tomato paste. Cover with fish stock, season
with salt, pepper, sugar, and bay leaf, and simmer
for 20 minutes. Add vinegar or lemon juice, cool,
and pour over fried sardines. Marinate for 2–3
hours and sprinkle with parsley and dill.

Fish Aspic ▷

Marinated Sturgeon à la King

OSETRINA MAIRNOVANNAYA PO KOROLEVSKY

Serves 4–6

2 pounds sturgeon, filleted
3 cups vinegar
1 tablespoon mustard
salt, pepper
¼ teaspoon whole cloves
2 bay leaves
¼ teaspoon cinnamon
peel of 2 lemons
4 oranges, peeled and sliced
4 lemons, peeled and sliced
1 cup grapes
1 cup fresh figs
1 cup raisins
2–3 small apples, quartered
½ cup oil

Poach sturgeon in lightly salted water 6–8 minutes until done. Drain.

Boil vinegar, mustard, salt, pepper, cloves, bay leaves, cinnamon, and lemon peel together. Strain. Pour over orange and lemon slices, grapes, figs, raisins, and apples and simmer for a few minutes. Strain again. Set liquid aside to cool.

Layer the sturgeon fillet alternately with the orange and lemon slices and figs, raisins, and grapes in a serving dish. Cover with reserved liquid. Sprinkle with oil.

Cover the dish and refrigerate a few hours before serving.

Carp Aspic

ZALIVNOYE IZ KARASEY

Serves 6

several fish heads and bones
1 bunch soup greens
1 bunch dill
1 bunch parsley
salt, pepper
bay leaf
2–2½ pounds fillets of carp
25 crayfish
1 egg white, beaten
6 tablespoons unflavored gelatin
lettuce leaves
1 small, fresh cucumber, cut in strips
5 boiled medium potatoes, diced
½ cup black or green olives

Ask for fish heads and bones at the fish market. Prepare a hearty broth using fish heads, fish bones, soup greens, half the dill, parsley, salt, pepper, and bay leaf covered with 2 inches of water. Simmer for 45 minutes. Strain. Discard heads and bones.

Poach carp for 10 minutes in the fish broth. Remove carp from broth and drain on paper towels.

Clarify broth with beaten egg white and prepare aspic with 3–4 cups fish broth and gelatin. Poach crayfish 8 minutes in broth. Drain. Peel. Set aside. Rinse a ring mold with cold water, coat with a layer of aspic and allow to set, and fill with layers of fish and crayfish. (Save several crayfish to use as garnish.) Overlap layers of fish and crayfish slightly. Cover each layer with aspic and allow to set before beginning the next layer. Pour the rest of the aspic over the fish layers and allow to set in the refrigerator.

To serve, immerse the mold briefly in hot water and invert on a platter covered with lettuce leaves. Fill the center with strips of cucumber, diced potatoes, and olives. Garnish with crayfish and sprinkle with dill.

Salmon and Crayfish Aspic ▷

Salmon and Crayfish Aspic

ZALIVNOYE IZ OSETRINY I RAKOV

Serves 6

salmon head and small fish for fish broth
  (approximately 1 pound)
3 celery stalks
1 medium onion, whole
salt, pepper
2 bay leaves
1 egg white, beaten
approximately 2 pounds salmon fillets
6 tablespoons unflavored gelatin
1 bunch parsley
2 parsley roots, peeled
1 lemon, sliced
½ pound crayfish
1 bunch watercress
1 bunch dill

Clean salmon head and small fish and prepare a broth with the celery, onion, salt, pepper, and bay leaves. Cook 45 minutes, covered. Strain. Clarify with beaten egg white and pour through a fine sieve or filter. (The broth must be completely clear.)

Cut salmon fillets into pieces (not too small) and poach over low heat in fish broth for approximately 8 minutes. Drain and cool. You may need to clarify with egg whites, once again. Reserve broth for aspic.

Prepare aspic using 3 cups fish broth and gelatin. Finely chop half the parsley and cut parsley roots into strips or diamond shapes.

Rinse a 12-inch mold with cold water and cover with a thin layer of aspic. Allow aspic to set. Decorate with parsley root strips, lemon slices, and parsley leaves. Add another layer of aspic. Allow to set again.

Layer crayfish, parsley, salmon, more parsley,

and salmon again. Cover each layer with aspic and allow to set before beginning the next layer. Pour remaining aspic over the top and put in refrigerator for several hours to set.

To serve, immerse the mold briefly in hot water, invert on a platter, garnish with watercress and dill, and serve with a horseradish sauce (see recipe, page 148).

Note: the fish bouillon should be highly spiced and well salted because the gelatin tends to dilute the flavor.

Fish Satsivi

SATSIVI IZ RYBY
Serves 4

1 pound pike or perch
peppercorns
3–4 bay leaves
1²/₃ cups shelled walnuts
2–3 cloves garlic
salt
¹/₂ teaspoon chili powder
1 teaspoon ground cloves
1 teaspoon ground coriander
1 teaspoon saffron
¹/₂ teaspoon cinnamon
3–4 medium onions, minced
2–3 cups vinegar
3 egg yolks

Cut fish into serving pieces and poach 8 minutes in salty water with peppercorns and bay leaves. Strain, reserving the broth, and arrange fish on a platter.

Mash nuts with garlic, salt to taste, and chili powder in a mortar, mix with the other spices, and add a small amount of fish broth to form a smooth paste.

Braise onions in the fish broth, add vinegar and mashed nuts mixture, and simmer 10 minutes until the mixture thickens.

Beat egg yolks with a small amount of fish broth. Whip vigorously for 2–3 minutes and stir into the sauce. Pour over fish and refrigerate.

Squid in Mustard Sauce

KALMARY V GORCHICHNOM SOUS
Serves 4

1–1¹/₂ pounds squid
2 cooked egg yolks
2 tablespoons mustard
2 tablespoons vinegar
salt
sugar

Rinse squid thoroughly and put in a pot covered with cold water. Bring quickly to a boil and simmer 2–3 minutes. Drain, cool, and cut into thin strips.

Mash egg yolks with mustard and vinegar. Stir until smooth and season to taste with salt and sugar. Mix squid with the sauce and marinate for 2–3 hours in the refrigerator before serving.

Aspic

STUDYEN
Serves 4

1 calf's head
4 calf's feet or pig's feet
1–2 carrots
1–2 medium onions
1 bunch parsley
8 black and white peppercorns
3–4 bay leaves
salt
1 head garlic, mashed
freshly ground black and white pepper
slices of lemon
1–2 carrots, sliced decoratively

Calves' heads, common items in European and Russian gastronomy, are not readily available in America. One needs to special order them from the butcher.

Rinse calf's head and feet. Cut into small pieces and cover with cold water. Simmer over low heat for 6–8 hours. During the last hour, add carrots,

Aspic ▷

Appetizer Platter

Smoked fish: herring, eel, sturgeon, sardines, bream, mackerel.
Stuffed eel, boiled sturgeon, anchovies, crayfish, shrimp.
Marinated mushrooms, olives, bell peppers stuffed with sauerkraut, pickled green and red tomatoes.
Stuffed eggs, dwarf pumpkin, pickled cucumbers, lemons.

onions, parsley (save some parsley leaves for later), peppercorns, and bay leaves to the broth and salt lightly.

Strain and reserve broth. Remove meat from bones and dice. Transfer to a pot, sprinkle with garlic, and cover well with strained (if necessary, filtered) broth. Season with salt and pepper. Bring to a rapid boil. Remove from heat. Cool. Rinse a mold with cold water.

Cover bottom of mold with a thin layer of broth, decorate with slices of lemon, parsley leaves, and fancy-cut carrot slices. Cover carefully with a small amount of broth and refrigerate to set. Add meat and rest of the broth and return to refrigerator for several hours to set.

To serve, immerse the mold briefly in hot water and invert the aspic on a platter.

Stuffed Carp Ukrainian-Style

KARP FARSHIROVANNY PO UKRAINSKY
Serves 4–6

1 carp (approximately 2 pounds)
extra fish bones
1 bunch soup greens
salt, pepper
1 or 2 medium onions, minced
1 tablespoon butter
¼ pound cooked ham
cold horseradish sauce (see recipe, page 148)

Rinse fish and remove scales. Slit open along the backbone, remove entrails and bones. Carefully separate the skin from the fish. (This may be done at the fish market.) Reserve skin.

Prepare a broth using fish bones, soup greens, salt, and pepper. Strain. Sauté onions in butter until light brown.

Chop fish and ham very fine (or run through a meat grinder) and mix with browned onions. Season with salt and pepper. Fill the skin of the carp with the chopped mixture. Wrap in a cheesecloth and simmer for about 40 minutes in the fish broth.

Remove cloth, refrigerate, and serve with cold horseradish sauce.

Liver Pâté with Vegetables

PECHONOCHNY PASHTET
Serves 4–6

1 pound calf or pork liver
½ pound bacon
2 carrots, diced
1 medium onion, diced
1 parsley root, peeled and diced
3–4 anchovy fillets
pepper
½ teaspoon nutmeg

Rinse liver and remove any membrane and fat. Cut into small pieces. (Soak pork liver in milk for 1 hour.)

Dice bacon and render. Sauté vegetables in the bacon fat. Add the liver and 1–2 tablespoons of water. Cook 3 minutes. Cool and add anchovies, pepper to taste, and nutmeg. Press through a sieve or process twice using the fine blade of a meat grinder.

Transfer the puree to a bowl placed over ice cubes and whip until it is light and foamy.

Using kitchen parchment, shape the mixture into a roll. Refrigerate for 3–4 hours. Slice and serve.

Poultry Satsivi

SATSIVI IZ DICHI
Serves 6–8

1 chicken (3 pounds) or equivalent amount of
    duck, goose, or turkey
1 bunch soup greens
salt, pepper
3 medium onions, minced
1⅔ cups shelled walnuts
2–3 cloves garlic
1 teaspoon ground coriander
1 teaspoon ground cloves
1 teaspoon cinnamon
1½ teaspoons saffron
2 tablespoons wine vinegar or pomegranate
    juice (available in health food stores)
2 egg yolks

Cover chicken and soup greens with cold water. Bring to a boil. Reduce heat and simmer for 20 minutes. Remove chicken from the liquid, season with salt and pepper, and transfer to a roasting pan with a small amount of broth. Roast in a 400°F oven for 20 additional minutes, or until done. Baste several times with pan juices.

Cool chicken. Cut into serving pieces and arrange on a deep platter. Braise onions in a small amount of skimmed pan juices until tender.

Mash nuts with garlic and spices in a mortar and add to the onions. Stir in a small amount of chicken broth and simmer for 10 minutes. Season with wine vinegar or pomegranate juice and return to a boil.

Blend egg yolks with a small amount of broth and beat vigorously into the hot sauce. Pour over the poultry, chill, and serve.

Duck Aspic

ZALIVNOYE IZ UTKI

Serves 6–8

1 duck (2–2½ pounds)
salt
4 cloves garlic, mashed
1 tablespoon oil
6–9 tablespoons unflavored gelatin
1 orange, sliced
grapes, sliced
1 cup cranberries marinated in sherry

Rinse and dry duck. Rub with salt and garlic, sprinkle with oil, and roast in a 375°F oven for 1 hour.

Remove meat from bones and cut into strips.

Cover the bones with water and boil for 30 minutes. Prepare an aspic with the broth and gelatin according to package directions.

Rinse a bowl with cold water and coat the bottom with a film of aspic. Allow to set. Add duck meat and cover with the rest of the aspic.

Allow to set in refrigerator at least 4 hours and decorate with slices of orange, grapes, and marinated cranberries.

This recipe may also be prepared using cooked chicken layered with cooked green peas.

Chicken Liver Pâté

PASHTET IZ KURINOY PECHONKI

Serves 4

½ pound chicken liver
1 clove garlic, minced
5 tablespoons butter
salt, pepper
lettuce

Rinse liver, remove membrane, and chop finely. Add garlic, pieces of butter, salt, and pepper. Cook 10 minutes in a double boiler, stirring constantly until the mixture is golden yellow. Refrigerate until cold. To serve, form into little balls using an ice-cream scoop and place on lettuce leaves.

Boiled Suckling Pig

POROSYONOK VARYONY KHOLODNY

Serves 10–12

1 suckling pig (approximately 6 pounds)
lemon juice
2–3 carrots, chopped
1 parsley root, chopped
2 medium onions, chopped
salt
cold horseradish sauce (see recipe, page 148)
2 pickled cucumbers
1 pound sauerkraut
a few marinated apples
1 cup parsley, chopped

Order the suckling pig from the butcher ahead of time and have it prepared so that it is ready to cook. Rinse thoroughly, dry, and rub all over with lemon juice. Wrap in a cheesecloth, put in a stock pot, and cover with cold water. Add vegetables. Simmer, covered, for 3 hours. Do not add salt until 20 minutes before the end of cooking time.

To marinate apples: Bring to a boil 1 quart water with 1 cup vinegar, ½ cup sugar, 1 teaspoon cinnamon, ½ teaspoon nutmeg, and ½ teaspoon ground cloves. Poach 4–5 whole apples for 6 minutes. Let apples cool in the "marinade."

Allow meat to cool in the broth. Slice into pieces and serve with horseradish sauce, pickled cucumbers, sauerkraut, `marinated apples, and parsley.

Pâté of Grouse in Aspic
PASHTET IZ RYABCHIKA V ZHELE
Serves 6–8

3–4 oven-ready grouse (or partridge) or 1 pheasant or 1 large chicken
salt
1 cup butter
3 slices white bread
1 cup heavy cream
5–7 eggs
2 ounces fresh bacon, diced
1/2 pound fresh calf's liver, diced
pepper
1–2 bay leaves
1 ounce truffles, grated
1/2 teaspoon nutmeg
1–2 quarts aspic (see basic recipes, pages 14 and 26)
10–20 crayfish or 1/4 pound cooked crayfish, peeled
1 bunch parsley

Rinse and dry the grouse thoroughly. Sprinkle with salt and brown in 1/2 cup butter until done. Let cool, remove meat from bones, and run through a meat grinder.

Soak bread in 1/2 cup heavy cream. Add 2 eggs and remaining 1/2 cup butter. Stir thoroughly into the ground meat (or mix briefly in food processor).

Sauté bacon with liver, pepper, and bay leaves. Let cool, process in a meat grinder, and add to the meat. Stir in the remainder of the cream, 3–5 eggs, and truffles. Season with salt, pepper, and nutmeg.

Butter a pâté or soufflé mold carefully. Fill with the mixture and bake in a 375°F oven for 1 1/2 hours. Allow the pâté to cool.

In the meantime, prepare the aspic. Rinse a mold or bowl with cold water. Pour 1/2 inch of aspic into the bowl. Arrange crayfish in bottom of bowl and decorate with parsley leaves. Cover carefully with aspic and put in refrigerator until set.

Using an ice-cream scoop, form balls of the pâté and layer them in the mold. Cover each layer with aspic and allow to set before adding another layer.

Finish with a layer of aspic and allow to set for several hours in the refrigerator.

To serve, invert the pâté on a serving dish.

Siberian Countryside in Winter ▷

Soups
and Stews

SUPY I SOLYANKI

A house without soup is an unlucky house, says a Russian proverb. And, indeed, a steaming soup kettle is a symbol of family warmth and security, especially during the long Russian winter. Soups are the pride of Russian cuisine, which boasts the greatest variety of soup recipes of any cuisine in the world.

Soups are the reason the Slavs settled in Russia. In order to make a strong, savory broth, vegetables and herbs are needed in addition to meat and fish. It takes time for these to grow, and it was therefore necessary to settle down to await the harvest. Doesn't the fact that spoons were in use four hundred years before forks proves that soup came first?

In greater Russia each region has its own traditional soup recipes. For example:

Shchi (central Russia, Urals, Siberia)
This short word evokes memories and strong feelings for everyone who has ever eaten shchi. There are over 80 different ways of cooking it. All have six basic ingredients: cabbage (or sauerkraut), meat (or fish), mushrooms, vegetables, flour, and sour cream (or buttermilk). Shchi is best when eaten with black bread and stuffed pirogi.

Ukha (Volga area, northern Russia, Siberia)
This fish soup is known as the mother of Russian soups. It is mentioned in literature as far back as the twelfth century. Ukha is usually made with several kinds of fish and there are innumerable variations. We distinguish between *White Ukha* (pike, whitefish, perch, etc.), *Black Ukha* (carp, Prussian carp, rosefish), and *Red* or *Amber Ukha* (sturgeon, salmon, and other Siberian fancy fish). Ukha is also served with black bread and pirogi.

Borscht (Ukraine, central Russia, north Caucasus, Baltic Republics)

Several European countries, as well as Ukraine, Russia, Poland, and Romania, lay claim to being the originators of this popular dish, which probably explains why there are about a hundred ways to prepare it. Borscht can consist of 36 different ingredients and requires at least 3 hours to prepare. It can be served hot or cold. Either way it is accompanied by sour cream, white bread, or specially baked pastries, but it is never served with black bread.

Rassolnik (central Russia and Byelarus)
This is a soup based on pickled cucumbers. The most important ingredients are innards of veal, beef, or poultry (or stewing beef), pickled cucumbers, potatoes, carrots, onions, leeks, celery, barley, rice, or buckwheat, and herbs and spices. It is served with sour cream and pirogi stuffed with meat.

Solyanka (central and northwest Russia, north Caucasus)
A thick, spicy soup (or stew) that can also be served as a main course. Solyanka consists of meat (innards, ham, smoked sausage) or fish, a variety of vegetables, marinated mushrooms, pickled cucumbers, olives, capers, herbs, and spices. It is served with sour cream, grated cheese, or bread crumbs.

Okroshka (central and south Russia, Siberia)
A refreshing cold delicacy based on *kvass* (or sauerkraut juice, sour milk, a marinade of pickled cucumbers, etc.), meat or fish, vegetables, herbs, and spices. It is served with sour cream and chopped hard-boiled eggs.

The queen of cold soups is *botvinya*, made from fancy fish, fresh vegetables, and herbs, and served cold with ice cubes in a special partitioned bowl.

Meat or Fish Stock

MYASNOY BOUILLON, RYBNY BOUILLON

(BASIC RECIPES)

In the Russian kitchen, meat and fish stock (bouillon) are prepared with great care. They are used as the basis for many soups and stews and are an important component of sauces, vegetable dishes, aspics, pâtés, and stuffing for pirogi.

MEAT BROTHS

For a hearty broth you need 1–1½ cups water, ½ pound beef with bones (shoulder, neck), ⅛ pound veal knuckle, and ½ cup soup greens (carrots, celery, parsley root, leek, onion). We distinguish between white, yellow, or red broth depending upon how it is prepared.

WHITE BROTH

Cut meat into pieces, add cracked bones, cover with cold water, and bring to a boil. Skim foam from broth several times. Add chopped soup greens and salt. Simmer 2½–3 hours over low heat. To keep the broth light (white), use only a few carrots.

YELLOW BROTH

Brown soup greens in a small amount of fat before adding to the meat.

RED BROTH

Chop meat and soup greens and crack bones. Add only a small amount of water and simmer covered until all the liquid has evaporated and the meat is glossy brown. (Stir frequently to prevent burning.) Add cold water to cover and simmer about 1½ hours until done.

Before using, strain meat stock and remove fat: Chill until fat hardens and remove with a spoon or cloth. If necessary, clarify the broth: Mix 1 or 2 egg whites with a small amount of cold water and simmer this mixture in the broth for a few minutes until the egg whites solidify. When the egg whites have caused the sediment to sink to the bottom, strain the broth once more through a fine sieve. This method clarifies the broth while enhancing the flavor.

GLAZE

This concentrated broth is used primarily to enrich sauces. Cover pieces of beef bone, veal knuckle, and chopped root vegetables with cold water. Bring to a boil and skim. Add salt, cover, and simmer for approximately 6 hours. Strain, remove fat, and continue to simmer the broth until it thickens and attains a jellylike consistency.

ASPIC

Simmer clarified meat broth with calf's feet and a calf's head. Season generously with salt, pepper, bay leaf, and vinegar. Strain and carefully remove fat. Dissolve gelatin in the broth according to package directions.

FISH STOCK

Simmer heads, skin, and bones of fish such as whitefish, pike, trout, etc., with any other fish pieces for 30–40 minutes. Add light-colored root vegetables (leek, celery, parsley root, onion), bay leaves, peppercorns, and dill (also slices of lemon if desired). Simmer for another half hour. Do not add salt until the end of the cooking time. Strain and clarify by simmering the stock for a few minutes with a mixture of 2 tablespoons of roe or caviar, 1 egg white, and a small amount of cold water. Pour the broth through a fine sieve.

Carrots should not be used in fish stock because they are too sweet.

Ukrainian Borscht

UKRAINSKY BORSHCH
Serves 8–10

---

³/₄ pound beef brisket
³/₄ pound marbled pork
¹/₂ pound soup greens (carrots, leeks, celery, parsley)
2 medium onions
salt
5–10 white peppercorns
2 bay leaves
2 quarts water
2 medium beets (about ³/₄ pound), peeled and julienned
4 tablespoons butter
vinegar
³/₄ pound white cabbage, sliced
5 medium boiled potatoes, diced
¹/₂ cup cooked kidney beans
3 tomatoes (or 1 tablespoon tomato paste)
¹/₄ pound cooked ham (or smoked sausage), diced
¹/₃ cup flour
2 tablespoons bacon fat
3 cloves garlic
1 bunch parsley, chopped
1 bunch dill, chopped
1 cup sour cream

Prepare a hearty broth using beef, pork, half the soup greens, 1 onion, salt, peppercorns, bay leaves, and 2 quarts of water. Simmer for 1¹/₂ hours, covered. Strain. Reserve broth and meat.

Braise beets in butter or fat skimmed from the broth. Season with salt and a dash of vinegar. Add a small amount of broth and simmer until done.

Chop the rest of the soup greens and onion and sauté them in butter.

In a kettle, simmer white cabbage in the strained broth for about ¹/₂ hour. Add braised and simmered beets, sautéed vegetables, diced boiled potatoes, kidney beans, peeled and chopped tomatoes (or tomato paste), and diced ham or smoked sausage. Cook thoroughly.

Mix flour with a little slightly cooled broth in a small bowl until smooth and pour rapidly into kettle, stirring well. Mash bacon fat with garlic and parsley (or chop very finely) and let steep in the soup for about 20 minutes.

Cut the meat into bite-sized pieces and heat in the soup.

Season with salt and vinegar and sprinkle with chopped dill. Top each portion with a tablespoon of sour cream before serving.

Borscht Poltava with Dumplings

BORSHCH POLTAVSKY
Serves 4–5

1¹/₄ pound chicken or goose
1 bunch soup greens
salt, pepper
1¹/₂ quarts water
1–2 medium beets (about ¹/₂ pound), peeled and julienned
vinegar
1 carrot
1 medium onion
1 parsley root, peeled
1¹/₂ tablespoons butter
1 tablespoon tomato paste
2 medium potatoes, diced
³/₄ pound white cabbage, sliced
2 tablespoons bacon fat
1 bunch parsley, chopped
1 bunch dill, chopped
1 cup sour cream

DUMPLINGS

³/₄ cup buckwheat flour   1 egg
¹/₂ cup water, boiling   salt

Make a broth using chicken or goose, soup greens, and salt to taste. Cover with water. Cook, covered, for 2 hours. Strain. Reserve broth.

Braise beets in a little broth and vinegar until tender.

Chop carrot, onion, and parsley root. Sauté in butter. Mix with tomato paste.

Simmer cabbage in the broth for 30 minutes. Add potatoes and cook 15 more minutes.

Ukrainian Borscht ▷

Mash bacon fat with parsley in a mortar (or chop parsley very finely). Add with root vegetables and beets to the broth. Season with salt and pepper and stir well.

In the meantime, prepare the dumplings. Mix ¼ cup buckwheat flour with ½ cup boiling water and let steep until cool. Stir in the rest of the buckwheat flour, egg, and a pinch of salt. Cut out dumplings using two spoons dipped in cold water. Cook dumplings in simmering salted water until they rise to the surface. Remove with a slotted spoon.

Remove poultry meat from bones and add to the soup with the dumplings. Garnish with chopped dill and serve with sour cream.

Polish Borscht

POLSKY BORSHCH
Serves 6

1¾ pounds beef (flank steak, London broil)
2 bunches of soup greens
2 quarts kvass (see recipes, pages 263–266)
½ pound cured smoked pork or lean smoked pork belly
½ pound smoked sausage, sliced
2 tablespoons dried wild mushrooms
1 medium onion, chopped
4 tablespoons butter
4 medium beets (about 1¼ pounds), peeled and julienned
¼ cup flour
salt, pepper
vinegar
sour cream

Kvass, smoked meat, and smoked sausages give Polish borscht a very special flavor. Tart apple cider, nonalcoholic malt beer, or a mixture of 2 cups beet juice and 1½ quarts water can be used instead of kvass.

Make a broth of beef, soup greens, and kvass (or any of the aforementioned substitutes). Cook 1 hour. Before the end of the cooking time, add smoked meat and soaked, well-rinsed dried mushrooms. Simmer together until done.

Strain the broth and reserve. Dice mushrooms and smoked meat. (Save beef for another meal.)

Sauté onion in butter or fat skimmed from soup. Add beets and sauté briefly, then add a small amount of broth and braise until tender. Dust with flour and stir continuously. When it is thick, add to the strained broth and bring to a full boil. Add smoked meat, mushrooms, and sausages. Cook until hot. Season with salt, pepper, and a dash of vinegar. Stir in sour cream and serve.

Fish Borscht

BORSHCH IZ KARASEY
Serves 4

1 quart water
1 carrot, chopped
1 parsley root, peeled and chopped
1 medium onion, finely chopped
¼ knob celeriac, peeled and chopped
¼ cup dried wild mushrooms or ½ pound fresh mushrooms
salt
10 white peppercorns
2 bay leaves
¾ pound white cabbage
1–2 medium beets (about ½ pound), peeled
½ cup butter
2 tablespoons flour or bread crumbs
2 cups beet juice (available in health food stores)
2 tablespoons green olives
vinegar
1½ pounds perch or whitefish

In a kettle, place water, carrot, parsley root, half the onion, and celeriac. Add mushrooms, salt, peppercorns, and bay leaves. Cover. Bring to a boil and simmer for 1½ hours. Strain.

Cut white cabbage and beets into small pieces. Add to broth and simmer until tender.

Sauté remaining onion in a small amount of butter. Stir in 1 tablespoon flour and add to soup.

Add beet juice and olives. Season with vinegar.

Cut cleaned fish into serving pieces. Coat lightly with remaining flour or bread crumbs, and sauté in a generous amount of butter. Drain on paper towels. Reheat fish in borscht immediately before serving.

Green Borscht

BORSHCH ZELYONY

Serves 4–5

1¼ pounds stewing meat
1 bunch soup greens
1½ quarts water
salt
1–2 medium beets (about ½ pound), peeled
   and julienned
sugar
vinegar
1 tablespoon tomato paste
1 carrot, chopped
1 parsley root, peeled and chopped
1 medium onion, finely chopped
2 tablespoons butter
1 tablespoon flour
¾ pound spinach
½ pound sorrel
¼ pound scallions
3 medium potatoes, cut in small pieces
pepper
bay leaf
2–3 hard-boiled eggs
1 bunch dill, chopped
1 cup sour cream

Following the basic recipe, prepare a broth using the meat, soup greens, water, and salt. Strain.

Braise beets, salt, sugar, a dash of vinegar, and tomato paste in a small amount of the fat skimmed from the broth.

Sauté carrot, parsley root, and onion in butter. Add flour and stir in ½ cup broth.

Rinse spinach, sorrel, and scallions carefully and cut into thin strips.

Cook potatoes 10–15 minutes in the remaining broth. Add all the vegetables. Season with salt, pepper, and bay leaf. Simmer until tender.

Cut cooked meat into bite-sized pieces. Put some meat in each soup bowl and cover with hot borscht. Garnish each portion with ½ hard-boiled egg, dill, and a dollop of sour cream.

Vegetarian Borscht Kiev with Wild Mushrooms

BORSHCH KIEVSKY S GRIBAMI

Serves 4

¼ cup dried wild mushrooms
1–1½ quarts water
salt, pepper
bay leaf
1 medium beet (about ¼ pound), peeled and
   julienned
1 parsley root, peeled
1 carrot
1 medium onion
4 tablespoons butter
1 tablespoon tomato paste
2 medium potatoes, diced
¾ pound white cabbage, sliced
2 cups beet juice (available in health food
   stores)
1 tablespoon flour
vinegar
sugar
½ cup sour cream
2 egg yolks
1 bunch parsley, chopped

Soak the wild mushrooms for 20 minutes in warm water. Add 4–6 cups of water, salt, pepper, and bay leaf and simmer until soft. Strain and reserve broth. Rinse and drain mushrooms well. Cut into small pieces.

Braise beets in mushroom broth until tender.

Coarsely chop parsley root, carrot, and onion. Brown in butter, add tomato paste, and stir.

Sauté mushrooms in butter.

Simmer potatoes and cabbage in 3 cups of the mushroom broth for 15 minutes. Add the beets, root vegetables, mushrooms, and beet juice. Bring to a boil and cook for 15 minutes.

Mix flour with a small amount of mushroom stock until smooth and stir in to thicken the soup.

Season with salt, pepper, vinegar, and sugar and simmer until all ingredients are cooked. Whisk sour cream with the egg yolks and add some to each dish of borscht. Sprinkle with parsley.

Shchi

(SAUERKRAUT SOUP)
SHCHI
Serves 4–6

1³/₄ pounds beef (shank, London broil, soup meat, brisket)
³/₄ pound ham
1 bunch soup greens
1¹/₂–2 quarts water
2 tablespoons dried mushrooms
1¹/₄ pounds sauerkraut
1 medium onion, chopped
1 tablespoon butter
3 bay leaves
10 black peppercorns
1 tablespoon flour
salt, pepper
1 cup sour cream

Prepare a broth using beef, ham, soup greens, and water. Strain. Reserve meat from broth and dice.

Soak dried mushrooms, rinse well, simmer for 10 minutes in a small amount of water, and strain.

◁ *Shchi (Sauerkraut Soup) with Variety of Meats*

Squeeze the sauerkraut (reserving the juice), blanch in boiling water, drain, and chop.

Sauté the onion lightly in butter, add sauerkraut, and cook 15 minutes. Season with bay leaves and peppercorns. Add broth and simmer until sauerkraut is tender, about 1 hour.

Mix flour with 1 tablespoon of mushroom broth and add to thicken the soup. Bring back to boil and simmer again for 5 minutes.

Season with salt and pepper. If the soup is not sour enough, add sauerkraut juice.

Chop the mushrooms and add with the diced beef and ham to the soup. Cook 10 minutes. Stir in sour cream or serve separately as a garnish. Shchi may also be served with buckwheat groats.

Shchi with a Variety of Meats

SHCHI SBORNIYE (PETROVSKIYE)
Serves 4

---

2 quarts water
¹/₂ pound beef (shank, London broil, brisket, soup meat)
¹/₂ pound lamb (leg or shoulder)
¹/₄ pound ham
¹/₄ pound chicken
¹/₄ pound duck or goose
2 medium onions
1 carrot
1 parsley root, peeled
salt
10 black peppercorns
1¹/₂ pounds sauerkraut, rinsed and squeezed dry
2 tablespoons butter
3 bay leaves
4 cloves garlic, crushed
1 bunch dill (or parsley), chopped
1 cup sour cream

Put meat in a kettle with the water, add 1 onion, root vegetables, salt, and pepper. Bring to a boil, reduce heat, and simmer 1¹/₂ hours, covered. Strain and reserve broth and dice the meat.

Braise sauerkraut in butter and add to broth.

Cut second onion into rings and sauté in butter. Add this onion and the diced meat to the broth. Season with bay leaves, salt, and pepper, and simmer over low heat until done (approximately 15 minutes).

Just before serving, stir in garlic, season to taste, and garnish each portion with dill (or parsley) and sour cream.

24-hour Shchi

SHCHI SUTOCHNIYE
Serves 4

$^3/_4$ **pound smoked pork ribs**
1$^1/_2$ quarts water
$^3/_4$ **pound beef brisket**
1$^1/_2$ pounds sauerkraut, rinsed and squeezed dry
4 tablespoons butter
1 carrot, chopped
1 parsley root, peeled and chopped
1 turnip, chopped
1–2 medium onions, chopped
salt
6 black peppercorns
3 bay leaves
4 cloves garlic
1 bunch dill, chopped
4 tablespoons sour cream

Cut the ribs apart, put in a pot with enough cold water to cover, and simmer for approximately 1 hour. Add beef brisket and continue to simmer for another 1–1$^1/_2$ hours.

In the meantime, braise the sauerkraut in a small amount of butter and in another pot sauté the root vegetables and onions lightly in butter. Add sauerkraut, vegetables, and onions to the simmering soup.

Season with salt, peppercorns, and bay leaves and continue to simmer for 1 hour more.

Let the soup steep for 3–4 hours after removing from heat. Chill overnight.

Reheat before serving. Cut meat into bite-sized pieces and season with finely chopped or crushed garlic. Garnish each portion with dill and sour cream.

Green Shchi

SHCHI ZELYONIYE
Serves 5

2 pounds beef brisket
1 bunch soup greens
2 quarts water
1$^1/_4$ pounds baby nettles
1 medium onion, chopped
$^1/_2$ cup butter
1 pound sorrel
1 tablespoon flour
$^2/_3$ cup sour cream
salt, pepper
2 smoked sausages
5 hard-boiled eggs

Make a broth using the brisket, soup greens, and water. Strain. Dice the meat and set aside in a covered dish.

Meanwhile, sort through the nettles and discard discolored ones, rinse thoroughly, blanch in hot water, and bring to a boil. Drain and chop.

Lightly sauté onion in butter. Add nettles and braise till almost tender.

Sort through the sorrel, rinse well, and chop. Add to nettles. Cover and braise 5–10 minutes or until done.

Make a light roux with 1 tablespoon butter and 1 tablespoon flour. Stir in a small amount of broth. Add to the vegetables. Pour the rest of the broth over the vegetables, stir well, and return to a simmer.

Add diced meat and sour cream to the soup and season to taste. Slice sausages and sauté in butter 5–10 minutes. Add sausages and halved eggs to the soup immediately before serving.

Shchi with Sorrel and Spinach

SHCHI S SHCHAVELYEM I SHPINATOM

Serves 4

¼ cup dried mushrooms
1 leek, chopped in small pieces
1 carrot, chopped
1 celery stalk, chopped
1 parsley root, peeled and sliced
⅓ cup semolina
1 quart water
salt, pepper
1 tablespoon butter
1–2 medium onions, chopped
1 tablespoon flour
1 pound spinach
1 pound sorrel
1 cup sour cream
2–3 hard-boiled eggs

Soak the mushrooms, rinse. In a kettle, put leek, carrot, celery, parsley root, semolina, water, salt, and pepper and cook, covered, 15 minutes. Strain. Reserve broth.

Drain mushrooms, cut into small pieces, and sauté in butter with onions. Dust with flour, sauté again, and blend with a small amount of broth. Add the rest of the broth and return to simmer.

Rinse spinach and sorrel thoroughly, put dripping wet in a pot, and steam till tender. Press spinach and sorrel through a sieve and add to the soup with the liquid in which they cooked. Stir, heat, and season to taste. Serve with sour cream and sliced hard-boiled eggs.

◁ *Shchi (Sauerkraut Soup) with Sorrel and Spinach*

Ukha with Fried Fish

UKHA OPEKANNAYA

Serves 4

3 pounds fish (cod, halibut, etc.)
2 medium potatoes, peeled and diced
1 carrot, sliced
1 parsley root, peeled and sliced
2 medium onions, finely chopped
salt
8 black peppercorns
3 bay leaves
1 quart water
1 egg, beaten
1 tablespoon flour
4 tablespoons butter
1 bunch each parsley and dill, chopped

Have the fish store fillet the fish. Keep the trimmings. In a kettle, put vegetables, onions, fish trimmings, salt, peppercorns, and bay leaves. Cover with water and simmer 30 minutes on low heat. Strain. Discard fish trimmings. Reserve broth.

Poach fish fillets for 5 minutes in the strained broth. Remove and pat dry. Turn fillets in egg. Coat with flour and fry in butter till brown.

Return broth to a boil. Salt to taste. Add fried fish and steep for 5 minutes. Garnish with parsley and dill.

Sauerkraut Soup with Fish Heads

SHCHI S OSETROVOY GOLOVOY ILI PROSTO S OSETRINOY

Serves 4

2½ pounds sturgeon or salmon heads
1½ quarts water
2–3 medium onions
salt, pepper
1¼ pounds sauerkraut, rinsed
3–4 tablespoons oil or butter
1 tablespoon flour
1 bunch parsley, chopped

Rinse fish heads. Put in a pot, cover with cold water, and bring to a boil. Reduce heat, cover, and simmer for 45 minutes. Skim broth. Season with a quartered onion, salt, and pepper, and simmer until the meat falls off the bones.

Strain the broth, remove fish, put aside in a covered dish. Reserve.

Squeeze sauerkraut lightly and sauté in oil or butter along with 1–2 chopped onions. Add to soup and simmer 30 minutes until sauerkraut is tender. Blend flour with a small amount of warm water and use this to thicken the soup.

Transfer fish to soup tureen, pour hot broth over it, and garnish with parsley.

Fish Soup Rachmanov

RACHMANOVSKIYE SHCHI

Serves 5

---

1 pound small fish or fish heads, tails, and bones
1 stalk celery, chopped
1 carrot, sliced
1 parsley root, peeled and sliced
1 bunch combined herbs (parsley, tarragon, dill)
salt
6 peppercorns
2 bay leaves
6 cups water
1¼ pounds fresh salmon
1 pound spinach
1 pound sorrel
4 tablespoons butter
1 tablespoon flour
1 cup sour cream
5 eggs

In a kettle put the fish trimmings, celery, carrot, parsley root, herbs, salt, peppercorns, and bay leaves and cover with water. Bring to a boil, reduce heat, and simmer 45 minutes. Strain. Reserve broth.

Poach salmon 5 minutes in broth. Remove fish, drain, cover, and set aside.

Rinse spinach and sorrel thoroughly. Blanch in boiling water. Drain. Braise in 3 tablespoons butter and a small amount of fish broth. Mash by hand or puree in food processor.

Make a light roux with 1 tablespoon butter and 1 tablespoon flour. Stir into the spinach-sorrel puree. Gradually add broth and bring to a boil. Remove soup from heat and stir in sour cream.

Meanwhile, soft-boil eggs for about 4 minutes. Plunge them into cold water, remove shells. Cut salmon in bite-sized pieces. Place in soup tureen along with the soft-boiled eggs. Fill the tureen with hot soup and serve.

Rassolnik with Pickled Cucumbers and Kidneys

RASSOLNIK S SALYONIMY
OGURSAMI I POTCHKAMI

Serves 4

---

2 calf's kidneys
1¼ pounds beef flank
Soup greens (carrots, parsley roots, celery, leeks), chopped
salt, pepper
1½ quarts water
5 medium pickled cucumbers, peeled and finely chopped
1 medium onion, chopped
4 tablespoons butter
3 tablespoons tomato paste
5 medium potatoes, diced
½ cup pearl barley
2 tablespoons pickle brine
2 tablespoons flour, or more as needed
½ cup crème fraîche

Rinse kidneys well. Blanch three times in three different boiling waters and rinse with warm wa-

Rassolnik with Pickled Cucumbers and Kidneys ▷

ter. Combine beef, blanched kidneys, half of the soup greens, salt, and pepper in a pot. Cover with cold water and cook 1½ hours, or until tender. Add peels of pickled cucumbers during the last 10 minutes. Strain.

Sauté the rest of the chopped soup greens and onion in butter. Stir in tomato paste. Add potatoes and cover with a small amount of broth. Simmer 15 minutes or until the potatoes are tender. Rinse pearl barley, cover with cold water, bring to a boil, and simmer for 20 minutes, until done. Transfer to a colander, rinse carefully, and drain.

Sauté cucumbers in butter, add a small amount of broth, and simmer 10 minutes. Cut the beef into bite-sized pieces, add with the other cooked ingredients and pickle brine to the broth, and bring to a boil. Thicken the soup with flour blended with a small amount of broth.

Shortly before serving, slice kidneys thinly against the grain. Heat them in the soup, but do not allow soup to boil again. (The kidneys would become rubbery.)

Garnish each portion with a spoonful of crème fraîche.

Rassolnik with Wild Mushrooms
RASSOLNIK S GRIBAMI
Serves 4

¼ **cup dried wild mushrooms**
1½ **quarts water**
1 **medium onion**
1 **carrot**
1 **parsley root, peeled**
2 **tablespoons butter**
2–3 **medium potatoes, diced**
3 **medium pickled cucumbers, peeled and sliced**
½ **cup pickle brine**
salt
8 **black peppercorns**
3 **bay leaves**
2 **tablespoons chopped dill**
¼ **cup sour cream**

Soak dried mushrooms for 1 hour in cold water. Boil until tender in the same water. Drain and reserve broth.

Rinse mushrooms and slice into strips. If necessary, strain liquid to get rid of sand residue.

Cut onion, carrot, and parsley root in strips. Sauté in butter and simmer with potatoes in the mushroom broth until tender.

Add sliced pickled cucumber and the pickle brine to the soup. Season with salt, peppercorns, and bay leaves. Add cooked mushrooms and simmer for another 10–15 minutes.

Garnish with chopped dill and serve with sour cream.

Vegetarian Rassolnik
RASSOLNIK VEGETARIANSKY
Serves 4

6–8 **pickled cucumbers, peeled and sliced**
1 **pound root vegetables (carrots, parsley roots, celery, leeks), chopped**
2 **medium onions, chopped**
4 **tablespoons butter**
1 **bunch parsley, chopped**
1 **bunch tarragon, chopped**
1 **bunch dill, chopped**
salt
8–10 **peppercorns (black and white)**
2 **bay leaves**
1½ **quarts water**
¼ **cup pearl barley**
3 **medium potatoes, diced**
½ **cup pickle brine**
1 **tablespoon flour**
1 **bunch dill, finely chopped**
1 **cup sour cream**

Sauté the cucumber slices, root vegetables, and onions in 3 tablespoons butter. Add parsley, tarragon, dill, salt, peppercorns, and bay leaves. Cover with water and prepare a broth. Strain.

Simmer rinsed pearl barley in water till tender. Transfer to a colander. Rinse with hot water and drain.

Simmer potatoes in the strained broth until tender. Add pickled cucumbers and pearl barley. Season with brine and return to boil. Make a light roux with 1 tablespoon butter and flour and add to soup to thicken.

Sprinkle soup with dill and serve each portion with a spoonful of sour cream.

Fish Rassolnik

RASSOLNIK IZ RYBY

Serves 6

1 pound turnips
1 parsley root
8 stalks celery
²⁄₃ pound carp or freshwater roach
²⁄₃ pound pike or whitefish
²⁄₃ pound sturgeon
8 medium pickled cucumbers, peeled
¹⁄₂ cup pickle brine
1 bunch parsley
1 bunch tarragon
1 bunch dill
1–2 medium onions, chopped
salt
10 white peppercorns
2–2¹⁄₂ quarts water
approximately ¹⁄₂ cup butter
²⁄₃ pound smoked salmon
2 tablespoons flour
1–2 bunches dill, chopped

Filet all fish, reserving skin and bones. Scrub root vegetables and celery, peel, and cut into decorative slices. Reserve clean peels. In a kettle combine the skin and bones of all the fresh fish, the peels and brine of the pickled cucumbers, root vegetable leaves and peels, herbs, onions, salt to taste, and peppercorns. Cover with water, bring to a boil, reduce heat, and simmer for 45 minutes. Strain.

Return broth to a boil, add fresh fish fillets, and poach 3–5 minutes, or until done. Drain. Set fish aside. Boil sliced root vegetables in a small amount of broth until they are cooked al dente, or about 5 minutes, and set aside.

Slice cucumbers and braise in 3 tablespoons butter.

In a pan, heat pieces of smoked salmon in a little butter.

Bring fish broth to a boil. In a saucepan, heat 2 tablespoons of butter. Stir in 2 tablespoons flour and 1 cup of broth. Add to broth with cooked fish, root vegetable slices, and braised pickled cucumbers. Return to a boil and turn heat off. Add the smoked salmon and let steep for several minutes.

Sprinkle with dill and serve.

This delicious fish soup may be varied according to taste: Different kinds of fish may be used and the roux can be made with crayfish butter. Slices of tomato may be added 10 minutes before serving. One-quarter cup of pearl barley (precooked in water) may also be added.

Rassolnik with Chicken Giblets

RASSOLNIK POTROKHAMI

Serves 4

1 pound beef (brisket, flank)
1 carrot, sliced
1 medium onion, finely chopped
1 parsley root, peeled and sliced
salt
8 black peppercorns
2 bay leaves
1¹⁄₂ quarts water
³⁄₄ pound chicken giblets
3 tablespoons rice
3 medium pickled cucumbers, peeled and sliced
3 cloves garlic, minced
1 tablespoon butter
1 bunch dill, chopped
1 bunch parsley, chopped
¹⁄₂ cup sour cream

Prepare a broth using beef, carrot, onion, parsley root, salt, peppercorns, and bay leaves. Simmer 1 hour. Add giblets and continue simmering for another hour.

Strain broth, reserving the meat. Add rice and simmer 15 minutes until done. Add cucumbers and simmer the soup another 5–7 minutes. Add diced meat and heat it in the broth.

Remove soup from heat. Mash garlic with salt and butter and add to soup.

Garnish with dill and parsley and serve with sour cream.

This soup can also be made with goose giblets. In that case, use ¹⁄₄ cup pearl barley instead of rice.

Crayfish Soup Moscow-Style

MOSKOVSKY RAKOVY SUP
Serves 4

1¼ pounds perch fillets
1¾ pounds carp or freshwater roach, etc.
3 carrots, sliced
½ pound parsley root, peeled and sliced
½ pound leeks
4 stalks celery, cut in small pieces
1 medium onion, finely chopped
1 bunch parsley
1 bunch tarragon
1 bunch dill
salt, pepper
bay leaf
1½ quarts water
1 cup heavy cream
2 egg whites
¾ pound canned crayfish meat
1 tablespoon crayfish butter
1 bunch dill, chopped

Prepare a hearty fish broth using fish heads and bones, root vegetables, celery, onion, herbs, seasoning, and water. Strain.

Puree perch fillets with cream, egg whites, and a little salt in food processor. Form little dumplings using two spoons repeatedly dipped in cold water. Simmer in fish broth about 8–10 minutes.

Add crayfish to soup and reheat. Garnish with crayfish butter (see recipe, page 154) and dill before serving.

Variation as shown in picture on the right: Prepare fish broth as described above. Strain. Cut perch fillets into thin slices. Dissolve ½ teaspoon saffron in 1 tablespoon vodka and add to broth. Add sliced fish fillets to saffron-flavored broth. You may, instead of crayfish, add the same amount of fresh shrimp. Simmer about 10 minutes.

Serve this soup with Rastegai (see recipe, page 218).

Crayfish Soup Moscow-Style ▷

Solyanka with Fish and Cabbage

SOLYANKA RYBNAYA S KAPUSTOY

Serves 4

1½ quarts water
1 pound carp or freshwater roach, etc.
heads and bones of 2 salmon
1 bunch parsley root, peeled and sliced
1 bunch celery, chopped
6 carrots, sliced
salt, pepper
2 bay leaves
1 medium onion, chopped
4 tablespoons butter
2 tablespoons flour
½ pound sauerkraut or white cabbage
½ pound sturgeon
½ pound perch
½ pound salmon
10 Kalamata olives, pitted
10 white mushrooms or ½ pound wild
   mushrooms
2 pickled cucumbers, peeled and diced
¼ pound fresh shrimp, peeled, deveined, and
   diced
½ cup pickle brine
3 tablespoons sour cream or heavy cream
1 bunch dill, chopped
1 bunch parsley, chopped

Prepare stock using water and the carp or other small fish, salmon heads and bones, soup vegetables, salt, pepper, and bay leaves. Strain.

Sauté onion in butter. Dust with flour and brown lightly. Stir into the broth. Return to a boil and strain again.

Blanch the sauerkraut or cabbage. Drain. Braise in remaining butter and a small amount of the broth. Cut sturgeon, perch, and salmon into pieces. Slice olives and mushrooms. Add all of these ingredients, together with cucumbers and shrimp, to the broth. Return to boil. Season with pickle brine. Simmer over low heat until done.

Serve with a dollop of sour cream or heavy cream, dill, and parsley.

◁ *Solyanka with Fish and Cabbage*

For a more intense flavor the soup pot can be covered with a pastry crust and baked in a 350°F oven for 25 minutes, which makes it especially decorative.

Solyanka with Assorted Meats

SOLYANKA SBORNAYA MYASNAYA

Serves 4

1–2 medium onions, chopped
4 tablespoons butter
¼ pound pickled cucumbers, peeled
3 tablespoons tomato paste
salt
peppercorns
bay leaf
2 tablespoons capers
¾ cup Kalamata olives, pitted
½ pound boiled or roasted beef, veal, or lamb
½ pound roasted calf's or beef kidneys
¼ pound cooked ham
¼ pound small sausages
1½ quarts meat stock
⅓ cup sour cream
1 lemon, peeled and sliced
1 bunch parsley, chopped
1 bunch dill, chopped

Lightly sauté onions in butter. Cut cucumbers into diamond shapes. Add to the onions along with the tomato paste and braise about 5 minutes. Season with salt, peppercorns, bay leaf, capers, and half the olives.

Slice meat, kidneys, ham, and sausages thinly. Add to onions. Cover with stock and simmer for 10 minutes over low heat.

Season soup to taste with salt and pepper and serve each portion with sour cream, the remaining olives, peeled lemon slices, and herbs.

This solyanka is excellent with leftovers. It can also be prepared with roasted or boiled poultry, venison, pickled tongue, etc.

Solyanka with Assorted Meats ▷

Cream of Lentil Soup
SUP PYURE IZ CHECHEVITSY
Serves 4

1³/₄ pounds stewing beef
¹/₂ pound ham
1 bunch parsley
salt, pepper
³/₄ pound lentils
1 carrot, sliced
1 medium onion, chopped
2 tablespoons bread crumbs
2 egg yolks
¹/₂ cup heavy cream
1 bunch dill, chopped

Put beef, ham, parsley, salt, and pepper in a kettle, and cover with water. Bring to a boil. Reduce heat and simmer for 1 hour, adding water as needed. Drain.

Dice ham. Reserve beef for another meal.

Rinse lentils, strain, and transfer to a pot along with carrot, onion, and bread crumbs. Season with salt and pepper. Cover with water and bring to a boil. Skim and cover pot. Cook until lentils are tender, about 30 minutes.

Press lentils through a sieve or puree in food processor or blender. Reheat the puree and add the meat broth. Stir well and simmer until thick.

Blend egg yolks and cream, add to soup. Heat, but do not allow to boil again.

Add diced ham and dill and serve.

◁ *Cream of Lentil Soup*

Botvinya with Fish

BOTVINYA IZ RYBY

Serves 4

1 pound spinach
1 pound sorrel
5 shallots, finely chopped
1 or 2 fresh cucumbers (approximately 1 pound)
1 large bunch herbs made of parsley, dill, tarragon, and chervil, finely chopped
salt, pepper
sugar
1 tablespoon grated fresh horseradish
1 tablespoon mustard
1 quart kvass (see recipes, pages 263–268)
ice cubes
2–2¹/₂ pounds cooked fish, such as trout, whitefish, or salmon, sliced
16 cooked crayfish

Rinse spinach and sorrel. Steam in a small amount of salted water for 5 minutes. Press through a sieve or puree in food processor.

Cool and mix with half the shallots, diced cucumber (set aside several cucumber slices for garnish), and herbs. Season 15 minutes before serving with salt, pepper, sugar, horseradish, mustard, and cold kvass.

Stir well and serve soup with ice cubes, cold fish garnished with crayfish tails, cucumber slices, remaining chopped shallots, and a little grated horseradish.

Mushroom Broth

GRIBNOY SUP

Serves 4

¹/₄ cup dried wild mushrooms
3 carrots
¹/₂ pound leeks
¹/₂ pound parsley root, peeled
4 stalks celery
1 medium onion
1 bunch parsley, chopped
salt, pepper
caraway seeds
1 tablespoon butter

Soak mushrooms for 1 hour in warm water, drain, and blanch in boiling water.

Drain again and cut into strips. Chop carrots, leeks, parsley root, celery, and onion. Add half of mixture to the mushrooms with parsley, salt, pepper, and caraway to taste and bring to a boil in approximately 1 quart water. Reduce heat and simmer 30 minutes.

Sauté the rest of the vegetables in butter and add them to the mushroom broth for the last 10 minutes of cooking.

Strain the broth and sprinkle with chopped parsley.

Clear mushroom broth can also be served with noodles, semolina dumplings, small stuffed ravioli, etc.

Potato Soup with Mushrooms

KARTOFELNY SUP S GRIBAMI

Serves 4–5

1 pound fresh mushrooms (cepes, chanterelles, mixed wild mushrooms)
2 tablespoons butter
3 carrots
4 stalks celery
¹/₂ pound parsley root, peeled
¹/₂ pound leeks
1 medium onion
1¹/₂ quarts water
5 medium potatoes, diced
salt, pepper
bay leaf
1 bunch parsley, chopped
1 bunch tarragon, chopped
¹/₂–1 cup sour cream
1 bunch dill, chopped
1 bunch scallions, chopped

Carefully clean and rinse mushrooms. Remove stems from caps. Slice stems and sauté them in 1 tablespoon butter.

Chop soup vegetables and onion and sauté in 1 tablespoon butter.

Slice mushroom caps into very thin slices and simmer in water with potatoes, salt, pepper, and bay leaf for 20 minutes. Add sautéed ingredients, parsley, and tarragon and continue to cook till tender.

Remove bay leaf. Season soup with salt and pepper.

Before serving top each portion with a spoonful of sour cream, dill, and scallions.

Black Bread Soup

SUP IZ CHORNOVO KHLEBA

Serves 4

2 carrots, diced
6 stalks celery, cut in 1-inch pieces
1 parsley root, peeled and diced
1 medium onion, chopped
1 tablespoon butter
1 quart water
salt, pepper
$^1/_2$ pound black bread
$^1/_2$ cup dried peas soaked overnight (green or yellow)
1 small black radish
1 carrot
2 stalks celery
6–8 stalks asparagus
$^1/_4$ pound spinach, chopped coarsely
1 bunch dill, chopped
1 leek, chopped (white part only)
1 bunch parsley, chopped

Sauté 2 carrots, the celery, parsley root, and onion in butter. Add 1 quart water, salt, and pepper and cook for $^1/_2$ hour.

Slice the bread and toast (or brown in oven at low heat). Transfer bread to soup pot. Simmer soup for an additional hour. Puree in a food processor. Return to pot. Heat soup again.

Boil peas for 1–1$^1/_2$ hours.

Coarsely grate the radish, carrot, and celery.

Cut asparagus into pieces.

Rinse spinach and add to soup with peas, grated radish, carrot, and celery, and asparagus. Cook 10 more minutes.

Season with salt and pepper, sprinkle with dill, and serve garnished with leeks and parsley.

Milk Soup with Vegetables

MOLOCHNY SUP S OVOSHCHAMI

Serves 4

4 medium potatoes, peeled
1 small head white cabbage
1 carrot, peeled
1 turnip, peeled
1 leek, white part only
1 slice celeriac, peeled
1$^1/_2$ quarts milk
$^1/_4$ pound asparagus, peeled and trimmed
$^1/_4$ pound spinach
approximately 2 tablespoons butter
$^1/_2$ cup heavy cream
3 egg yolks
salt
1 bunch dill, chopped
1 bunch parsley, chopped

Dice all the vegetables except asparagus and spinach. Simmer in milk till tender, about 15 minutes.

Cut asparagus into pieces. Cut spinach into strips and simmer another 5–10 minutes over low heat. Thicken soup with blended butter, cream, and egg yolks. Season with salt and garnish with herbs.

Cold Lenten Soup

OKROSHKA POSTNAYA

Serves 4–5

1 medium potato, peeled and diced
1 medium beet (about ¼ pound), peeled and diced
½ cup beans (fresh green beans, dried kidney beans, or dried red beans)
1 fresh cucumber (about ¾ pound) or 2–3 pickled cucumbers, peeled
¼–½ pound marinated mushrooms
¾ pound stewed fruit (apples, plums, cherries, peaches, grapes)
1 tablespoon olive oil
½ tablespoon mustard
salt, pepper
5 cups kvass (or tart apple cider or nonalcoholic malt beer: see Polish borscht, page 38)
5 cups sauerkraut juice
ice cubes
1 bunch parsley, chopped
1 bunch dill, chopped
1 bunch scallions, chopped

Cook potato, beet, and beans in separate pots until tender. Drain and cool.

Slice cucumber, drained mushrooms, and fruit. Combine in a soup tureen with potato, beet, and beans.

In another container mix olive oil, drop by drop, with mustard and salt, stirring until it forms a thick sauce.

Add kvass and sauerkraut juice to olive oil mixture. Stir well and pour over the fruit and vegetable mixture in the tureen. Season with salt and pepper to taste. Refrigerate. Serve with ice cubes, herbs, and scallions.

Cold Soup Polish-Style

OKROSHKA PO POLSKY SO SMETANOY

Serves 4–5

4 medium beets (about 1¼ pounds)
salt
2 bunches dill
1 bunch scallions
1 cup beet juice (available in health food stores)
1–1½ cups sour cream
1½ quarts water or meat stock
pepper
vinegar
4–5 hard-boiled eggs
3 pickled gherkins or 1 fresh cucumber
15–20 cooked crayfish or ¼ pound cooked beef, diced
ice cubes
1 lemon for garnish

Rinse beets. Boil in salted water until tender. Peel and chop finely. Mash 1 bunch dill and scallions with salt in a mortar (or food processor) and put in a soup tureen with the beets.

Stir beet juice into sour cream and dilute with water or strained meat stock. Season with salt, pepper, and vinegar. Chill well.

Slice eggs and gherkins or cucumber and add to soup. Add crayfish or cooked beef and a few ice cubes.

This refreshing dish is served with lemon slices, chopped dill, and a separate bowl of ice cubes. As a variation, 2 cups buttermilk may be used instead of beet juice.

Cold Soup Polish-Style ▷

Meat

MYASNIYE BLYUDA

Beef is the most important meat in Russian cuisine. Formerly it was necessary to salt meat to preserve it, after which it was prepared in a special way. Most recipes for salted beef have been forgotten because modern cold storage has eliminated the need for this method of preservation.

Ivan the Terrible drafted strict regulations for the slaughter of beef and took measures to make certain that calves were not killed and eaten. Calves were for petting, to be loved, and to be played with. Those who disagreed did not fare well in Russia. Dmitry the Pretender ruled for a mere two years. While in power, he served veal and tried to introduce the use of the fork. That proved to be too much for the boyars. They called him an imposter and staged the so-called calf's putsch, forcing him to abdicate.

Beef Stroganoff is named for Count Stroganoff (1795–1891), mayor of Odessa, who was famous for feeding his people. As long as they were halfway decently dressed, he would feed anyone who came to the door free of charge. It was for this reason his chefs invented a recipe that could be prepared ahead of time and was easy to serve in individual portions.

The Caucasus and central Asia provided our kitchens with many dishes using lamb—e.g., shashlik and pilaf. But actually, lamb is not particularly well suited to Russian cooking because it does not go well with the traditional pickled cucumbers or sauerkraut—not to mention vodka.

As for pork, the opposite of what I have said about beef is true; preference is given to the young animal, the suckling pig.

Ground meat did not become popular until the mid-nineteenth century, after the Americans introduced the meat grinder. Until then, older pigs had never been used for anything other than ham.

Beef Stroganoff

BEF STROGANOV
Serves 4

---

2 pounds fillet of beef
salt, pepper
2 tablespoons flour
1 large onion
¹/₂ cup butter
6 tablespoons tomato paste
1 cup meat broth
¹/₃ cup crème fraîche or sour cream

Slice beef fillet ³/₄ inch thick against the grain. Pound lightly to tenderize. Cut slices into 1¹/₂–2-inch-long strips. Season with salt and pepper and toss with flour.

Slice onion into thin rings. Sauté in butter in a large, heavy skillet until transparent. Add meat. (The skillet must be large enough to allow strips to fit in a single layer.) Sauté quickly over high heat until brown. Remove meat and onion from skillet, cover, and keep warm. Braise tomato paste briefly in the pan drippings. Add broth and crème fraîche. Add meat and onions. Stir well and simmer 5–10 minutes. Season with salt and pepper and serve with sautéed potatoes.

Note: Keep Beef Stroganoff warm in a chafing dish.

Roast Loin of Beef
Hussar-Style

ZHARKOYE IZ GOVYADINY V TYESTYE

Serves 6–8

2 pounds loin of beef, tenderloin
salt, pepper
$^1\!/_2$ cup butter
1-2 cups beef broth
1-2 medium onions, chopped
$^1\!/_2$ pound mushrooms or wild mushrooms,
   sliced
$1^1\!/_2$ cups bread crumbs from black bread
1 cup sour cream
$^1\!/_2$ cup grated Parmesan
2 pounds rye bread dough (order from baker
   ahead of time)

or make as follows:

1 package dry yeast
1 cup lukewarm water
1 cup unbleached flour
$^1\!/_2$ cup whole wheat flour
$1^1\!/_2$ cups rye flour
$^1\!/_2$ teaspoon salt

Dilute yeast in $^1\!/_4$ cup lukewarm water. Let it become foamy. Mix in the three flours, water, and salt. Knead into a ball. Cover and let rise $1^1\!/_2$ hours. Punch down and use for recipe.

1 egg, lightly beaten for glaze
$^1\!/_2$ cup heavy cream
ground rosemary
1 bunch parsley, chopped for garnish

Preheat oven to 400°F. Wash and dry meat. Make an incision with a knife in the center of the roast. Sprinkle with salt and pepper. Brown on all sides in butter. Pour off any butter remaining in pan, and add 1 cup broth.

   Prepare stuffing: Sauté onions, mushrooms, and bread crumbs in butter. Stir in sour cream and a small amount of broth if needed to make a moist and smooth mixture. Add salt and pepper to taste. Season with Parmesan and cool. Stuff filling into roast cavity. Roast in oven 15 minutes.

Roast Loin of Beef Hussar-Style ▷

66

When meat is cool, slice thinly against the grain. Spread stuffing on each slice and put slices back together in the original shape of the loin. Roll out the rye bread dough to the thickness of a finger and place meat on the dough. Wrap carefully so that no juice will escape during baking. Place on a buttered baking sheet. Brush top with cold water and egg to get a nice glaze and bake in a 350°F oven for approximately 20 minutes.

In the meantime, deglaze the roasting pan with cream and simmer briefly. Season with salt, pepper, and ground rosemary. Place the baked bread with meat on a serving dish and cut top of the dough horizontally to make a lid. Carefully pour cream sauce over the meat and sprinkle with parsley. To serve, replace the lid and surround with roast potatoes.

Beef Casserole

ZAPECHONOYE GOVYASHCHYE FILE
Serves 6–8

---

3 pounds fillet of beef
salt, pepper
5 tablespoons butter
8–10 small potatoes, peeled
1 large onion, chopped
³/₄ pound mushrooms, sliced
1 cup sour cream
approximately 2 cups broth
pastry crust made with 3¹/₂ cups flour (optional)

Rinse meat and pat dry. Cut into long strips and pound to tenderize. Season with salt and pepper. Brown in 3 tablespoons butter. Thinly slice potatoes. Blanch for 5 minutes and strain. Sauté onions and mushrooms in 2 tablespoons butter. Layer meat, potatoes, and onion-mushroom mixture in a buttered, ovenproof casserole dish.

Deglaze pan where meat was browned with sour cream. Season with salt and pepper. Pour sour cream mixture over top of casserole and add enough broth to come nearly to the top.

Cover well and bake in a 350°F oven for approximately 20 minutes.

Serve with green salad or a vegetable of your choice.

This beef casserole is particularly festive when covered with a pastry crust. Press the edges down well, decorate with leftover pieces of dough, brush with egg yolk, and bake approximately 40 minutes.

Roast Beef "Hussar's Liver"

ZHARKOYE IZ GOVYADINY
"GUSARSKAYA PECHEN"
Serves 6–8

---

3 pounds roasting beef (sirloin, eye round, or chuck)
salt, pepper
4 tablespoons oil
2 medium onions, finely chopped
¹/₂ cup butter, softened
2 egg yolks
1 cup bread crumbs
¹/₂ cup grated cheese
milk

Rinse and dry meat and rub with salt and pepper. In a skillet, brown on all sides in oil. Transfer to an ovenproof dish and roast in a preheated 400°F oven for 15 minutes. Baste occasionally with a spoonful of water and turn several times.

In the meantime, prepare the filling: Mix onions well with butter, egg yolks, bread crumbs, and cheese. This can be done in the food processor. Season with salt and pepper. The mixture should be spreadable. If it is too thick, stir in a few tablespoons of milk.

Cool the roast and cut ¹/₂-inch slices. Spread the filling between the slices and wrap the roast lengthwise with twine.

Transfer to top of the stove and moisten with pan juices from roasting and a small amount of water. Braise for 10 minutes. Before serving, remove twine, slice, and cover with pan drippings. Serve with potatoes or rice.

This dish is particularly attractive covered with a pastry crust decorated with leftover pieces of dough and baked in a 375°F oven for half an hour.

Roast Beef "Hussar's Liver" ▷

Roast Beef with Horseradish Stuffing

ZHARKOYE IZ GOVYADINY S KHRENOM
Serves 4–6

2 pounds roasting beef (sirloin, London broil, eye round, or chuck)
salt, pepper
2 tablespoons flour
4 tablespoons oil
4 tablespoons prepared horseradish
6 tablespoons sour cream
2 eggs
3 tablespoons bread crumbs
sugar

Rinse and dry meat. Rub with salt and pepper and coat with flour. Brown in hot oil in a Dutch oven. Add 1 cup water and braise covered for 1 hour. Add more water as necessary.

For the filling, mix horseradish, sour cream, eggs, and bread crumbs. Season with salt, pepper, and sugar.

Remove the roast from the pan, let cool, and cut in ½-inch-thick slices nearly to the bottom.

Spread filling between slices. Tie lengthwise with twine. Return meat to the Dutch oven and braise 15 minutes. Before serving, remove twine and pour pan drippings over meat. Serve with mashed, boiled, or sautéed potatoes.

Roast Beef with Herring Stuffing

ZHARKOYE IZ GOVYADINY "GUSARSKAYA PECHEN" S SELYODKOY
Serves 4–6

2 pounds roasting beef (loin, eye round, or chuck)
salt, pepper
3 tablespoons butter
1 medium onion, chopped
2 carrots, sliced
1 salted herring
1 egg
4 scallions, chopped
½ pound rye bread, grated (or 2–3 cups bread crumbs)
1 cup beef broth

Rinse and dry meat. Rub with salt and pepper and brown on all sides in 1½ tablespoons butter.

Add onion, carrots, and a small amount of water. Braise, covered, for approximately 1 hour. Add water as necessary.

In the meantime, prepare the filling: Rinse herring, drain, and chop very fine. Mix well with egg, 1½ tablespoons softened butter, scallions, and ½ cup bread crumbs. Pepper generously.

Remove meat from pot, let cool, and slice ½ inch thick nearly to the bottom.

Spread filling between slices and wrap the meat lengthwise with twine. Return to pot, add broth, and braise for 30 minutes. Remove meat and untie. Thicken sauce with the remaining bread crumbs, bring to a boil, and pour over meat.

Serve with mashed or boiled potatoes.

◁ *Roast Beef with Horseradish Stuffing*

Stuffed Ground Meat Roulade

RULYET IZ GOVYADNY FARSHIROVANNY

Serves 6

---

3 slices stale white bread
1 cup milk
1 medium onion, chopped
½ cup butter
2 pounds ground beef or sirloin
ice water or chopped ice
salt, pepper
1 egg, beaten
1 tablespoon bread crumbs

FILLING

1 medium onion, chopped
½ pound white mushrooms or wild mushrooms, thinly sliced
2 tablespoons butter
1 tablespoon bread crumbs
1 cup sour cream
salt, pepper
1 bunch parsley, chopped
1 bunch dill, chopped
small amount of beef broth, if needed

To prepare the filling: Sauté onion and mushrooms in 2 tablespoons butter. Add bread crumbs and sour cream, blend well, and season with salt, pepper, and herbs. (If the mixture is too thick, stir in a small amount of broth.)

To prepare roulades: Soak white bread in milk and squeeze thoroughly. Sauté onion in 2 tablespoons butter. Combine bread, onions, and ground beef. Stir well. Add enough ice water or chopped ice to make a smooth mixture. Season with salt and pepper.

Spread meat mixture finger-thick on a dampened dishcloth. Spread filling over the meat mixture. Lift one end of the cloth and roll the meat and filling up like a jelly roll to form an oblong roast like you would a meat loaf.

Place meat roll on a greased baking sheet. Brush with egg and sprinkle with bread crumbs. Melt remaining butter, drizzle some over meat roll, and bake in a 375°F oven for about 1 hour. Baste with more melted butter as it bakes.

Serve with tomato sauce (see recipe, page 150) and roasted potatoes or potato pancakes.

Ground Beef Croquettes

KLASSICHESKIYE MYASNIYE KOTLYETY

Serves 8

---

2 stale white rolls (crusts removed)
1 cup milk
1½ cups butter
2 pounds lean ground beef or sirloin
ice water or chopped ice
1 large onion, chopped
salt, pepper
3 tablespoons flour
2 eggs, beaten
6 tablespoons bread crumbs

Soak rolls in milk. Combine with ½ cup softened butter and ground beef. Stir well. Add enough ice water or chopped ice to make a moist (but not watery) mixture. Sauté onion in 1 tablespoon butter and add to the meat mixture. Season with salt and pepper and stir well.

With moistened hands shape palm-sized patties. Place on a dampened wooden board. Place 8 tablespoons butter in the freezer to chill for 5 minutes. Top each patty with a dab of iced butter. Pull up the edges of the meat mixture and press gently together.

Shape into small oval loaves, coat with flour, egg, and bread crumbs.

Brown all sides in remaining butter that is not too hot. Bake 30 minutes until done in an oven at 375°F. (The croquettes will swell as they bake.) Serve with sautéed potatoes, vegetables, or salad.

Ice water or chopped ice make the cutlets especially juicy because the water from the melted ice evaporates during the cooking process instead of the meat juices. When using this method, do not add eggs to meat mixture.

Ground Beef Croquettes ▷

Braised Veal with Caviar Sauce

TELYATINA TUSHONAYA S
SOUSOM IZ IKRY
Serves 10

4¹⁄₂ pounds veal shank
salt
¹⁄₂ pound bacon
¹⁄₂ pound cooked ham
10 anchovy or sardine fillets, well rinsed
1 medium onion, finely chopped
1 parsley root, peeled
1 leek, white part only
¹⁄₂ knob celeriac
1 cup dry white wine
juice and grated peel of 1 lemon
10 black peppercorns
approximately 1 quart beef broth
2 tablespoons black caviar
1 tablespoon butter

Soak veal for 2 hours in salted water. Remove from water, dry, and lard all over with strips of bacon, ham, and anchovy fillets. Cut vegetables into small pieces and spread out on the bottom of a Dutch oven. Add larded meat, moisten with wine and lemon juice, and sprinkle with grated lemon peel, salt, and peppercorns.

Add enough broth to cover meat. Cover and braise for 2¹⁄₂–3 hours.

Remove meat when done, and keep warm. Strain the braising liquid, pour into a small pot, bring to a boil. Turn off heat and stir caviar in sauce. Bind with butter. Pour over the meat. Serve with rice or potato croquettes.

◁ *Braised Veal with Caviar Sauce*

Veal Cutlets with Calf's Brains

KOTLYETY IZ TELYATINY S
SOUSOM IZ MOSGOV
Serves 4

4 veal cutlets
salt, pepper
½ cup butter
1 calf's brain (approximately ¾ pound)
vinegar
4 tablespoons bread crumbs
1 medium onion, chopped
1 bunch parsley, chopped
1 tablespoon flour
3 tablespoons sour cream
2 egg yolks, beaten

Rinse and dry veal cutlets. Sprinkle with salt and pepper and brown on both sides in 3 tablespoons butter. Transfer to an ovenproof dish and moisten with the hot butter.

Soak brain for 30 minutes in cold water, drain, and cut in half. Simmer half of the brain in salted water with a dash of vinegar for approximately 15 minutes. Remove from water, slice thinly, and cover the cutlets with half the slices of brain. Drizzle with 2 tablespoons melted butter, sprinkle with 2 tablespoons bread crumbs, and bake in a preheated 400°F oven for 15 minutes.

In the meantime, sauté the onion and parsley in 1 tablespoon butter. Puree the remaining half of the brain in food processor and brown with the onion. Dust with flour, sauté lightly, and add sour cream. Stir well and bring to a boil. Let cool slightly, stir in egg yolks, and season with salt and pepper.

Top the veal cutlets with this mixture. Sprinkle with the remaining bread crumbs, dot with remaining butter, and brown in a 400°F oven for approximately 15 minutes. Serve with sautéed potatoes and salad.

Stuffed Breast of Veal

FARSHIROVANNAYA TELYACHYA
GRUDINKA
Serves 6

3 pounds breast of veal
¾ pound calf's heart
¾ pound calf's lung
1 medium onion, chopped
½ cup butter
6 tablespoons tomato paste
salt, pepper
2 hard-boiled eggs, chopped
1 tablespoon flour
2 cups broth
peeled whole potatoes

Rinse and dry the breast of veal and using a sharp knife cut a deep pocket (or ask your butcher to prepare it). Rinse heart and lung. Cut in half. Remove veins, tendons, and fat (again, your butcher might do this). Blanch several times in boiling water. Rinse with cold water and dry. Cut heart and lung into thin strips (or run through meat grinder). Brown with onion in butter. Season with tomato paste, salt, and pepper. Add eggs.

Prepare a roux with 1 tablespoon butter and 1 tablespoon flour. Add a small amount of broth and pour over the browned heart and lung.

Stir well. Bring to a boil and let thicken.

Let cool. Then fill the pocket of the breast with this mixture. Stitch together. Rub breast with salt and pepper and coat with melted butter.

Roast in a 375°F oven for 1½ hours, basting frequently with pan juices and adding broth as necessary. During the last hour, surround the breast with peeled potatoes and roast until done.

Before serving, remove twine, cut breast open, moisten with pan juices, and serve with roasted potatoes.

Breast of veal can also be stuffed with a meat mixture: Mix 1 pound ground veal, ½ cup heavy cream, ½ cup thinly sliced smoked or pickled tongue, and ¼ pound diced bacon. Season with salt and pepper.

Stuffed Breast of Veal ▷

Veal and Herring in Scallop Shells

RUBLENNAYA TELYATINA
ZAPECHONAYA S SELYODKOY

Serves 6

---

1 salted herring
1 pound roasted veal
1 medium onion, chopped
$1/2$ cup butter
approximately 1 cup beef broth
$1/2$ cup sour cream
2 egg yolks
4 tablespoons bread crumbs
salt, pepper
$1/2$ teaspoon nutmeg
2 tablespoons grated cheese

Run herring and veal through meat grinder.

Sauté onion in butter. Add the meat-fish mixture and a few tablespoons of beef broth. Stir and braise for 5 minutes. Stir in sour cream and return to boil, then turn heat off. Let cool slightly. Add egg yolks and 2 tablespoons bread crumbs. If the mixture is too dry, add a small amount of broth.

Season with salt, pepper, and nutmeg. Spoon into six buttered scallop shell molds.

Mix the remainder of the bread crumbs with cheese and sprinkle over the top.

Bake in a 400°F oven for 15 minutes and serve as an hors d'oeuvre.

Shashlik

SHASHLIK

Serves 4

$1^{3}/_{4}$ pounds lamb from the leg or shoulder
salt, pepper
2 bunches parsley
2 bunches cilantro
3 medium onions, finely chopped
3–4 tablespoons vinegar
oil for grilling

Cut meat into cubes measuring 2 inches and sprinkle with salt and pepper. Chop half the herbs and stir into onions. Add vinegar and stir again.

Marinate meat in this mixture for 8–12 hours. Keep in a cool place and turn several times.

Drain the meat, thread onto four skewers, brush with oil, and grill. Serve remaining herbs whole with the grilled shashlik.

Grilled tomatoes, strips of green peppers, or a tangy tomato sauce with rice go well with this meal.

Eggplant Stuffed with Shashlik

SHASHLIK S BAKLAZHANAMI

Serves 4

---

4 large eggplants (8–10 inches long)
$1^{3}/_{4}$ pounds lamb from the leg or shoulder
salt, pepper
4 tablespoons oil
1 bunch parsley, chopped
1 bunch cilantro, chopped
tarragon
thyme

In this recipe shashlik is grilled in eggplant halves. It is important to use eggplants that are about the same size (two halves per person).

Halve eggplants lengthwise and remove some of the flesh so that they look like small boats.

Cube lamb into 2-inch pieces, sprinkle with salt and pepper, and turn in the oil.

Push wooden skewers through the narrow part of eggplant halves, spear cubed lamb, sprinkle eggplant and meat with parsley and cilantro, then push skewers through the opposite end of the eggplant. The meat should be suspended over the hollowed eggplant so that the juices can collect there.

Brush the eggplant boats with oil and grill under the broiler until the meat is done.

Serve with rice and whole herbs such as tarragon or thyme.

Lamb with Pumpkin

BARANINA S TIKVOY
Serves 4

1¼ pounds lamb from the leg or shoulder,
  cubed in 2-inch pieces
3–4 tablespoons butter
2 pounds pumpkin meat, cubed
½ cup chopped onions
salt, pepper
½ pound tomatoes, halved
1 bunch parsley, chopped

Brown meat on all sides in butter. Cover with water and braise for 15 minutes.

Sauté pumpkin with onions in butter and add to meat.

Season with salt and pepper. Preheat oven at 375°F.

Add tomatoes, cover, and braise in a 375°F oven 1 hour until done.

Sprinkle with parsley and serve with rice.

Stuffed Breast of Lamb

BARANYA GRUDINKA FARSHIROVANNAYA
Serves 4

---

2 ounces bacon (2 strips)
2 medium onions, sliced in rings
1 pound lamb's or calf's liver, sliced
1 cup buckwheat groats
salt, pepper
2 tablespoons butter
1 hard-boiled egg, chopped
2 pounds breast of lamb
4 tablespoons oil

Dice bacon and sauté with onion rings. Add liver to bacon and onions and continue to sauté for approximately 5 minutes. Let cool and run through meat grinder.

Bring 2 cups water to a boil with a pinch of salt. Stir in the buckwheat groats. Reduce heat and cook 20 minutes. Stir in butter. Let cool and stir into the liver mixture.

Season with salt and pepper and add the hard-boiled egg.

Rinse and dry the breast of lamb and, using a sharp knife, cut a deep pocket along the bone. Stuff with the prepared mixture and secure closed with twine or skewers. Sprinkle with salt and pepper and rub with oil.

Bake in a 375°F oven for approximately 2 hours. Baste frequently with pan juices. Should the meat brown too quickly, add a small amount of water or broth.

Slice the finished roast, remove twine, moisten with pan juices, and serve with either rice or potatoes and vegetables.

Breast of lamb can also be stuffed with a rice filling: Mix 2½ cups cooked rice with 2 beaten eggs, 2 chopped onions sautéed in butter, chopped parsley, salt, and pepper, and proceed as with buckwheat/liver filling.

Roast Leg of Lamb

BARANINA PO DOMASHNEMU
Serves 4–6

---

3 pounds leg of lamb
salt, pepper
6–7 cloves garlic
½ cup butter
6 medium potatoes, peeled, cut in half, cooked
  in water, and drained
2–3 apples, peeled, cored, and quartered
1 cup whole, cooked cranberries

Rinse and dry leg of lamb. Rub with salt and pepper and spike all over with slivers of garlic.

Melt butter in roasting pan. Add leg of lamb and roast in a 475°F oven for approximately 20 minutes. Baste occasionally with pan juices.

Add potatoes and apples to the leg of lamb, reduce temperature to 375°F, and continue roasting another 45 minutes until done.

Arrange meat, potatoes, and apples on a serving dish. Moisten with pan juices and serve with cranberries.

Roast Leg of Lamb ▷

Hunter's Shashlik

OKHOTNICHY SHASHLIK
Serves 4

1¹/₂ pounds lamb from the leg or shoulder
salt, pepper
¹/₂ pound mushrooms
4 bell peppers (red, green, yellow, or any
    combination)
4 tablespoons oil

Cut meat into 2-inch cubes and season with salt and pepper.

Clean mushrooms and remove stems. (Use only the heads.)

Rinse bell peppers, remove seeds, and cut into cubes the same size as the lamb. Thread peppers, meat, and mushrooms alternately onto four skewers, brush with oil, and broil or grill. Serve with rice.

Lamb Croquettes

BARANY FRIKADELI
Serves 4

1¹/₄ pounds lamb from the leg, shoulder, or
    breast, cut into pieces
1 medium potato, peeled
4 cloves garlic, minced
salt, pepper
¹/₂ teaspoon paprika
1 egg
1–2 tablespoons mustard
2 tablespoons flour
6 tablespoons butter

Run lamb and raw potato through meat grinder. Stir in garlic, salt, pepper, and paprika. Run again through meat grinder.

Beat egg into mixture and add cold water to make a smooth, moist (but not watery) mixture.

Moisten hands and shape small patties. Brush on a thin coating of mustard and dredge in flour.

Sauté in hot butter until desired doneness and serve with tomato sauce, rice, or potatoes.

Shashlik Platter ▷

Lamb Stew

BARANINA TUSHONAYA
Serves 4

1 pound lamb from the leg or shoulder
3 tablespoons oil
4 medium onions, chopped
1 pound ripe, juicy tomatoes
3 medium potatoes, peeled and sliced
$\frac{1}{2}$ bunch parsley, chopped
$\frac{1}{2}$ bunch basil, chopped
$\frac{1}{2}$ bunch cilantro, chopped
4–5 cloves garlic, finely chopped
1 small hot pepper, cut into strips
salt

Cut lamb into small pieces and brown in hot oil.

Add onions and sauté along with meat. Blanch tomatoes for 2 minutes in boiling water. Then peel and dice.

Add tomatoes and potatoes to meat. Braise covered a good hour until done.

Five minutes before the end of cooking time, stir in herbs, garlic, and hot pepper. Season with salt.

Lamb Stew with Fruit

BARANINA TUSHONAYA S FRUKTAMI
Serves 4

$1\frac{1}{4}$ pounds lamb from the leg or shoulder
2 medium onions, chopped
5 tablespoons butter
3 apples, peeled, cored, and quartered
$\frac{1}{4}$ pound prunes, pits removed
1 tablespoon flour
2 tablespoons tomato paste
beef broth (small amount)
salt, pepper
sugar

Cube lamb into medium-sized pieces and brown in a pot with onions. Cover with water. Braise for 20 minutes.

Add apples and prunes. Braise 40 minutes longer.

Make a light roux with butter and flour. Add tomato paste and 1–2 tablespoons broth. Stir until smooth and use to thicken stew. Season with salt, pepper, and sugar. Simmer until meat is tender. Serve with rice.

One or two quinces can be used instead of prunes: Peel, remove seeds, and cube. When using quinces, season with fresh parsley.

Lamb Stew with a Variety of Vegetables

BARANINA S OVOSHCHAMY V GORSHOCHKE
Serves 4–5

1 pound lamb from the leg or shoulder, cubed
$\frac{1}{2}$ cup butter
3 medium potatoes, peeled and sliced
1 carrot, sliced
2 medium onions, finely chopped
1 small zucchini, diced
1 small eggplant, peeled and diced
2 tablespoons tomato paste
$\frac{1}{2}$ cauliflower, cut into florets
1 small bell pepper, cut into strips
10–20 green beans, cut in pieces
salt
2 tomatoes, sliced
3–4 cloves garlic, crushed
1 bunch dill, chopped
1 bunch parsley, chopped

Brown lamb on all sides in butter. Cover with boiling water and stew for 20 minutes. Sauté potatoes, carrot, and onions in butter and add to meat.

Sauté zucchini and eggplant for a few minutes in butter and add to the stew. Simmer 10 minutes longer. Stir in tomato paste, add cauliflower, bell-pepper, and green beans. Return to boil and season with salt.

Cover stew with tomato slices. Stir in garlic and sprinkle with herbs. Cover and cook in a 400°F oven for an additional 40 minutes.

Lamb with Celery

BARANINA S SELDEREEM

Serves 4

1¼ pounds lamb from the leg or shoulder
½ cup butter
1–2 medium onions, chopped
4 stalks celery, diced
salt, pepper
1 bunch cilantro, chopped
2 egg yolks
juice of 2 lemons
celery leaves, chopped

Cube lamb into bite-sized pieces and brown on all sides in 4 tablespoons butter. Sauté onions in 2 tablespoons butter. Sauté celery with the onions.

Put the browned lamb into a pot, reserving the pan juices. Add the onion-celery mixture, season with salt, pepper, and cilantro, and cover with boiling water.

Cover pot tightly and stew over low heat until meat is tender, about 1 hour. When meat is done, remove to serving platter.

In the meantime, prepare sauce: Melt remaining 2 tablespoons butter, beat in egg yolks, lemon juice, and pan juices from browning the lamb. Stir well and heat. Pour sauce over the meat and sprinkle with chopped celery leaves if desired. Serve with rice.

Lamb Dumplings

BARANY FRIKADELI

Serves 4

---

1 pound soup bones
1 carrot, sliced
1 medium onion, chopped
1 knob celeriac, peeled and chopped
salt, pepper
bay leaf
1 pound lamb from the leg or shoulder
2 eggs
5 tablespoons semolina
½ cup butter
1 bunch parsley, chopped

Prepare a broth using soup bones, vegetables, salt, pepper, and bay leaf. Strain.

Cut lamb into pieces and run twice through a meat grinder. Add eggs and semolina and stir until the mixture is smooth. Season with salt and pepper.

Moisten hands and shape dumplings the size of eggs. Put a small piece of cold butter in the middle of each dumpling and make sure it is covered all over with the meat mixture.

Cook dumplings in simmering broth until they rise to the surface. Remove with a slotted spoon, drain well, and sprinkle with parsley. Serve with tomato sauce and boiled or mashed potatoes.

Pilaf

PLOF

Serves 4

Pilaf is one of the best known and loved dishes of central Asia (Uzbekistan, Turkmenistan, Tadzhikistan, Azerbaijan, Kirghizia). A special meal with family and friends, whether it is a wedding feast or a funeral dinner, is unthinkable without pilaf. But pilaf is every bit as welcome at the everyday table. It can be prepared in many ways.

TRADITIONAL INGREDIENTS

Lamb, rice, onions, carrots, raisins, dried apricots, red bell peppers, and barberries (mirabelle plums may be substituted for barberries) are the traditional ingredients. In many areas, pheasant, partridge, or chicken is used in place of lamb. Wheat or dried lentils may be used instead of rice.

TRADITIONAL PREPARATION

Heat oil, sauté meat and vegetables, add liquid and rice, and braise till done.

Butter or clarified butter is used only if rice is cooked separately.

Pilaf should be cooked in a heavy, cast-iron pot with a curved bottom. Woks are also suitable.

The oil must be very hot, but not so hot that it burns. The temperature is just right when salt crystals pop in the oil. Meat should be cut into ¹/₂-inch cubes. Slice the onions in very thin rings and the carrot into thin strips.

To begin, brown meat on all sides. Add onions and carrots, let brown, add hot water, and season with salt and pepper. After 10–15 minutes, add rice. The water should be about ¹/₂ inch above the rice. The amount of water depends on the quality of the rice and diameter of the pot. As a general rule, there should be 1 quart of water to 2 cups rice.

Cover the pot tightly and steam pilaf over low heat. Do not stir. If the rice is not tender after 25 minutes, sprinkle a little more boiling water over it through a slotted spoon, and make a hole down the middle, using a cooking spoon or long knife, so that the steam can rise from bottom to top.

When ready the pilaf should be grainy and moist but not mushy.

To serve, invert the pilaf on a large serving dish so that the meat and the vegetables are on top. Serve with a green salad.

Pilaf ▷

Uzbek Pilaf

UZBEKSKY PLOF

Serves 6

1¼ pounds lamb from the leg or shoulder,
    cubed
4 medium onions, chopped
12 carrots, diced
5 cups rice
½ cup oil
salt, pepper

Follow directions for traditional preparation (see recipe, page 85).

Buchara Pilaf

BUKHARSKY PLOF

Serves 6

---

1 pound lamb from the leg or shoulder, cubed
3 medium onions, chopped
5–6 carrots, diced
4 cups rice
¼ pound dried apricots or raisins
½ cup oil
salt, pepper

Follow directions for traditional preparation (see recipe, page 85).

Azerbaijan Pilaf

AZERBAIDZHANSKY PLOF

Serves 4

---

4 cups rice
4 tablespoons butter
dill, chopped
salt
1¼ pounds lamb or chicken, cubed
½ cup oil
4 medium onions, chopped
juice of ½ lemon
1 teaspoon saffron
2 tablespoons cinnamon
pepper
4 eggs, beaten

In this recipe the rice is cooked separately and when done is mixed with butter, dill, and salt.

In a skillet, sauté meat in oil until light brown, add onion, and then season with lemon juice, saffron, cinnamon, salt, and pepper. Braise a good hour until tender. Transfer to ovenproof dish. Add eggs to meat, combine with prepared rice, brown lightly in the oven, and serve.

Chicken with Pilaf

PLOF S KURITSEY

Serves 4

---

1 oven-ready chicken, whole
salt, pepper
several pinches of cinnamon
½ pound sweet chestnuts
1 medium onion, chopped
½ cup butter
¾ pound mirabelle plums (fresh or canned)
½ cup shelled almonds
2–3 cloves garlic, minced
¾ cup pomegranate juice (available in health
    food stores)
¾ pound rice
½ teaspoon saffron
watercress leaves
mint leaves

Rinse chicken and rub cavity with a mixture of salt, pepper, and cinnamon.

Cut an X in the chestnuts and bake in a 350°F oven until the shells open. Peel. Cook 15–20 minutes in water until soft. Chop and sauté with onions in butter. Remove pits from plums and add to chestnuts.

Chop almonds coarsely and mix with garlic. Add to chestnuts and cook for 5 minutes more, mixing well. Stuff the chicken with this mixture, stitch closed, and brush with melted butter. Roast 1 hour in a 375°F oven, basting several times with pomegranate juice.

Cook rice separately with saffron. Arrange chicken and rice on a serving dish and garnish with cress and mint leaves.

Cooked Suckling Pig with Meat Stuffing

VARYONNY FARSHIROVANNY
POROSYONOK
Serves 10

1 suckling pig, boned (bones reserved)
2 medium onions, chopped
2 tablespoons butter
6 slices stale white bread
1 cup milk
1/2 pound bacon, diced
1 bunch parsley, chopped
1 1/4 pounds veal, rump, or eye round, ground
6 eggs
salt, pepper
1/2 teaspoon nutmeg
1/2 pound cooked ham (or smoked tongue), diced
soup greens

Order suckling pig ahead of time. Have the butcher bone it. Rinse thoroughly. Dry.

For the stuffing: Sauté onions in 1 tablespoon butter until light brown. Soak white bread in milk and squeeze well. Mix onions, bread, bacon, and parsley well with the ground veal. Add 2 eggs and season with salt, pepper, and nutmeg. Prepare two omelets using remaining 4 eggs.

Stuff pig with meat mixture, layer with diced ham (or tongue), and top with the omelets.

Stitch closed, rub with salt, wrap in a large cotton or linen cloth, and tie together.

Place two wooden sticks along the edge of a large pot, and suspend the wrapped pig from the sticks with twine in such a way that the pig does not touch the bottom of the pot.

Add enough water to cover. Add soup greens, pig backbone, ribs, and innards, salt, and pepper. Cook in simmering water for approximately 2 hours. Drain.

Serve hot or cold.

Roast Suckling Pig

POROSYONOK FARSHIROVANNY
KISLOY KAPUSTOY
Serves 8

1 small suckling pig (approximately 9 pounds) with innards
salt, pepper
4 medium onions, chopped
4 tablespoons butter
3–4 pounds sauerkraut, rinsed
6 hard-boiled eggs
1 bunch parsley
1 bunch dill
garlic to taste, crushed
4 tablespoons oil
1 cup sour cream

Have the butcher bone suckling pig. Rinse thoroughly. Dry. Salt and pepper the body cavity generously.

For the stuffing: Sauté onions in 1 tablespoon butter. Thoroughly rinse the liver, heart, kidneys, and lung. Cut into small pieces and brown with the onions. Let cool and run everything through a meat grinder together. Squeeze sauerkraut and braise in butter; add innards. Chop eggs and herbs, stir into the mixture, season with salt and pepper, and add crushed garlic.

Stuff pig with sauerkraut stuffing and stitch closed. Rub the outside with salt and brush with oil and sour cream.

Place the pig, belly side down, on a roasting pan rack. Roast in a 375°F oven for 2 hours until

cooked and crisp. Baste frequently with pan juices.

Serve roast suckling pig with boiled potatoes, a variety of vegetables, and garlic sauce (see recipe, page 156).

Roast Pork with Prunes

SVINOYE ZHARKOYE S SOUSOM
IZ CHERNOSLIVA
Serves 4

2 pounds pork roast, loin preferably
salt
3 tablespoons bacon fat
1 tablespoon vinegar
1 bay leaf
5 peppercorns
½ pound prunes, pits removed
6 tablespoons bread crumbs
1 tablespoon butter
1½ teaspoons sugar
1 tablespoon cinnamon

Rinse and pat meat dry. Rub with salt and brown well on all sides in hot bacon fat.

Add 1 cup water, season with vinegar, bay leaf, and peppercorns. Braise the roast, covered, for 1½ hours.

In the meantime, cover the prunes with water, cook until soft, and press through a sieve or run through a food processor. Sauté bread crumbs lightly in butter and mix with the prune purée. Add sugar and cinnamon.

Transfer the cooked meat from the pot to a serving dish and keep warm.

Pour the braising juices through a sieve into the prune puree, stir well, and bring to a boil. Pour prune sauce over sliced roast and serve with boiled or roasted potatoes.

◁ *Roast Pork with Prunes*

Ham Roulade

RULYETY IZ OKOROKA ILI VETCHINY
Serves 4

2 medium onions, chopped
1 tablespoon butter
8 slices cooked ham (very thinly sliced)
2 medium pickled cucumbers, cut in strips
2 cooked carrots, cut in strips
2 slices black bread, cut in strips
4 tablespoons flour
¼ cup cooking oil
2 cups broth
½ cup sour cream
salt, pepper

Sauté onions in butter.

Cover each slice of ham with 1–2 strips cucumber, carrot, bread, and onions. Roll together and tie with twine or fasten with small skewers.

Dredge the ham rolls in flour and brown on all sides in hot oil.

Add broth, stir, and let simmer for approximately 10 minutes.

Add sour cream and let steep for a few more minutes.

Season with salt and pepper.

Before serving remove twine or skewers, arrange the roulades on a serving dish, and cover with sauce.

Serve with mashed or boiled potatoes.

Ham Roulade ▷

Innards

BLYUDA IZ SUBPRODUKTOV

In recording all aspects of classic Russian cuisine as I know it, I am well aware that the chapter dealing with innards—so popular in Russian cooking—might provoke negative reactions and perhaps even turn a few readers away momentarily. If that is the case, I apologize to my readers. Nothing could be further from my intentions.

According to a sixteenth-century manual on housekeeping, a good housewife, or to be precise, a good cook, never throws anything away. Because we Russians respect the wisdom of our forebears, and allow no waste in our kitchens, we have invented some particularly delicious recipes using innards. In fact, no banquet is complete without them. They were, and are, popular with every stratum of society. In times past there were special, always overcrowded, inns in which, for a set price, one could eat as much as one wanted. The menus (*kartki*) consisted primarily of innards. The tables were jammed with coachmen and the nouveau riche as well as with exacting gourmets.

Liver, kidneys, heart, sweetbread, and brains, which are also popular in the West, are not the only innards we prepare in a variety of imaginative ways. We also stuff stomachs with groats, mushrooms, bacon, or eggs; we boil or roast tripe as well as the stomachs of beef or lamb with vegetables and onions; we prepare delicious dishes of lungs; we even stuff intestines to make our famous *Nyanya*. (For those who might be put off, remember that intestines are used as casings for all sausage!)

In addition, numerous recipes using giblets play an important part in Russian cuisine. Hors d'oeuvres and vol-au-vents made with chicken, goose, or turkey liver are always a great success with my guests, even those who tell me they do not eat innards. Why ignore these delicious rarities?

◁ *Village on Lake Baikal*

Stuffed Beef Tongue

FARSHIROVANNY YAZIK
Serves 6–8

1 beef tongue
1 bunch soup greens, chopped
salt
2 slices white bread
1/2 cup milk
1 medium onion, chopped
1 tablespoon butter
1 egg
1 bunch parsley, chopped
pepper

Wash beef tongue and submerge in cold water. Add soup greens and simmer until soft—about 1 hour. Do not add salt until the tongue is almost done.

Plunge tongue into cold water, then peel skin off. Slice the underside of the tongue lengthwise and hollow it out. Put this meat through grinder.

Soak bread in milk. Squeeze dry.

Sauté onion in butter.

Thoroughly mix ground tongue meat, bread, onion, egg, and parsley. Season with salt and pepper.

Fill the tongue with this mixture, wrap with twine, and fasten.

Simmer the stuffed tongue for 10 minutes in its own broth. Remove twine and slice.

This dish can be served cold or hot (with Madeira sauce, for example: see recipe, page 149). As a variation, the sliced tongue can be allowed to cool and then covered with aspic.

Stuffed Beef Stomach

FARSHIROVANNY GOVYAZHI ZHELUDOK
Serves 6–8

1 small beef stomach, about 2 pounds
1 bunch soup greens

STUFFING FOR STOMACH

3–4 medium onions, chopped
2 tablespoons butter
5–7 slices white bread, diced
2 pounds cooked ham, diced small
salt, pepper
nutmeg
ginger

Rinse and dry stomach thoroughly. To prepare stuffing, sauté onions in 1 tablespoon butter. Remove onions and sauté bread in same butter

Mix ham well with onions and bread. Season with salt, pepper, nutmeg, and ginger.

Fill the stomach with this mixture and stitch closed. Simmer with soup greens in salted water until done, approximately 1 hour.

Remove stomach from broth, coat with 1 tablespoon melted butter, and brown in a 400°F oven for 20 minutes. Serve with sautéed potatoes.

If the stomach is large, either increase the amount of filling, or use only part of the stomach and stitch closed all the openings.

Pig's Stomach with Potato Stuffing

FARSHINOVANNY SVINOY ZHELUDOK

Serves 8–10

15 medium potatoes, peeled and grated
2 cups milk
2 medium onions, minced
3 tablespoons butter
approximately ³⁄₄ pound bacon, diced
salt, pepper
2 bay leaves, ground
1 pig's stomach

Squeeze liquid out of grated potatoes. Cover with hot milk. Sauté onions in butter, add bacon, and sauté until light brown. Mix onions and bacon well with the potatoes. Season with salt, pepper, and bay leaves.

Carefully wash and dry the stomach, stuff, and stitch closed.

Place in roasting pan and add a little butter if needed. Roast in a 350°F oven for 1 hour. Baste frequently with pan drippings. Add a tablespoon of water when necessary to maintain moisture around the meat.

Before serving, remove twine, slice, and serve. A green salad goes well with this dish.

Liver Shashlik

SHASHLIK IZ PECHENI

Serves 3–4

1 pound liver (calf, pork, or lamb), cut in 1-inch cubes
¹⁄₄ pound bacon, diced
2–3 medium onions, quartered or cut in pieces for skewers
2–3 tablespoons oil
salt, pepper

Thread liver, bacon, and onions alternately onto three or four skewers, brush all over with oil, and sprinkle with pepper. Broil or roast in a hot oven at 450°F until done, about 5 minutes on each side.

About 2 minutes before the end of the cooking time, sprinkle the liver with salty water (¹⁄₂ teaspoon salt to ¹⁄₂ cup water).

Serve with rice and tomato sauce.

Liver Croquettes

FRIKADELI IZ PECHONKI

Serves 3–4

---

1 pound liver (calf or beef)
¼ pound bacon
1 egg
2–3 tablespoons bread crumbs
salt, pepper
2–3 tablespoons flour

Rinse and dry liver. Remove membrane if necessary. Cut into pieces and run through a meat grinder. Dice half the bacon very fine and stir with egg and bread crumbs into ground liver. Mix well and season with salt and pepper. Render the rest of the bacon in a frying pan. Drain on absorbent paper.

Shape the liver mixture into patties, dredge with flour, and fry on both sides in bacon fat until crisp.

Sprinkle cooked bacon over croquettes. Serve with mashed potatoes.

Liver Pancakes

OLADYI IZ PECHENI

Serves 4

---

1 pound liver (calf or beef)
milk
½ small white cabbage
4 tablespoons flour
2 eggs, separated
¼ pound grated Vermont cheddar or Gruyère
  cheese
5 tablespoons sour cream
salt
4 tablespoons butter

Cover liver with milk and let stand for approximately 20 minutes. Remove from milk, dry, and remove membrane if necessary.

Cut cabbage into pieces, combine with liver,

◁ *Liver Pancakes*

and run through meat grinder. Add flour, egg yolks, grated cheese, and sour cream. Stir well and season with salt. If the mixture is too dry, add a small amount of milk.

Beat egg whites until stiff and fold into the liver mixture.

Drop the mixture from a spoon into hot butter and cook on both sides until golden brown.

Serve with sour cream or moisten with melted butter.

Sautéed Calf's Liver with Lung Sauce

ZHARKOYE IZ TELYACHYEI PECHONKI
POD SOUSOM IZ LYOKHKIKH

Serves 8

1¼ pounds calf's liver
milk
salt, pepper
flour for dredging
2–3 tablespoons butter
1 bunch dill, chopped

SAUCE

1¼ pounds calf's lung
1 bunch soup greens
1 medium onion, peeled
2 bay leaves
peppercorns
salt
5 hard-boiled eggs, chopped
3–5 scallions, thinly sliced
1 tablespoon flour
1 tablespoon butter
1½ cups beef broth
½ cup sour cream

Prepare sauce first. Place rinsed lung, soup greens, whole onion, bay leaves, peppercorns, and salt in a pot. Cover with water and cook 30 minutes until tender. Drain lung and slice into noodle-sized strips. Mix with eggs and scallions.

Sauté flour in butter, dilute with broth, and simmer until thick.

Add lung mixture and sour cream and season with salt.

Soak liver in milk for 20–30 minutes. Dry and remove membrane if necessary.

Cut liver into small pieces, season with salt and pepper, dredge with flour, and brown in hot butter. Transfer to a bowl, cover with hot lung sauce, and sprinkle with dill.

Serve with boiled or mashed potatoes.

Braised Calf's Liver in Clove Sauce

TELYACHYA PECHONKA POD
GVOZDICHNYM SOUSOM

Serves 3–4

---

1 pound calf's liver
salt, pepper
¼ pound bacon, diced in 1-inch pieces
3 tablespoons flour
1 tablespoon butter
1 cup beef broth
½ cup dry white wine
½ teaspoon ground cloves
½ teaspoon grated lemon peel
2 pinches ground ginger
2 teaspoons sugar

Remove membrane from liver if necessary.

Wash and dry liver and cut into strips. Season with salt and pepper and let stand for 15 minutes.

Dice bacon and render in a frying pan. (Reserve 1 tablespoon bacon and chop very fine.) Reserve fat.

Prepare a roux using 1 tablespoon flour and 1 tablespoon butter. Dilute with the broth and simmer until thick. Add wine, the remaining finely chopped bacon, lemon peel, spices, and sugar. Stir well, bring to a boil, and season to taste.

Dredge liver strips in flour and sauté in bacon fat 3 minutes.

Transfer liver to a serving platter, cover with sauce, and serve with rice or mashed potatoes.

Calf's Liver Pudding

PUDING IZ TELYACHYEI PECHONKI

Serves 4

1½ pounds calf's liver
3–4 tablespoons butter
1 medium onion, chopped
6 slices white bread
1 cup milk
4 eggs, separated
2 tablespoons cognac
1½ tablespoons currants
salt, pepper
nutmeg

SAUCE

1 tablespoon butter
1 tablespoon flour
1 cup broth
½ cup dry white wine
1 tablespoon lemon juice
2 tablespoons raisins
1 teaspoon capers
2–3 teaspoons sugar
salt, pepper

Sauté rinsed and dried calf's liver in butter. Let cool and puree in food processor.

Sauté onion in butter.

Soak white bread in milk and squeeze dry.

Stir onion, bread, egg yolks, cognac, and currants into the liver puree. Season with salt, pepper, and nutmeg. Beat egg whites until stiff and fold carefully into the puree.

Butter an 8-inch mold and fill with the mixture. The mold should be only three-fourths full. Cover tightly, place in a larger pan with water, and steam in a 350°F oven for 1½ hours.

To prepare the sauce, make a roux of butter and flour, add broth and wine, and simmer until thick. Strain, add lemon juice, raisins, capers, and sugar, bring to a boil, and season with salt and pepper.

To serve, invert the pudding on a dish and cover with the sauce.

Serve with rice or mashed potatoes.

Calf's Liver with Mushrooms

TELYACHYA PECHONKA S SHAMPINONAMI

Serves 4

1½ pounds calf's liver
salt, pepper
2 tablespoons flour
½ cup butter
½ pound mushrooms, thinly sliced
1½ cups beef broth
½–1 cup sour cream

Wash and dry liver and cut into strips. Season with salt and pepper, dredge with 1 tablespoon flour, and sauté quickly in 2 tablespoons hot butter. Sauté mushrooms briefly in 1 tablespoon butter and salt lightly.

Prepare a roux with 1 tablespoon butter and 1 tablespoon flour. Add broth, stir until smooth, and bring to a boil. Reduce heat to avoid curdling and add sour cream. Do not allow to boil. Season the sauce with salt and pepper.

Preheat oven at 375°F. Alternate layers of mushrooms and liver in a casserole, cover with cream sauce, and bake for 20 minutes.

Serve with boiled or mashed potatoes.

Calf's Brain Pudding

PUDING IZ TELYACHYKH MOSGOV

Serves 4

---

4 halves of calf's brains
salt
1 tablespoon vinegar
5–6 eggs, separated
1 bunch dill, chopped
2 tablespoons butter
white pepper
nutmeg
1–2 tablespoons bread crumbs

Soak brains in water for 2 hours. Drain, remove membrane and small veins. Simmer brains for 10 minutes in salted water with vinegar. Let cool, and puree in food processor. Mix well with egg yolks, dill, and 1 tablespoon soft butter. Season

with salt, pepper, and nutmeg. Beat egg whites until stiff and fold carefully into the mixture.

Butter an 8-inch pudding mold, sprinkle with bread crumbs, and fill with the brain mixture. Steam in a pan with water or steamer, or bake in a 350°F oven, in a pan containing 1–2 inches water, for approximately 20 minutes.

Invert the pudding on a platter and serve with mushroom or crayfish sauce (see recipes, pages 151 and 154).

Deep-Fried Calf's Brain

MOSGI V KLYARE

Serves 4

---

salt
vinegar
1 calf's brain
batter for frying (see recipe, page 206)
oil
1 bunch parsley

Bring salted water and a dash of vinegar to a boil, remove from heat, and immerse calf's brain. Let steep until water is tepid. Rinse brain with fresh water, drain, remove membrane and small veins, and cut into bite-sized pieces. Spear each piece with a fork, dip into batter, and fry in hot oil. Serve with deep-fried parsley. (Fry parsley in hot oil for 3 minutes until crisp. Drain on absorbent paper.)

This is a popular accompaniment to soups (particularly shchi).

Larded Liver

SHPIGOVANNAYA SALOM PECHONKA

Serves 4

1¾ pounds liver (calf or beef)
¼ pound bacon
3 medium onions
3 tablespoons butter
salt, pepper
1 bunch dill, chopped
1 bunch parsley, chopped

Cut rinsed and dried liver into finger-thick slices and lard with thin strips of bacon.

Slice onions into rings and sauté in 2 tablespoons butter. Melt a small amount of butter in a deep skillet or casserole. Alternate layers of liver (sprinkled with salt and pepper) and onion rings. Dot with remaining butter, cover, and braise over low heat for 10–15 minutes.

Sprinkle the finished dish with herbs and serve with sautéed or roasted potatoes.

Calf's Brains au Gratin
MOSGI, ZAPECHONIYE V RAKOVINAKH
Serves 4

2 calf's brains
salt
vinegar
1 medium onion, chopped
2 tablespoons butter
2 egg yolks, mixed with $1/2$–1 cup sour cream
1 bunch parsley, chopped
1 bunch dill, chopped
4 tablespoons bread crumbs
pepper
nutmeg
$1/4$ cup beef broth
cooked cauliflower florets or crayfish for
  garnish

Soak brains, remove membrane and small veins, and wash thoroughly.

Bring salted water and a dash of vinegar to a boil, turn off heat, and let brains steep for about 10 minutes. Drain and cut into strips.

Sauté onion in 1 tablespoon butter. Cool and mix thoroughly with strips of brain, egg yolk and sour cream mixture, herbs, and 3 tablespoons bread crumbs. If the mixture is too dry, stir in a small amount of broth.

Season with salt, pepper, and nutmeg and pour into scallop molds. Sprinkle with remaining bread crumbs and dot with remaining butter. Let brown in a 400°F oven for about 15 minutes.

Add cauliflower florets or crayfish for the last 5 minutes of cooking time. Serve as a warm hors d'oeuvre.

◁ *Calf's Brains au Gratin*

Calf's Brains with Crabmeat Sauce

MOSGI POD RAKOVYM SOUSOM

Serves 4

2 calf's brains
salt, pepper
vinegar
1 tablespoon flour
2 tablespoons butter
1½ cups heavy cream
½ pound mushrooms, sliced
¼ pound crabmeat
20 asparagus stalks, cooked and diced
1 bunch parsley, chopped
1 bunch dill, chopped
nutmeg

Soak brains, remove membrane and small veins, rinse, and simmer in salted water with a dash of vinegar for approximately 10 minutes. Drain.

In the meantime, prepare the sauce: Cook flour lightly in 1 tablespoon butter, gradually add cream, stir well, and bring to a boil. Cook mushrooms in butter, add crabmeat and asparagus, add to sauce, and return to a boil. Season with herbs, salt, pepper, and nutmeg. Cut brain into strips and steep for several minutes in the sauce. Serve with rice.

Braised Udder with Apples and Rice

TUSHONOYE VIMYA S RISOM I YABLOKAMI

Serves 4

1½–1¾ pounds udder
2 carrots, chopped
2 medium onions, chopped
2 parsley roots, chopped
2 bay leaves
1 teaspoon sugar
salt, pepper
2 tablespoons butter
1 cup rice
2 large apples, peeled and grated

Wash udder thoroughly and soak for 2–3 hours in cold water. Wash again, cover with boiling water, and simmer for approximately 20 minutes.

Add vegetables, bay leaves, sugar, salt, and pepper. Cover and simmer over low heat until tender. Remove udder from broth and cut into cubes. Sauté in butter for 10 minutes, then add rice, and let rice cook briefly. Add enough udder broth to cover the rice. Cover and steam over low heat, adding more broth if necessary. Mix apples into the rice and season with salt and pepper.

Kidneys au Gratin

POCHKI ZAPCHONIYE GRIBAMI I VECHINOY

Serves 4

1 pound kidneys (calf or beef)
¼ cup vinegar
6 tablespoons butter
¼ pound cooked ham
¼ pound cooked tongue
¾ cup mushrooms, thinly sliced
1 tablespoon flour
1 cup beef broth
2 tablespoons tomato paste
salt, pepper
1 cup sour cream
¼ cup grated cheese
1 bunch parsley, chopped
1 bunch dill, chopped

Slice kidneys lengthwise and soak for 2 hours in cold water with vinegar. Rinse. Remove membrane and fat and trim. Blanch in boiling water twice, rinse with cold water, dry, and cut into noodle-sized strips. Sauté quickly in 2 tablespoons hot butter. (If necessary, divide into several batches so that there is only one layer in the skillet.) Cut ham and tongue into small strips and brown briefly in butter. Last, sauté mushrooms.

Prepare a roux of 1 tablespoon flour and 1 tablespoon butter, add broth, and stir until smooth. Simmer. Add tomato paste, stir well, and season with salt and pepper. At the last minute stir in the sour cream. Do not boil.

Preheat oven to 400°F. Fill an ovenproof mold with one layer each of kidney, ham, tongue, and mushrooms, and pour sauce over the top.

Sprinkle with grated cheese and dot with 1 tablespoon butter. Bake in 400°F oven until the top is golden brown and crusty. To serve, moisten with remaining melted butter and sprinkle with herbs.

Serve with roasted potatoes and salad.

Braised Heart
TUSHONOYE SERTSE
Serves 4

1¼ pounds beef heart
¼ pound smoked pork belly
2–3 tablespoons butter
1 medium onion, chopped
1 carrot, chopped
1 bunch parsley, chopped
1 cup beef broth
2 tablespoons tomato paste
salt, pepper
1 tablespoon flour
½ cup sour cream

Cut rinsed and dried heart into ½-inch slices and lard with thin strips of pork belly. Sauté on both sides in a little butter. Add onion, carrot, and parsley, and cook briefly. Stir in ½ cup broth and tomato paste. Season with salt and pepper. Braise over low heat 15 minutes until heart is tender.

Prepare a light roux with flour and 1 tablespoon butter, add remaining broth, stir until smooth, and use this to thicken the stew.

Turn heat off and stir in sour cream, season again with salt and pepper, and let steep for 5–10 minutes.

Serve with boiled or fried potatoes.

Kidneys with Zucchini or Eggplant
POCHKI S KABACHKAMI ILI BAKLAZHANAMI
Serves 4

---

1 pound calf's kidneys
¼ cup wine vinegar
1 medium onion, sliced into rings
3–4 tablespoons oil
½ pound zucchini or eggplant, peeled and sliced
½ pound wild mushrooms or white mushrooms, thinly sliced
1 pound tomatoes, sliced
salt, pepper
butter
1 bunch dill, chopped
1 bunch parsley, chopped

Cut kidneys in half lengthwise and soak for 2 hours in cold water mixed with vinegar. Blanch in boiling water twice. Rinse. Drain.

Meanwhile, prepare vegetables: First, sauté onion rings in 1 tablespoon oil. Add zucchini or eggplant to onions. In another pan briefly braise mushrooms in 1 tablespoon oil.

Brush an ovenproof casserole dish with 1 teaspoon oil and cover the bottom with half the tomato slices. Add mushrooms and vegetables and cover with remaining tomatoes. Carefully season each layer with salt and pepper.

Dot with butter and braise in a 375°F oven for 25–30 minutes. Shortly before the end of the cooking time, dry the kidneys, remove membrane and fat, trim, and cut into small pieces. Season with salt and pepper and cook quickly in remaining hot oil. (There should never be more than a single layer of kidneys in the skillet. If necessary, brown in several batches.)

To serve, spread kidneys on top of vegetables, sprinkle with herbs, and serve with sautéed potatoes.

Poultry and Game

BLYUDA IZ DICHI

In the category of game we include all the creatures living in our immense forests, steppes, and moors. Wildfowl, of which we have more than 30 kinds, are known as "white game." All other animals hunted for food—such as hare, doe, stag, wild boar, bear, etc.—are called "red game." Domestic fowl—chicken, goose, duck, and turkey—are usually referred to as poultry.

Game and poultry are invariably associated with festive occasions, since, according to ancient tradition, they are served only on holidays—goose at Christmas, turkey at weddings, chicken on birthdays.

Roasted, braised, and grilled—marinated, larded, stuffed—Russian recipes for venison and poultry are legion. Many dishes evoke the names of people. For example, the German ambassador to the court of Tsar Alexander I told the following story about our Chicken Cutlets Pozharsky (see recipe, page 117).

When Alexander's coach broke down in the small town of Ostashkov during a journey, the tsar showed up unexpectedly for breakfast. Traditionally, veal cutlet was served with breakfast. Pozharsky, the innkeeper of the town, was in great distress, since there was no veal to be found on such short notice. Luckily, he had an inventive wife who suggested that he use chicken instead and disguise their subterfuge with a coating of bread crumbs. The tsar was so delighted with the crisp, juicy "veal" cutlet, he honored the capable innkeeper with a medal.

Terrified that their deception would be discovered, the innkeeper and his wife confessed the truth. Grateful for the pleasure the meal had given him, the tsar generously forgave them, and from then on "Pozharsky Cutlet" was always served to the tsar. Pozharsky dubbed himself "supplier to the court of his majesty the tsar," became rich, and opened a second restaurant in another town.

◁ *A River in Central Russia*

Turkey with Stuffing
FARSHIROVANNAYA INDEYKA
Serves 6–8

1 oven-ready turkey, about 12 pounds
salt, pepper
1/2–3/4 cup butter, softened

Rinse and dry turkey. Rub inside and out generously with salt and pepper. Stuff lightly with any one of the stuffings listed below and stitch closed.

Brush with butter and roast in the oven for approximately 2–3 hours, depending on size (about 20 minutes per pound). Baste frequently with pan juices, adding broth or water, a spoonful at a time, if necessary.

Serve roast turkey with its own pan juices, or deglaze the roasting pan with water or chicken broth and season with heavy cream, sour cream, or Madeira.

Serve with rice or potatoes, your choice of vegetables, and salad.

Stuffed turkey may also be braised. Place turkey on a bed of finely cut root vegetables (carrots, celery, parsley root, leek), onion rings, and 2–3 crumbled bay leaves.

Fill pot with boiling water until it covers half the turkey. Season with salt and pepper. Cover and braise for 1 1/2–2 hours. When it is done it may be browned, uncovered, under the broiler for a few minutes. Serve with a dark sauce (see recipe, page 147) made with liquid from braising.

CALF'S LIVER AND RAISIN STUFFING

1/4 pound bacon, diced
1 pound calf's liver, rinsed and cut in small
   pieces
pepper
1 bay leaf, ground
2 slices white bread
1 cup milk
3 eggs
1/4 cup raisins
salt

Sauté bacon. In skillet, add liver and cook 2 minutes. Season with pepper and ground bay leaf.

Let cool and run through meat grinder. Soak bread in milk and squeeze dry. Add bread, eggs, and raisins to liver mixture. Season with salt and pepper.

One-quarter pound diced calf's tongue and thinly sliced truffles braised in Madeira may be used instead of raisins.

TURKEY GIBLETS STUFFING

2 medium onions, minced
4 tablespoons butter
turkey giblets, rinsed, dried, and cut in small
    pieces
1 cup rice
½ cup raisins
1 small bunch parsley, chopped
salt, pepper

Sauté onions in butter. Add giblets to onions and continue cooking over low heat for 15 minutes.

Add rinsed rice and sauté until transparent. Cover with boiling water and braise over low heat until rice is tender and all the liquid has been absorbed. Stir in raisins and parsley. Season with salt and pepper.

RICE STUFFING

½ cup rice
½ cup dried apricots
½ cup raisins
4 tablespoons butter
½ cup almonds, chopped
1 small bunch parsley, chopped
salt
several pinches each of ground cloves and
    cinnamon

Simmer rinsed rice in water. Do not allow it to get too soft. (Check after 15 minutes; it should be al dente). Drain rice. Chop apricots and braise with raisins in butter. Mix with almonds, stir into rice, and season with parsley and spices.

CALF'S LIVER AND WALNUT STUFFING

1 pound calf's liver, rinsed, dried, and cut in
    small pieces
2–3 tablespoons butter
1 pound walnuts, chopped
1 roll or 3 slices of bread, soaked in 2 cups milk
    and squeezed dry
3 eggs
salt, pepper

Cook liver in butter until tender, about 3–5 minutes. Let cool and run through meat grinder. Add walnuts, bread or roll, and eggs. Season with salt and pepper.

Turkey Meat with Apricots
INDEYKA S ABRIKOSAMI
Serves 4

1¾ pounds turkey breast, cut into strips
3–4 tablespoons butter
2 medium onions, chopped
2 tablespoons tomato paste
½ cup dry white wine
salt, pepper
cinnamon
1 tablespoon flour
1 cup chicken broth
½ pound fresh apricots, halved and pitted
2–3 bay leaves
3 cloves garlic, crushed
1 bunch dill, chopped
1 bunch parsley, chopped

Brown turkey strips on all sides in 1 tablespoon butter. Set aside.

In a separate pan, sauté onions in 2 tablespoons butter. Stir in tomato paste and add white wine. Bring to a boil, season with salt, pepper, and cinnamon, and add the turkey. Stir and continue cooking over low heat for approximately 30 minutes.

Prepare a light roux with 1 tablespoon butter and 1 tablespoon flour and the broth. Add apricots and 2–3 bay leaves to the turkey mixture along with the roux. Stir well. Season with salt and pepper and cook an additional 5 minutes.

Shortly before serving, mix in garlic and herbs. Serve with rice and salad.

Turkey Cutlets with Sour Cherry Puree

FILET IZ INDEYKI POD
VISHNOVYM SOUSOM

Serves 4

1³/₄ pounds turkey breast cutlets
salt
¹/₂ cup Madeira
1³/₄ pounds sour cherries
¹/₄ cup sugar
pinch of cinnamon
pinch of cardamom
pinch of nutmeg
pinch of ground cloves
¹/₂ cup butter
1 baguette
pepper

Pound turkey cutlets to tenderize and rub with salt. Cover with Madeira and marinate for 30 minutes. In the meantime, rinse and remove pits from sour cherries. Cook cherries over low heat with sugar and spices for 15 minutes.

Crack approximately 20 cherry pits with a hammer, cover with water, and boil for a few minutes. Strain, discard pits, and add this broth to sour cherries. Add another pinch of cinnamon, cardamom, nutmeg, and cloves and cook until the cherries are the consistency of a thick puree.

Remove meat from marinade, drain, and dry. Sauté cutlets in butter. Add salt and pepper.

Pile the cherry puree in the middle of a serving dish, surround with slices of toasted bread, and arrange sautéed turkey cutlets on the toast.

Stuffed Duck

FARSHIROVANNAYA UTKA

Serves 4

1 oven-ready duck
salt, pepper
¹/₂ teaspoon ground cloves
¹/₄ pound bacon
1 carrot, chopped
1 parsley root, peeled and chopped
1 leek, chopped
1 slice of celeriac, peeled and chopped
2–3 bay leaves
2 tablespoons butter, softened
2 cups chicken broth
1 tablespoon flour
¹/₂ cup Madeira

Rinse and dry duck. Open along the back and remove backbone. Rub duck inside and out with salt, pepper, and ground cloves. Stuff the opening across the back with either of the stuffings listed below and stitch closed. Line a roasting pan with thin slices of bacon. Add vegetables and 2–3 bay leaves and place the duck on top. Brush with butter and roast in a 400°F oven for approximately 1¹/₂ hours. Baste frequently with pan juices. Remove excess fat. When the duck is brown and crisp, remove from pan, add ¹/₂ cup of the broth by the spoonful, and mix well to form the gravy.

Place roast duck on a serving dish and keep warm.

Press the pan juices and vegetables through a sieve or process in a food processor and transfer to a saucepan. Stir flour into 2 tablespoons broth until smooth and thickened. Stir in remaining broth and add to saucepan. Bring to a boil, and season with Madeira. (This sauce is particularly elegant with a few slices of truffles heated in it.)

Carve duck, pour some sauce over it, saving some to pass around at the table, and serve with boiled potatoes and a green salad.

GROUND VEAL STUFFING

2 slices white bread
1 cup milk
1 pound ground veal
1 medium onion, chopped
2 tablespoons butter
6 eggs
salt
nutmeg

Soak white bread in milk, squeeze, and mix with ground veal. Sauté onion in butter, add 4 beaten eggs, and make an omelet. Let cool. Break up omelet and add along with 2 raw eggs to the meat mixture. Stir.

Season with salt and nutmeg.

MUSHROOM AND NOODLE STUFFING

¹/₄ cup dried wild mushrooms
homemade noodles made with ¹/₂ cup flour (see basic recipe, page 206)
1 egg
salt, pepper

Pour boiling water over dried mushrooms to cover and let steep for 1 hour. Rinse carefully and simmer in water until soft. Drain, cut into strips, and mix with cooked noodles and egg. Season with salt and pepper.

Duck with noodle stuffing can also be boiled. Use broth in which mushrooms were cooked, add chopped soup greens, chopped herbs, salt, and pepper. Cover duck with liquid and simmer over low heat for 1¹/₂–2 hours.

Boiled duck is served with a sauce prepared with some of the broth that has been thickened with a light roux and enriched with sour cream.

Stuffed Wild Duck

ZHARENNAYA DIKAYA UTKA
Serves 4

1 oven-ready wild duck
salt
¹/₄ cup raisins
¹/₄ pound dried apricots, chopped
2–3 small onions, chopped
3–4 tablespoons olive oil (or corn, peanut)
4 cloves garlic, crushed
pepper
¹/₂ cup rice
¹/₂ teaspoon saffron
¹/₂ teaspoon paprika

Rinse and dry wild duck and rub inside and out with salt.

For the stuffing, soak raisins and apricots in hot water for 20 minutes. Drain.

Sauté onions, apricots, and raisins in 2 tablespoons oil. Add 3 of the garlic cloves, salt, and pepper, and cook over low heat, covered, for approximately 10 minutes.

Stuff duck with this mixture and stitch closed. Brown duck on all sides in remaining oil. Stir ¹/₂ cup boiling water by the spoonful into pan drippings. Place in a 375°F oven and cook for 50 minutes, basting frequently with pan drippings, until done.

Remove the duck, cover, and keep warm.

Briefly sauté rice in pan with 3 tablespoons drippings. Season with saffron and paprika and cover with 1¹/₂ cup water. Cover pot and cook over low heat until rice is tender and the liquid has been absorbed. Arrange the rice on the sides of a serving platter, place roasted duck in the center, and let everything steep for another 2 minutes. Serve with salad.

Stuffed Wild Duck ▷

Duck with Rutabaga

UTKA S REPOY

Serves 4

1 oven-ready duck
salt, pepper
2 tablespoons butter
2 large onions, chopped
2–3 cups chicken broth
2 pounds rutabaga (or kohlrabi)
1–2 tablespoons sugar
1 cup Malaga wine
2 teaspoons potato flour (if needed)

Rinse and dry duck. Rub inside and out with salt and pepper. Place duck and onions in pan and roast in a 375°F oven for approximately 60–80 minutes. Turn occasionally and baste frequently with pan juices. After it has browned, moisten, a spoonful at a time, with the broth.

In the meantime, peel rutabaga, cut into long slices, cover with water, and cook until soft. Add broth if necessary. Use as little liquid as possible, so that the vegetable is quite dry when it is done.

In a skillet, melt the butter, add 1–2 tablespoons sugar, and brown lightly, stirring constantly. (Do not let the sugar get too dark or it will be bitter!) Add sliced, cooked rutabaga and the onions from the roasting pan, stir well, and let caramelize for several minutes.

Serve roast duck with onions and rutabaga. Remove fat from pan juices, pour juices in a saucepan, add a small amount of broth and Malaga wine, and bring to a boil. Thicken with potato flour if desired. Pour sauce through a strainer and serve separately.

◁ Pressed Chicken Georgian-Style

116

Pressed Chicken Georgian-Style

TSYPLYATA TABAKA

Serves 4

1 oven-ready chicken
salt, pepper
1/2 cup butter
3–5 cloves garlic
5 shelled walnuts

Rinse and dry chicken. Make an incision the entire length of the breast side of the chicken. Spread chicken, with its inside facing down, on a flat surface, preferably between two sheets of wax paper. Flatten with a meat pounder. Rub with salt and pepper.

Melt butter in a pan large enough to accommodate the flattened chicken. Place chicken in the pan, cover with a flat plate to weigh it down, and put a pot filled with water on top of the plate. Brown over medium heat, turn (weigh down again), and repeat for browning the other side. Cook for 1 hour.

Grate garlic and walnuts with a small amount of salt and mix with 1 tablespoon hot water. Shortly before the end of the cooking time, brush chicken with this paste.

Serve with salad.

Roast Chicken Grouse-Style

ZHARENNAYA KURITSA, KAK RYABCHIK

Serves 6

3 young, small, oven-ready chickens (2–3 pounds each)
salt, pepper
2 tablespoons juniper berries, crushed
1/4 pound bacon
2 tablespoons vinegar
1/2 cup butter
3 tablespoons sour cream
2–3 tablespoons bread crumbs

Rinse and dry chickens. Rub vigorously inside and out with salt, pepper, and juniper berries.

Refrigerate for 12–15 hours to allow spices to steep.

Rinse and dry chicken again. Lard chicken with thin strips of bacon and moisten with vinegar.

Melt butter in a large skillet on top of the stove. Brown each chicken on all sides, transfer to roasting pan, and roast in a 350°F oven until done, about 50–60 minutes. Turn repeatedly and baste with pan juices.

Pour sour cream over the roasted chickens and continue browning for a few more minutes. Sprinkle with bread crumbs and let crisp briefly.

Arrange chickens on a serving dish and cover with pan juices. Serve with fresh salad.

Chicken Cutlets Pozharsky

ZNAMENITIYE POZHARSKIYE KOTLYETY

Serves 4

1 oven-ready chicken
¼ pound white bread (approximately 4 slices)
1 cup heavy cream
½ cup butter, softened
salt, pepper
2 eggs
3 tablespoons bread crumbs

Cut rinsed chicken into pieces. Remove meat from bones (save thigh and wing bones). Run chicken through meat grinder.

Soak white bread in cream, squeeze, reserving the cream, and mix with 4 tablespoons butter. Add chicken meat and run mixture through the meat grinder.

Sprinkle with salt and pepper. Add all but a dash of the reserved cream and work into a soft dough.

Moisten hands and form four cutlet-shaped patties. Stick a wing or thigh bone into each so that they look like veal cutlets. (A little meat on and around the bones will keep them from falling out.)

Beat eggs with a dash of cream and turn the patties in the eggs. Dredge patties in coarse bread crumbs and brown in hot butter on both sides. Place the browned patties on an oven-proof serving dish and let them crisp under the broiler for a few minutes.

Serve with vegetables or salad.

Chicken Croquettes "Novomikhailovsky"

NOVOMIKHAILOVSKIYE KURINIYE KOTLYETY

Serves 6–8

4 chicken breasts, boned
½ cup milk
1 cup butter
1½ cups heavy cream
salt, pepper
2 egg yolks
8–10 tablespoons bread crumbs

In the food processor, grind the chicken meat. Add 6 tablespoons milk, ½ cup butter, cream, salt, and pepper. Shape into patties.

Dip patties into egg yolks beaten with 2 tablespoons milk, dredge with crumbs, and sauté in the rest of the butter until they are golden brown.

Serve with vegetables, salad, or rice.

These celebrated patties were first served in 1852 at the St. Petersburg Agriculture Club. The club was located on Mikhailov Street; hence, the name of the dish.

Chicken Kiev

KOTLYETY PO KIEVSKY

Serves 2

1 oven-ready roasting chicken
4 tablespoons butter
2 eggs, beaten
2 tablespoons bread crumbs
salt, pepper
2 tablespoons flour
2 tablespoons oil

Halve chicken. Cut 1 whole fillet with wing joint attached from each half, and cut the tendon between the large and small part of each half. You now have two large pieces with wing bone and two smaller pieces.

Place chicken pieces between two sheets of wax paper or kitchen parchment (leaving bone to stick out) and pound until flat. Place 2 tablespoons of butter on each large slice and place the smaller pieces on top. Pull the edges up and roll the meat into a pear shape.

Put eggs and bread crumbs in two separate bowls.

Season the chicken with salt and pepper, dredge in flour, and dip into eggs and bread crumbs.

Finally, sauté and brown on all sides in hot oil for 3–4 minutes. Roast another 5–10 minutes in a 400°F oven and serve with thin french-fried potatoes and green peas.

Chicken Pudding

PUDING IZ KURITSY

Serves 6

2 oven-ready chickens
salt, pepper
1 cup butter
white bread
2–3 cups milk or heavy cream
approximately ¼ **pound crayfish or lobster**
    meat, chopped
6 eggs, separated
½ teaspoon nutmeg

Rinse and dry chickens. Rub with salt and pepper. Brown in 2 tablespoons butter until done. Let cool. (For ease of preparation, preroasted chickens may also be used.)

Remove bones and run chicken meat through meat grinder. Weigh ground chicken and mix with an equal amount of bread soaked in milk or cream.

Stir in ½ cup softened butter, crayfish meat, and 6 egg yolks. Season with salt, pepper, and

◁ *Chicken Kiev*

nutmeg. Mix well. Whip 6 egg whites until stiff and fold carefully into the chicken mixture.

Carefully butter a large soufflé mold and fill with the mixture. The mold should be filled only three-fourths full.

Place mold in a preheated 375°F oven in a pan with water (the water should come halfway up the sides of the soufflé mold). Cook 1½ hours. Remove from oven. Invert on a platter and serve with béchamel or crayfish (or lobster) sauce. (See recipes, pages 147 and 154.)

Chicken Roulades Stuffed with Mushrooms

KURINIYE RULYETY
FARSHIROVANNIYE GRIBAMI

Serves 3–4

¼ pound wild mushrooms or white mushrooms
3 tablespoons butter
2 tablespoons sour cream
salt
2 ounces white bread (approximately 2 slices)
½ cup milk
1 pound boneless chicken
2 eggs
2 tablespoons flour
2–3 tablespoons bread crumbs

For the stuffing, cut rinsed mushrooms into small pieces and sauté in 1 tablespoon butter.

Stir in sour cream, season with salt, and cook about 15–20 minutes.

Soak white bread in milk, squeeze, and mix with chicken. Run this mixture through a meat grinder.

Stir in 1 egg and season with salt.

Moisten hands and form flat patties. Cover with mushroom mixture and roll up. Dredge roulades in flour, dip in beaten egg, and coat with bread crumbs. Sauté roulades in remaining butter until done and crisp.

Serve with an assortment of vegetables or salads.

Braised Rabbit
with Pumpkin

TUSHONY KROLIK S TIKVOY

Serves 4

1 pound rabbit meat, cut into pieces
salt
1 tablespoon thyme or herbes de Provence
2 medium onions, chopped
2 carrots, chopped
1 parsley root, peeled and chopped
1 slice celeriac, peeled and chopped
2 tablespoons butter
1 pound pumpkin meat, grated
2 tart apples, diced
1 tablespoon flour
1 bunch parsley, chopped
1 bunch dill, chopped

Place meat in a pot and cover with water. Season with salt and thyme (or herbes de Provence), and cook over medium heat until done, about 25–30 minutes.

Sauté onions and root vegetables in butter. Add to cooked rabbit. Add pumpkin and apples.

Stir flour with some cooking liquid in a bowl until smooth. Add to pot and thicken the sauce by simmering for another 10–15 minutes.

Season, garnish with herbs, and serve with potatoes.

◁ *Braised Rabbit with Pumpkin*

Stuffed Venison Fillet

FARSHIROVANNOYE FILE LOSYA
ILI KOSULI

Serves 4–6

¹/₄ pound prunes
1 bunch parsley, chopped
1 pickled cucumber, diced in small pieces
2 pounds deer or stag fillet
salt, pepper
3 tablespoons butter or oil
1 medium onion, chopped
1 parsley root, peeled and chopped
1 cup broth
¹/₄ pound mushrooms, thinly sliced
1 cup sour cream
1 teaspoon potato flour

Soak prunes 30 minutes in water to cover. Drain. Remove pits and cut into small pieces. Mix well with parsley and cucumber.

Rinse and pat meat dry and cut a pocket lengthwise. Rub inside and out with salt and pepper. Spread the filling inside the pocket and wrap the meat with twine.

Brown stuffed fillet in hot butter (or oil) on all sides. Briefly sauté onion and parsley root with the meat. Add broth a little at a time, cover, and braise until tender. Remove the fillet, untie, and keep warm.

Cook mushrooms in the drippings, add sour cream, and thicken with potato flour. Continue cooking 5 minutes, stirring. Season to taste and serve with rice, salad, and optional cranberry sauce.

Stuffed Saddle of Venison

Saddle of venison may be larded and prepared with the same ingredients as the fillet. Make cuts along the backbone and between the ribs and fill with sliced cucumbers and prunes.

Stuffed Saddle of Venison ▷

Shashlik Northern Style

SHASHLIK PO SEVERNOMU
Serves 4–6

2 pounds venison
salt, pepper
1 medium onion, cut into rings
2 bay leaves, crumbled
1 bunch parsley, chopped
1 chili pepper, finely chopped
¼ cup cognac
approximately 3 cups wine vinegar
4 tablespoons oil

SAUCE

1 bunch scallions
1 bunch dill
1 bunch parsley
4 cloves garlic
2 cups thick tomato juice or 16 ounces canned
   pureed tomatoes
salt
cayenne pepper

Rinse and dry venison. Cut into cubes and sprinkle with salt and pepper. Transfer venison to a pottery or china dish and cover with onion rings, bay leaves, parsley, and small pieces of chili pepper.

Pour cognac over meat and add enough wine vinegar to cover.

Marinate for 12 hours. Stir several times.

Drain and dry meat, thread onto skewers, brush with oil, and grill.

To prepare the sauce, finely chop scallions, herbs, and garlic, mix, and stir with tomato juice or pureed tomatoes. Season with salt and cayenne and serve separately.

Roast Bear

ZHARENNAYA MEDVEZHATINA
Serves 4

1¾ pounds bear meat
1 carrot, chopped
1 medium onion, sliced
1 parsley root, peeled and chopped
1 slice celeriac, peeled and chopped
4 tablespoons lard
salt, pepper
1 pound soup bones
1 tablespoon flour
1 egg, beaten
1 tablespoon bread crumbs

MARINADE

1 quart vinegar
salt, pepper
1 onion, sliced
6 bay leaves
10 black peppercorns
20 juniper berries

To prepare the marinade, bring vinegar seasoned with salt, pepper, onion, spices, and juniper berries to a boil.

Rinse meat, transfer to a pottery or china dish, cover with hot marinade, and refrigerate for three days. Turn occasionally. Remove meat from marinade and put in a roasting pan. Sauté vegetables in 1 tablespoon lard. Spoon vegetables over top of meat.

Boil rinsed soup bones in equal parts marinade and water. Strain and pour the broth over the meat. Add salt and pepper. Braise over low heat for 5–6 hours. Replace evaporated liquid with water and more marinade.

Let the meat cool and cut into slices. Dredge with flour, dip into egg, and coat with bread crumbs. Cook until crisp in butter or cooking oil.

Serve with pickled vegetables or marinated fruit.

Roast Wild Boar

ZHARKOYE IZ DIKOY SVINYI

Serves 4

approximately 2 quarts vinegar
3 medium onions, chopped
10 bay leaves
15 black peppercorns
15 juniper berries
2 pounds wild boar meat
$^1/_4$ pound bacon
1 carrot, chopped
1 parsley root, peeled and chopped
1 slice celeriac, peeled and chopped
15 white peppercorns
1 cup dry white wine
2 cups broth
1 tablespoon black bread crumbs
1 tablespoon grated cheese
$^1/_2$ teaspoon cinnamon
2 teaspoons sugar
1 cup cherry juice
salt

Bring vinegar seasoned with onions, 6 bay leaves, black peppercorns, and juniper berries to a boil. Place rinsed meat in a suitable pottery or china dish, add hot marinade, cover, keep in refrigerator for 2–3 days. Turn several times and prick often with a fork. After 2–3 days, remove meat from marinade. Dry with absorbent paper.

Cover the bottom of a heavy pot with slices of bacon. Add a layer of root vegetables, white peppercorns, and remaining bay leaves. Place the marinated, dried meat on top. Brown in a 400°F oven, then lower temperature to 350°F.

Add wine and broth and cover. Braise for 2$^1/_2$–3 hours. Replace evaporated liquid by the spoonful with water or strained marinade. When done, slice roast and arrange on an ovenproof serving dish. Sprinkle with a mixture of black bread crumbs, cheese, cinnamon, and sugar, and put into a 500°F oven for 5–10 minutes, or under the broiler, to crisp the topping.

Strain the braising liquid into a saucepan, add cherry juice, and bring to a boil. Salt to taste and serve with sliced roast.

Potatoes and red cabbage are suitable accompaniments.

Chicken Giblet Ragout

RAGU IZ KURINYIKH POTROKHOV

Serves 4

$^1/_2$ pound each chicken hearts, livers, and
    gizzards
4 tablespoons butter
2 medium onions, sliced into rings
$^1/_4$ cup raisins
1 tablespoon flour
$^1/_2$–1 cup chicken broth
2 tablespoons tomato paste
several pinches of saffron
$^1/_3$ cup vodka
2 tart apples, peeled and diced
1 bunch parsley, chopped
1 bunch dill, chopped
salt, pepper

Carefully rinse and dry giblets. Quarter gizzards. Sauté separately in butter. Sauté onion rings in butter and add raisins, gizzards, hearts, and livers.

Prepare a roux with 1 tablespoon butter and 1 tablespoon flour. Add broth, stir in tomato paste, and bring to a boil.

Dissolve saffron in vodka and add to onions and giblets.

Add apples and herbs to the ragout. Season with salt and pepper. Braise over low heat for 20 minutes.

Serve with mashed potatoes or rice. The ragout may also be served as an appetizer in small, warm pastry shells (vol-au-vents).

Fish

BLYUDA IZ RYBY

Russia is a country of rivers and lakes, and the vastness of the land finds its match in the immense dimensions of its rivers and lakes. The longest river in Europe, for example, the Volga, flows into the world's largest inland sea, the Caspian Sea.

The wealth of fish, which never fails to provide us with lavish meals, and the convenient, efficient, and rapid transportation on rivers and lakes enticed the first settlers to live along the shore. These settlers quickly learned to prepare many kinds of fish in a great variety of ways. Since strict religious fasts denied them the enjoyment of meat and dairy products, imaginative fish dishes became the high point of a festive meal. Chroniclers report that as far back as the tenth century, platters of sturgeon weighing 40 to 60 pounds were served up at the court of the tsars.

During Peter I's reign, at the beginning of the eighteenth century, the first saltwater fish were brought to Moscow and St. Petersburg from far-off northern coasts. It was at this time that salting, smoking, and drying—methods of preservation with a long tradition in Russian cuisine—became important. Fish preserved using these methods could be stored for long periods while becoming more flavorful at the same time. The backbones of larger fish were also dried and chopped and, like ground dried fish, used for aromatic flavoring.

Typically, fish is baked in the oven in its own juices or with vegetables, mushrooms, or sauerkraut. It can also be braised, stuffed with groats, or baked inside pastry.

Among the wealth of fish in my homeland, one specialty has become famous: salted fish roe, or caviar. This was formerly everyday fare but is now a luxury for the export market. When I was a student in the sixties, it was still not unusual, even in most modest restaurants, to be offered eight to ten kinds of caviar. It was served with bread and butter, hot potatoes, or bliny and was a popular, affordable appetizer.

The color and size of the roe determine the type of Russian caviar: Black caviar comes from salmon-type fish (of which the very finest is *payusnaya*), red caviar comes from sturgeon, and pink caviar is the roe of the whitefish family. *Chastikovaya* caviar, from pike or perch, is one very popular dish, often prepared at home in wooden baskets.

In Russia, by the way, caviar is always accompanied by a small glass of vodka or other clear, distilled spirits—never champagne!

◁ *On the Volga River*

Braised Sturgeon

TUSHONAYA OSETRINA

Serves 4

2½-pound sturgeon
salt
½ cup butter
1 cup Madeira
½ cup pickle brine
1 bunch parsley, chopped
bay leaf

SAUCE

½ pound celeriac, peeled, chopped, and
  cooked 15 minutes in water
¼ pound pickled cucumbers (approximately 4
  medium-sized), chopped
⅓ cup marinated mushrooms, sliced
½ cup Kalamata olives, pitted and chopped
1–2 tablespoons capers
1 tablespoon butter
1 tablespoon flour
salt, pepper

Carefully rinse cleaned and dressed sturgeon, rub with salt, and let sit for 1 hour.

Melt butter in a casserole dish and add Madeira, pickle brine, parsley, and bay leaf. Bring to a boil. Add sturgeon, cover, and braise over low heat for 20 minutes.

Transfer fish to a serving dish and keep warm.

To make the sauce, heat celeriac, pickled cucumbers, mushrooms, olives, and capers in the braising liquid. Blend butter and flour together and thicken sauce. Season with salt and pepper and pour over fish.

Serve with boiled or fried potatoes.

Sautéed Sturgeon or Salmon

ZHARENNAYA OSETRINA

Serves 4

2½-pound sturgeon or salmon
salt, pepper
1 medium onion, finely chopped
2 tablespoons olive oil
2–3 tablespoons butter

Blanch cleaned and dressed fish, drain, remove skin, rinse, dry again, and cut into serving-sized pieces. Salt and pepper the fish, sprinkle with onion, and pour olive oil over the top.

Marinate for approximately 2 hours in oil.

Sauté on both sides in hot butter, and serve with mustard or walnut sauce (see recipes, page 156).

This type of fish can also be prepared whole and baked in the oven. Brush with 1–2 tablespoons melted butter before baking.

Baked Sturgeon with Mustard Sauce

OSETRINA S GORCHICHNYM SOUSOM

Serves 4

2½-pound sturgeon
salt
4 tablespoons butter or oil
1 carrot, sliced
2 medium onions, sliced
1 bunch parsley, chopped
2 eggs, lightly beaten
3 tablespoons bread crumbs
½ cup white wine
1 cup fish stock
2–3 tablespoons vinegar
1–2 teaspoons hot (English) mustard

Blanch cleaned and dressed sturgeon in boiling water, drain, remove skin, rinse well, dry, and rub with salt.

Coat a roasting pan with ½ tablespoon butter or oil. Cover bottom with slices of carrot and 1 onion. Add parsley and place the fish on top.

Sauté second onion in 2½ tablespoons butter or oil and let cool.

Beat sautéed onion together with eggs and brush this mixture on the fish. Sprinkle with bread crumbs and drizzle with the rest of the butter or oil. Bake in a 400°F oven for 20 minutes.

Transfer fish to a serving dish and keep warm.

Pour wine, fish stock, and vinegar into roasting pan. Bring to a boil with the vegetables. Stir in mustard, season to taste, and strain the sauce over the fish.

Serve with potatoes.

Sturgeon in Chablis

STERLYAD S VINOM
Serves 4

2½-pound sturgeon
salt
1–2 parsley roots, peeled and chopped
bay leaf
1 clove garlic, minced
2 cups Chablis
½ cup pickle brine
juice of 1 lemon
pickled mushrooms
olives
truffles
1 tablespoon flour
1 tablespoon butter

Rinse, clean, and dress sturgeon. Make incisions at the head and tail and carefully remove the spine. (This can be done at the fish market.) Slice the fish on the diagonal, salt, and place in a buttered pan. Sprinkle with parsley root.

Season with bay leaf and garlic, then add wine, pickle brine, and lemon juice. Cover and cook 15–20 minutes until done.

Transfer fish to a serving dish and keep warm. Garnish with pickled mushrooms, olives, and truffles.

In a small saucepan, reduce the cooking liquid somewhat.

Prepare a roux with flour and 1 tablespoon butter. Add strained reduced cooking liquid, bring to a boil, and season to taste.

Pour sauce over the fish, reserving some to serve at the table.

Serve with boiled potatoes.

Sturgeon in Red Wine and Cherry Sauce

OSETRINA S VISHNYOYYM SOUSOM
Serves 4

2–2½-pound sturgeon
salt
2 carrots, sliced
2 leeks, white part only, chopped
1 parsley root, peeled and sliced
2 medium onions, chopped
20 peppercorns
3–4 bay leaves
2 cups pickle brine or ½ cup vinegar plus 1½ cups water

SAUCE

2 tablespoons sugar
1 tablespoon butter
1 tablespoon flour
½ cup Madeira
½ cup cherry juice
½ teaspoon ground cloves
½ teaspoon cinnamon
vinegar or lemon juice
salt
2 tablespoons chopped Kalamata olives (or 1 tablespoon chopped capers)

Blanch cleaned fish in boiling water, remove skin, rinse and dry thoroughly, and rub with salt. Let stand approximately 1 hour.

Prepare a sour broth using carrots, leeks, parsley root, onions, spices, and brine or vinegar. Simmer fish (whole or cut into serving pieces) in broth over low heat 15–20 minutes until done.

Transfer to a serving dish and keep warm. Pour braising liquid through a strainer.

To prepare sauce, brown the sugar briefly in a hot pan and add several spoons of fish broth. Thicken with flour and butter, stir in Madeira and cherry juice, and bring to a boil. Add just enough fish broth to make a thick sauce. Season with cloves, cinnamon, vinegar or lemon juice, and salt. Add olives or capers to sauce, bring to a boil, pour over fish, and serve with boiled potatoes.

Stuffed Sturgeon with Almond Béchamel

FARSHIROVANNAYA OSETRINA S
BESHAMEL SOUSOM

Serves 4

2½-pound sturgeon
2 tablespoons walnut oil
2 slices bread
½ cup milk
1 bunch chives, chopped
salt, pepper
½ teaspoon nutmeg
1 tablespoon flour
1 tablespoon butter or oil
1½ cups almond milk
10–12 boiled shrimp
1 bunch parsley, chopped
1 bunch dill, chopped

Cut half of the fish into slices the size of a cutlet. Reserve for later. Cut the rest of the fish into pieces. Sauté fish pieces lightly in 1 tablespoon oil and run through meat grinder.

Soak bread in milk, squeeze, and mix thoroughly with ground fish. Season with chives, salt, pepper, and nutmeg.

Salt and pepper the slices of fish. Cover with stuffing, roll up seam down, and put in an ovenproof casserole.

Prepare béchamel sauce: Sauté flour lightly in 1 tablespoon butter or oil. Stir in almond milk, season to taste, and pour over the fish rolls. Bake in 350°F oven for 20–30 minutes.

Garnish with shrimp and sprinkle with herbs. Serve with boiled or sautéed potatoes.

Carp with Rice and Mushroom Stuffing

FARSHIROVANNY KARP

Serves 2

1¾–2-pound carp

STUFFING

3 tablespoons dried mushrooms
½ cup rice
¼ cup chopped onions
1 tablespoon butter
2 eggs, beaten
salt, pepper
cayenne pepper (or 2 ground hot peppers)
1 clove garlic, minced

BREADING

½ cup flour
2 eggs, beaten
1 cup bread crumbs
2 tablespoons butter, melted

Adjust the quantity of stuffing to the size of the fish.

Clean and dress carp, taking care not to tear the stomach cavity. Make deep incisions around the back fins and remove bones and innards. (Be careful not to tear the skin.) Separate the backbone at the head and tail and remove. Finally, remove the gills and thoroughly rinse the fish once more. All this can be prepared at the fish market.

Prepare the stuffing. Soak dried mushrooms in 1 cup hot water until soft, drain and rinse mushrooms and cut into small pieces. Reserve liquid.

Boil rice in the mushroom liquid. Sauté onions in 1 tablespoon butter.

Mix rice thoroughly with mushrooms, onions, and eggs. Season with salt, pepper, cayenne, and garlic.

Stuff fish at the incision along the back and stitch closed with twine or skewers. Dredge stuffed fish in flour, dip in eggs, and coat with bread crumbs. Brown on both sides in hot butter. Place in a roasting pan and bake in a preheated 375°F oven 20–30 minutes, depending on size.

Place on a platter, remove twine, cut into serving pieces, and pour 1 remaining tablespoon melted butter over fish.

Serve with buttered carrots. Buckwheat groats can also be used as stuffing for fish prepared in this way.

Baked Carp with Buckwheat Groat Stuffing

KARP FARSHIROVANNY
GRECHNEVOY KASHEY

Serves 4

½ pound buckwheat groats (see basic recipe, page 178)
1 carp (approximately 3 pounds), cleaned and scales removed
2 medium onions, chopped
1½ cups butter
4 hard-boiled eggs, mashed
salt
1 tablespoon flour
1 bunch parsley, chopped
1 bunch dill, chopped
4 tablespoons sour cream

Boil buckwheat groats and let cool.

Rinse fish thoroughly.

Sauté onions in 1 tablespoon butter, add the boiled buckwheat groats, and brown lightly. Let cool. Mix in hard-boiled eggs.

Salt the fish, stuff with slightly cooled groat mixture, and stitch closed.

Melt remaining butter. Pour half into a roasting pan. Place the fish in the pan, dust with flour, and drizzle with the rest of the melted butter. Bake in a 350°F oven for 20–30 minutes.

Stir herbs into sour cream. Pour over fish and bake 5 minutes more.

Serve with boiled potatoes.

Baked Carp with Buckwheat Groat Stuffing ▷

Bream Stuffed with Buckwheat Groats

LYESHCH FARSHIROVANNY
GRECHNEVOY KASHEY

Serves 4

2½-pound pan-ready bream or porgy
salt
1–2 medium onions, chopped
2 tablespoons butter
approximately 2 cups cooked buckwheat groats
  prepared the day before (see basic recipe,
  page 178)
3 hard-boiled eggs, chopped
2 bunches parsley, chopped
pepper
1 tablespoon flour
1 tablespoon bread crumbs
4 tablespoons sour cream

Clean fish and rub inside and out with salt.

To prepare stuffing, sauté onions in 1 table-spoon butter, add buckwheat groats, and brown briefly. Let cool, mix in eggs and 1 bunch chopped parsley, and season with salt and pepper. Stuff the fish with this mixture and stitch or secure closed with twine. Place in buttered roasting pan, sprinkle with a mix of flour and bread crumbs, and melt the rest of the butter and drizzle it over. Pour 2 tablespoons water around the sides of the fish and bake in a preheated 350°F oven for 20–25 minutes.

Arrange on a serving dish and remove twine. Deglaze roasting pan with sour cream and pour this sauce over the fish.

Sprinkle with parsley and serve with sautéed or boiled potatoes.

Braised Pike with Cream and Cheese Sauce

SHCHUKA VARYONAYA S SYROM

Serves 4

2½-pound pike, cleaned and scales removed
salt
1 leek, white part only, chopped
1 celery stalk, chopped
1 parsley root, peeled and chopped
1 medium onion, chopped
bay leaf
10 peppercorns (black and white)
1 cup heavy cream or sour cream
2 tablespoons butter
2 tablespoons grated cheddar or Swiss cheese
lemon juice
pepper

GARNISH

¾ pound pike fillet
1 small onion
2 slices bread, soaked in milk
1–2 eggs
salt, pepper
½ teaspoon nutmeg

Rinse pike, cut into pieces, and rub with salt.

Cover fish with water and simmer with vegetables, half the chopped onion, bay leaf, and 5 peppercorns until half done, about 10 minutes.

Remove fish and put in another pot. Pour cream over fish and add butter, remaining peppercorns, onion, and cheese. Braise over low heat until tender, shaking the pot occasionally.

To prepare the garnish: Run pike fillet and onion through meat grinder twice or puree in food processor. Blend fish-onion mixture with squeezed bread and eggs until smooth. Season with salt, pepper, and nutmeg. Shape into a long roll (like a sausage), wrap in cheesecloth brushed with butter, and tie the ends tightly together. Simmer in the cooking liquid for 15–20 minutes, unwrap, and slice. Place braised fish on a serving dish surrounded by slices of garnish.

Season cream-and-cheese sauce with lemon juice, salt, and pepper. Pour over fish.

Serve with boiled potatoes and salad.

Pike Jewish-Style

SHCHUKA PO YEVREYSKY S
SHAFRANOM

Serves 4

2½-pound pike, cleaned and scales removed
salt
1 carrot, chopped
1 parsley root, peeled and chopped
1 slice celeriac, peeled and chopped
2 tablespoons raisins
2–3 slices lemon, peeled and seeded
1 cup white wine
vinegar
1 tablespoon flour
1 tablespoon butter
½ teaspoon saffron
1 teaspoon sugar
1½ teaspoons honey

Rinse fish and pat dry. Cut into serving pieces. Salt and let sit 1 hour.

In the meantime, cook vegetables in lightly salted water 15 minutes until they are half done. Strain. Reserve broth.

Place fish, vegetables, raisins, and lemon slices in a casserole. Add wine, a dash of vinegar, and enough vegetable broth to cover the fish. Braise until done. Drain fish and place on a serving dish. Keep warm.

Strain the broth, pick out raisins and lemon slices, and place on top of fish.

To prepare sauce, mix flour with butter, saffron, and sugar. Stir into broth until smooth and simmer for a few minutes. Season with honey and pour over fish.

Serve with boiled potatoes.

Baked Pike with Sauerkraut

SHCHUKA ZAPECHONAYA S
KISLOY KAPUSTOY

Serves 4

2½ pounds pike fillets
salt, pepper
3 tablespoons flour
2 eggs, beaten
4 tablespoons bread crumbs
4–5 tablespoons butter
1¼ pounds sauerkraut, rinsed and squeezed
   dry
1 cup sour cream
¾ cup grated cheese

Salt and pepper the fillets, dredge with flour, dip into eggs, and coat with 3 tablespoons bread crumbs. Sauté on both sides in 2 tablespoons butter.

In the meantime, in a kettle, melt 1 tablespoon butter and cook sauerkraut, covered, adding a little water if it sticks. Sauerkraut should simmer 30–40 minutes or until tender.

Butter an ovenproof casserole and layer fish and sauerkraut alternately. Drizzle each layer of fish with sour cream, each layer of sauerkraut with cheese.

Cover the final layer with remaining bread crumbs and grated cheese and dot with remaining butter. Bake in a preheated 375°F oven approximately 30 minutes and serve with sautéed potatoes.

Stuffed Pike

FARSHIROVANNAYA SHCHUKA
Serves 4

2½-pound pike, cleaned and scales removed
1 medium onion, quartered
2–3 sardines
2 slices bread
½ cup milk
1–2 eggs
salt, pepper
½ teaspoon nutmeg
3 tablespoons butter, melted
1 cup sour cream

Rinse fish well. Dry. Cut along the back and remove meat from the bones, taking care to avoid further cutting the skin. Run pike meat, onion, and cleaned sardines through a meat grinder. Soak bread in milk, squeeze, mix with eggs, and stir into the fish mixture.

Mix well and season with salt, pepper, and nutmeg. Stuff the pike with this mixture, reconstituting the fish; stitch the skin closed with twine or skewers, and sprinkle the fish with salt.

Place in a buttered roasting pan and pour melted butter over it. Bake in a 400°F oven for approximately 30–40 minutes, basting frequently with pan juices.

Arrange fish on a serving dish and remove twine.

Deglaze roasting pan with sour cream. Season with salt and pepper and pour over fish.

Serve with boiled potatoes and green salad.

Stuffed Pike ▷

Perch or Pike Pudding

Perch or Pike Pudding

PUDING IZ SUDAKA

Serves 4

2-pound perch or pike, skinned and boned
3 slices white bread
1 cup milk
1 medium onion, chopped
3/4 cup butter
3 eggs
salt, pepper
1 carrot, sliced
1 parsley root, peeled and sliced
bay leaf
1 tablespoon flour
1 bunch parsley, chopped
crayfish (optional), cooked and shelled

Clean fish and cut into pieces. Reserve scraps. Soak white bread in milk and squeeze. Sauté onion in 1 tablespoon of butter.

Run fish, bread, and onion through meat grinder twice (or puree in food processor). Mix well with eggs and 1/2 cup butter. Season with salt and pepper.

Place the mixture in a buttered mold. Place mold in a baking pan with 2 inches water and bake at 375°F for approximately 1 hour.

In the meantime, prepare fish broth using fish scraps, carrot, parsley root, bay leaf, salt, and pepper.

Prepare a light roux with flour and 1 tablespoon butter. Add strained fish broth and simmer until it thickens. Season with salt and pepper.

Invert fish pudding on a serving dish, garnish with parsley and crayfish, and serve with sauce, rice, and green peas.

Perch with Bliny

SUDAK V BLINCHIKAKH
Serves 4

Bliny are medium-thin pancakes that are slightly thicker than crepes but thinner than ordinary breakfast pancakes and 5–7 inches in diameter.

2½ cups flour
3 eggs
approximately 2 cups milk
salt
1 teaspoon sugar
½–¾ cup butter
2-pound perch, bones and skin removed
2 tablespoons bread crumbs

Prepare a bliny batter using flour, 2 eggs, and milk. Season with salt and sugar. Let sit for ½ hour. Cook thin pancakes in hot butter.

Rinse fish and cut into thin slices. Add salt and brown fish in hot butter.

Layer each pancake with fish, fold pancake together like an envelope, brush with remaining beaten egg, and sprinkle with bread crumbs. Place on a buttered ovenproof platter (or baking sheet) and bake in a 400°F oven for 10 minutes until crisp. Serve with tomato sauce (see recipes, page 150).

Perch in Sour Cream

SUDAK SO SMETANOY
Serves 4

2-pound perch, skinned and filleted
6 medium potatoes, thinly sliced
½ cup butter, melted
salt, pepper
2 cups sour cream
1 bunch parsley, chopped

Cut fish into serving pieces.

Brush a casserole or ovenproof mold with butter and layer with potatoes and perch. Season each layer with salt and pepper.

Drizzle with remaining melted butter and pour sour cream over it.

Bake in a 375°F oven for 30 minutes. Sprinkle with parsley and serve.

A Snack of Pike or Perch

FORSHMAK IZ SHCHUKI ILI SUDAKA
Serves 6

1¼ pounds pike or perch fillets
2–3 tablespoons oil (olive or other)
¼ cup dried mushrooms
1 medium onion, finely chopped
3 eggs
1½ cups heavy cream
1 cup bread crumbs
½ cup grated Swiss cheese
salt, pepper
¾ cup butter

Rinse and dry fish fillets. Sauté lightly in oil. Check to see that all bones are removed and chop very finely or run fillets through meat grinder.

Cover mushrooms with boiling water and simmer 15–20 minutes until soft. Drain, reserving liquid, and cut into small pieces. Add mushrooms, onion, eggs, cream, and ½ cup bread crumbs to the ground fish. Season with ¼ cup cheese, salt, and pepper. Mix with approximately ½ cup mushroom broth until soft. Brush an ovenproof dish with oil and sprinkle with 1 tablespoon bread crumbs. Fill with fish mixture, sprinkle with remaining cheese and bread crumbs, dot with butter, and bake in a 400°F oven for 20 minutes.

Serve as a snack or appetizer with remaining melted butter and a baguette.

Bream with Scallions

LYESHCH POD ZELYONYM LUKOM

Serves 2–3

---

1 pan-ready bream or porgy (approximately 1³/₄
   pounds), cleaned and scaled
salt
2 bunches scallions, finely chopped
1¹/₃ cups sour cream
pepper
1 tablespoon butter, melted

Rinse fish and dry thoroughly. Salt lightly inside
and out.

Mix scallions with sour cream and season with
salt and pepper.

Brush an ovenproof dish with butter. Fill with
half the scallion mixture and cover with fish. Top
with the rest of the scallions and bake in a 350°F
oven for 15–20 minutes.

Serve with boiled potatoes.

Bream with Scallions ▷

Eel in Red Wine

UGOR VARYONY V KRASNOM VINYE

Serves 4

2½ pounds eel, skin removed
salt
2 medium onions, chopped
½ lemon, sliced
5 black peppercorns
3 cloves
1 small piece ginger
1 bottle red wine
1 tablespoon flour
1 tablespoon olive oil or butter
pepper

Clean and dress eel, rinse well. Cut into pieces, add salt, and put in a Dutch oven with onions, lemon slices, and spices.

Cover with red wine, bring to a boil, and simmer for 20–30 minutes.

Transfer eel to a serving dish and keep warm. Strain wine. Brown flour in oil or butter, add red wine, and bring to a boil. Season to taste and pour sauce over eel.

Serve with mashed potatoes.

Catfish Croquettes and White Beans

FRIKADYELY IZ SOMA

Serves 2–3

2½ cups dried white beans
salt, pepper
1 pound catfish fillets
½–1 cup heavy cream
2–3 tablespoons bread crumbs
3 tablespoons butter
1 large onion, chopped
2–3 tablespoons tomato paste

Soak beans overnight. Rinse. Cover beans with fresh water, add ½ teaspoon salt, and cook, covered, for about 1 hour, or until soft. Add water if needed. Drain and set aside for later.

Meanwhile, run fish fillets through meat grinder or food processor. Add cream and stir until smooth. Season with salt and pepper.

Shape into flat patties, coat with bread crumbs, and sauté in 2 tablespoons butter.

Sauté onion in 1 tablespoon butter. When onion is lightly browned, add tomato paste and beans, stir well, and heat.

Arrange croquettes and beans on a serving dish and pour pan drippings from croquettes over them.

Marinated Sprats

MARINOVANNIYE SHPROTY

Serves 8

---

2 pounds fresh sprats, heads and tails removed
salt
flour
oil

MARINADE

¼ cup sliced carrots
¼ cup finely chopped onions
2 tablespoons peeled and chopped parsley root
1 tablespoon oil
2 cups water or fish broth
2 tablespoons sugar
2 bay leaves
3 cups vinegar

Immerse sprats 8–10 minutes in a solution of ¾ cup salt and 1 quart water. Dry carefully with paper towel, dredge with flour, and fry in oil. Remove from pan and let cool.

To prepare marinade, sauté carrots, onions, and parsley root briefly in oil. Add water or fish broth, sugar, and bay leaves and boil for 10–15 minutes. Remove from heat, add vinegar, and cool.

Transfer fried sprats to a glass bowl and cover with the cold marinade. Cover, weight lightly, and let marinate for 1½–2 days. Serve with beet or potato salad.

Sprats with Potatoes and Leeks

SHPROTY S OVOSHCHAMI

Serves 6

1 pound salted herring fillets
½ cup butter
3 medium potatoes, cut into strips
1 pound fresh sprats
1 pound smoked sprat fillets
1 pound leeks, white part only, chopped
2 eggs
2 bunches dill, chopped
4–6 cups milk
salt, pepper

Soak herring fillets in water and cut into pieces.

Brush an ovenproof dish thickly with butter. Layer potatoes, fish (sprats and herring mixed), and leeks. Begin and end with potatoes.

Beat eggs and dill together with milk. Season with salt and pepper and pour over the fish. Dot generously with butter and bake in a 350°F oven for approximately 1 hour. (Do not cover.)

Serve with salad.

Sprats in Bacon Sauce

SHPROTY SO SVINYM SALOM

Serves 4

½ pound bacon, sliced in strips
2 medium onions, chopped
2 tablespoons flour
2–3 cups milk
salt
1¾ pounds fresh sprat fillets
2 tablespoons heavy cream
dill, chopped

Render bacon. Sauté onions in bacon fat. Add flour, stir, and brown lightly. Add milk and stir well so that there are no lumps. Add salt and simmer over low heat until thickened.

Cook sprat fillets in sauce for 8–10 minutes. Shortly before serving, add cream and garnish with dill.

Serve with boiled or mashed potatoes.

Stuffed Herring

FARSHIROVANNAYA SELYODKA

Serves 4

4 salted herring
½ cup herring roe
1 medium onion, finely chopped
2 eggs
4–5 tablespoons butter
4–5 tablespoons bread crumbs
pepper

Soak herring in water for 24 hours, rinse, pat dry, and clean. Do not remove skin. Chop herring roe and mix with onion, 1 egg, 1–2 tablespoons butter, 1–2 tablespoons bread crumbs, and pepper.

Stuff herring with this mixture, close with toothpicks, dip into second egg, beaten, and coat with bread crumbs.

Brown slowly on all sides in butter and serve with boiled potatoes or borscht.

Sauces

SOUSY

The influence of French cuisine on sauces used in Russian cuisine should not be underestimated. In the nineteenth century, French chefs were in charge of preparing culinary delights at the court of the tsars and at the estates of landed nobility. The first translations of French cookbooks appeared during the eighteenth and nineteenth centuries, notably the renowned classic work of M. A. de Carême, a master chef employed at the tsar's court. The French were already famous for their sauces, as witnessed by Talleyrand's response when he was asked to describe the difference between the English and the French. "England has three hundred religions and three sauces," he said. "France has three hundred sauces and three religions . . . "

But the celebrated French chefs also learned from their Russian apprentices and colleagues: for example, to serve each course in proper sequence, not to put everything on the table at once, as was common in France until then. Fruitful cooperation brought about completely unique sauces, which eventually became part of Russian tradition: *Mukovniki*, pan juices thickened with flour; or *Vsvari*, a sweet-and-sour spicy marinade; or the sauce resulting when herbs and berries are simply braised along with the meat.

During strict fasting seasons, vegetable oils, poppy and nut oils, or the brine from pickled vegetables were (and still are) used as the base for sauces.

And let us not forget our cold sauces—a must with appetizers, cold meats, aspics, etc. They are based on kvass, our national drink, and prepared with herb vinegars, sour cream, and creative seasonings.

Sauces play a very important role in Russian cuisine. Meat, fish, vegetables, and pâtés—roasted, baked, or braised—are always served with generous quantities of sauce.

Among hot sauces we distinguish between light (white) and dark (red) sauces. They are usually based on a roux made of butter and flour and thinned with some kind of liquid (4 tablespoons butter, 1/2 cup flour, cooked for 1–2 minutes, to which 2–4 cups liquid are added. The yield is four servings). The liquid must always be heated and should always be added to the roux, never the other way around.

In order to keep a light sauce truly light, butter should be hot, but never browned, and the flour should be stirred in quickly and not allowed to color. A small amount of liquid should be added at once and stirred until smooth. Then the rest of the liquid is added gradually. The sauce should be left to simmer over low heat for 10 minutes until the flour is completely dissolved.

Dark sauces are prepared the same way, except the flour is browned first in butter.

Depending on what is being served with the sauce, the liquid in the recipe can be meat broth, fish broth, or stock made of bones, vegetables, milk, wine, beer, etc.

For light sauces it is important to use a light-colored stock that has been carefully clarified to remove all fat.

Dark sauces, on the other hand, are prepared using concentrated stock, meat glaze, or pan drippings. The basic sauce prepared in this way is then seasoned with appropriate ingredients—spices and herbs—and often enriched with heavy cream, sour cream, or egg yolks.

The final consistency of the sauce depends on how it will be used. It should be creamy if it is going to be served separately. If the dish is going to be braised in the sauce, then the sauce should be milky. A sauce should be thick (the consistency of sour cream) if the dish is going to be served in the sauce. And if the dish is going to be covered with the sauce and baked, the sauce should be very thick (reduced).

◁ *Church in Northern Russia*

White Sauce

BELY SOUS

BASIC RECIPE

½ cup flour
4 tablespoons butter
2 cups meat broth (chicken or beef)
½ cup cream (heavy or light)
lemon juice
salt, pepper

Stir flour into melted butter (do not brown). Add a small amount of hot broth and stir until smooth. Stirring constantly, gradually add the rest of the hot broth and simmer for approximately 5 minutes. Add cream and continue to simmer over low heat for another 5 minutes until the sauce thickens. Pour through a fine-meshed sieve and season with lemon juice, salt, and pepper.

This sauce is particularly good enriched with 1–2 egg yolks or a lump of butter at the last minute. Do not allow to boil again.

Dark Sauce

TYOMNY SOUS—OSNOVNOY RETSEPT

BASIC RECIPE

½ cup flour
4 tablespoons butter
2–3 cups strong stock (or meat glaze)

Slowly brown flour in hot butter. Add a small amount of hot stock and stir until smooth. Stirring constantly, gradually add the rest of the stock and simmer the sauce over low heat for about 10 minutes until it thickens. Pour through a fine-meshed strainer and use as a base for savory dark sauces.

Sour Cream Sauce

SMETANNY SOUS

BASIC RECIPE

1 tablespoon butter
1 tablespoon flour
1½ cups stock or milk
1 cup sour cream
salt, pepper
chopped parsley

Prepare a light roux using butter and flour. Add hot stock or milk and simmer for several minutes. Stir in sour cream and simmer over low heat 5 minutes longer. Season with salt, pepper, and chopped parsley. (It is important to use stock or milk in sour cream sauce; if used alone, sour cream might curdle.)

Béchamel Sauce

BESHAMEL SOUS

4 tablespoons butter
½ cup flour
2 cups milk (or 1 cup milk and 1 cup heavy cream)
salt
½ teaspoon nutmeg

Prepare a roux using butter and flour and add hot milk. Simmer for 7–10 minutes, stirring constantly. Season with salt and nutmeg.

Onion Sauce

LUKOVY SOUS

1 medium onion, chopped
2 tablespoons butter
1–2 tablespoons flour
2 cups stock
2 tablespoons sour cream
salt, pepper
2 tablespoons chopped scallions

Sauté onions in butter. Add flour. Stirring constantly, add hot stock and simmer 3–5 minutes. Fold in sour cream, season with salt and pepper, and heat scallions briefly in the sauce.

This sauce goes well with ground-meat dishes, lamb, and pork. It can be varied by adding dill, parsley, and celery leaves (all finely chopped), making it suitable for venison and roast lamb.

Light Onion Sauce
SVETLY LUKOVY SOUS

5 medium onions, chopped
1/2 cup butter
1/2 cup stock
1/2 cup flour
1 cup milk
salt, pepper

Blanch onions in boiling water and drain well. Braise, covered, in 4 tablespoons butter and stock (preferably lamb broth) for 10 minutes over medium heat.

  Prepare a light roux with remaining butter and flour. Add hot milk and simmer for 3–5 minutes, stirring constantly. Add braised onions, bring to a boil, and strain through a sieve. Reheat and season with salt and pepper.

This is particularly good with roast lamb. The aroma and flavor of the onions are brought out if they are braised, covered, rather than fried.

Butter Sauce Polish-Style
MASLYANNY SOUS PO POLSKY

3/4 cup butter
2 hard-boiled eggs, finely chopped
lemon juice
salt
1 bunch parsley, chopped

Melt butter and stir in eggs. Season with lemon juice, salt, and parsley. Serve hot with fish.

148

White Sauce with Mustard, Horseradish, or Capers
BELY SOUS S GORCHITSOY, KHRENOM I KAPERSAMI

2 cups white sauce (see basic recipe, page 147)
1 tablespoon prepared mustard, 1 tablespoon prepared horseradish, or 1–2 tablespoons capers
sugar
vinegar or lemon juice

Bring white sauce to a boil and stir in mustard, horseradish, or capers. Season to taste with sugar and vinegar (or lemon juice). Serve with boiled meat.

Horseradish Sauce
SOUS IZ KHRENA

5 tablespoons butter
1/2 cup flour
approximately 2 cups stock
1 medium-sized horseradish root, or 1 jar prepared horseradish
1/2 cup sour cream
salt
sugar
vinegar or lemon juice

Prepare a light roux with 4 tablespoons butter and flour, add hot stock, and simmer, stirring constantly, until it thickens.

  Grate horseradish root. To prevent discoloring, immediately brown lightly in 1 tablespoon butter. Stir into the sauce, bring to a boil, add sour cream, stir, and turn off heat. Season highly with salt, sugar, and vinegar (or lemon juice).

Always grate fresh horseradish immediately before using. Do not soak horseradish in water because it will lose its flavor. To prevent discoloring, rub root with vinegar. Always sauté horseradish lightly in butter. This improves both flavor and aroma. Use a light chicken or vegetable stock that does not clash with the taste of horseradish.

  Serve with boiled beef, tongue, ham, or lamb.

Madeira Sauce

MADERA SOUS

1½ cups stock made from wildfowl
½ cup meat glaze made from adding water to
    roast beef pan drippings
1 tablespoon potato flour or cornstarch
scant ¾ cup Madeira
¼ cup chopped truffles (fresh or canned)
salt, pepper
lemon juice
4 tablespoons butter

Bring stock and glaze to a boil and strain. In a small bowl, mix potato flour and Madeira until smooth and thick. Pour into saucepan with stock. Simmer 3–5 minutes.

Season with truffles, salt, pepper, and lemon juice. Just before serving, add butter. Serve with wildfowl (pheasant, wild duck, partridge, quail, etc.).

Aurora Sauce

AVRORA SOUS

½ cup prunes
1 cup red wine
2 cups dark sauce (see basic recipe, page 147)
½ cup walnuts, chopped
2 tablespoons raisins
salt
sugar
1 tablespoon butter

Simmer prunes in a small amount of water until soft. Strain, remove pits, and cut into small pieces.

Add red wine to strained dark sauce and bring to a boil. Add prunes, walnuts, and raisins. Season with salt and sugar and simmer for a few more minutes. Shortly before serving, add butter.

Hunter's Sauce

OKHOTNICHY SOUS

¼ pound mushrooms, thinly sliced
1 medium onion, chopped
1½ tablespoons bacon fat
2 cups dark sauce (see basic recipe, page 147)
½ cup red wine
1 small bunch parsley, chopped
1 small bunch tarragon, chopped
salt, pepper
2 tablespoons butter

Sauté mushrooms and onions in bacon fat. Stir into heated dark sauce and cook over low heat for 5–7 minutes. Add red wine and herbs and season with salt and pepper. Shortly before serving, add butter. Serve with lamb or roast fowl.

Yeast–Sour Cream Sauce

SMETANO-DROZHZHIVOY SOUS

1 tablespoon yeast
1 cup water
1 teaspoon butter
1 teaspoon flour
1½ tablespoons milk
1 cup sour cream
2 egg yolks, beaten
salt, pepper

Dissolve yeast in cold water and simmer for 10 minutes over low heat.

In a saucepan make a roux with butter and flour. Stir in milk. Add sour cream and yeast mixture. Simmer for a few minutes. Remove from heat, stir in egg yolks, and season with salt and pepper. Serve.

Dark Beer Sauce

TYOMNY PIVNOY SOUS

1 cup meat stock
2 tablespoons dark roux
1 medium onion, grated
1 parsley root, peeled and grated
salt
sugar
pepper
2–3 cloves
1 bay leaf
½ cup dark beer
lemon juice

Add hot stock to roux. Stir in onion, parsley root, salt, sugar, pepper, cloves, and bay leaf. Boil for 15 minutes. Strain sauce into another pot. Reheat with beer and season with lemon juice.

Light Beer Sauce

SVETLY PIVNOY SOUS

½ cup meat or fish stock
1 cup light beer
2 tablespoons light roux
salt
sugar
cinnamon
lemon juice
2 egg yolks, beaten
¼ cup sour cream

Add hot stock and beer to roux and boil for 5 minutes.

Season with salt, sugar, cinnamon, and lemon juice.

Beat egg yolks into sour cream. Remove sauce from heat and stir in egg yolk–sour cream mixture. Do not allow to boil again.

Sour Cream–Tomato Sauce

SMETANO-TOMATNY SOUS

1 medium onion, chopped
2 tablespoons tomato paste
2 tablespoons butter
2 cups sour cream sauce (see basic recipe, page 147)
salt, pepper

Sauté onion and tomato paste in butter until light brown. Stir into hot sour cream sauce, simmer for 5 minutes over very low heat, and strain. Season with salt and pepper. Serve with roasted meat and fish or vegetable dishes.

Simple Tomato Sauce

PROSTOY TOMATNY SOUS

6 tablespoons tomato paste
1 tablespoon butter
2 cups dark sauce (see basic recipe, page 147)
½ cup white wine
lemon juice

Sauté tomato paste in butter and stir into heated dark sauce. Add white wine, cover, and cook for 5 minutes. Season with lemon juice.

Serve with roasted meat or fish.

Leek Sauce

SOUS IZ LUKAPOREYA

2 leeks, white part only, chopped
1 cup water
vinegar
3 egg yolks
½ cup butter, diced
1 clove garlic, crushed
½ teaspoon salt
1 teaspoon sugar
½ cup tarragon, chopped

Boil leeks in water with a dash of vinegar 10 minutes or until tender. Strain. Pureé in food processor and place in a double boiler. Stirring constantly, add the egg yolks and the butter. Beat vigorously until the sauce is thick and creamy. Season with garlic, salt, sugar, and tarragon.

Mushroom Sauce

GRIBNOY SOUS

¼ cup dried mushrooms
2 medium onions, chopped
9 tablespoons butter
½ cup flour
salt

Wash dried mushrooms thoroughly and soak in at least 2 cups boiling water for 1 hour. Simmer for 10–15 minutes and strain. Pour the mushroom stock through a fine sieve or filter. Rinse, drain, and dice the mushrooms. Sauté onions in 2 tablespoons butter until lightly brown, add mushrooms, and continue cooking for 10 more minutes. Prepare a roux with 6 tablespoons butter and flour. Add roux to the mushroom mixture and stir. Sauté a little longer. Add 1½ cups hot mushroom stock and simmer 2–3 minutes, stirring constantly. Season with salt and add 1 tablespoon butter.

Saffron Sauce

SHAFRANOVY SOUS

6 tablespoons butter
½ cup flour
1 quart meat stock
⅓ cup chopped onion
1 parsley root, peeled and chopped
⅓ cup chopped celery
1 teaspoon saffron
⅓ cup vodka
white wine
salt

Prepare a light roux using 4 tablespoons butter and ½ cup flour. Stir in hot meat stock and bring to a boil. Sauté onion lightly in the rest of the butter. Add onion, parsley root, and celery to the broth. Simmer 30 minutes and strain.

Dissolve saffron in the vodka, stir into sauce, and return to a boil. Season with white wine and salt. Serve with poultry.

Sweet-and-Sour Raisin Sauce

KISLO-SLADKY SOUS S IZYUMOM

2 tablespoons oil
2 tablespoons flour
2 cups fish stock
½ cup white wine
salt
1 tablespoon honey
juice of ½ lemon or 1 tablespoon wine vinegar
¼ cup raisins, blanched
20 slivered almonds (optional)

Heat the oil, stir in flour. Dilute with hot fish stock, stir until smooth, and simmer for 5 minutes. Add white wine, salt, honey, and lemon juice or vinegar for sweet-sour seasoning. Add blanched raisins and optional almond slivers and heat in the sauce. Serve with fish, potato, and rice dishes.

Sauerkraut Sauce

SOUS IZ KISLOY KAPUSTY

1 pound sauerkraut, rinsed and squeezed dry
   (reserve liquid)
½ cup butter
1 medium onion, chopped
1–1½ cups sauerkraut juice
salt, pepper
2 tablespoons vinegar
1 tablespoon honey

Puree sauerkraut in a food processor and braise in butter. Sauté onions in butter and add to sauerkraut. Add sauerkraut juice, cover, and stew for 30 minutes. (Do not add juice all at once or the sauce will not thicken.) Season with salt, pepper, vinegar, and honey for a sweet-sour taste.

Serve with roast goose or duck.

Marinated Cucumber Sauce

SOUS IZ MARINOVANNYKH OGURTSOV

1 medium onion, chopped
4 tablespoons butter
1 tablespoon vinegar
6 tablespoons tomato paste
2 cups meat stock
1 tablespoon light roux
⅔ cup marinated mushrooms, sliced
⅔ cup cornichons, chopped
pepper

Sauté onions in 2 tablespoons butter. Add vinegar, cover, and simmer until all liquid has evaporated. Sauté tomato paste lightly in 1 tablespoon butter, add to onions, and stir. Add stock and simmer over low heat until creamy. Strain sauce, add roux, and reheat.

Sauté mushrooms and cornichons briefly in remaining butter. Stir into the sauce, bring to boil, and season with pepper. Serve with dishes made of poultry.

Pickled Cucumber Sauce

SOUS IZ SOLYONYKH OGURTSOV

1 pickled cucumber (medium), finely diced
1 small pimento, finely chopped
2 cups onion sauce (see recipe, page 147)
1 tablespoon tomato paste
2 tablespoons prepared mustard or grated
   horseradish

Cook cucumber and pimento in hot onion sauce for 3 minutes. Stir constantly.

Season with tomato paste and mustard (or grated horseradish). Serve with boiled meat.

Red Currant Sauce

SOUS IZ KRASNOY SMORODINY

1 pound fresh red currants, or 1 cup dried red
   currants covered with water for 15 minutes
1 cup white wine
1 cup pan juices from a baked fish
1 tablespoon flour
sugar
1 teaspoon cinnamon

Rinse currants and pureé in food processor. Mix with wine and pan juices and bring to a boil. Dilute flour with a small amount of cold water, add to the currant mixture, and stir until smooth and thick. Simmer a few more minutes and season with sugar and cinnamon.

Serve with baked fish.

Cherry Sauce

VISHNYOVY SOUS

This sauce is prepared like the red currant sauce (see above). Use same amount of cherries. Serve with baked fish.

Sweet-and-Sour Prune Sauce

KISLO-SLADKY SOUS IZ CHERNOSLIVA

½ pound prunes
¼ cup raisins
4 tablespoons butter
½ cup flour
½ cup white wine or Madeira
juice of 1 lemon

Rinse prunes and raisins. Cover with water and cook until soft. Strain and remove prune pits. Reserve juice.

Prepare a dark roux with butter and flour, add 2½ cups hot prune broth, and simmer approximately 10 minutes until sauce thickens.

Add white wine or Madeira, bring to a boil, stir. Add prunes and raisins and heat in the sauce. Season with lemon juice.

Pickled Cucumber Sauce for Fish

SOUS IZ SOLYONYKH
OGURTSOV K RYBE

3–6 pickled gherkins
¼ cup oil
1 bunch parsley, chopped
1 tablespoon light roux
2 cups fish stock
½ cup pickle brine
1 tablespoon honey

Drain gherkins. Reserve brine.

Cut gherkins lengthwise into strips and sauté lightly for 3 minutes in oil with parsley. Stir into roux and add hot stock and brine. Cook for several minutes and season with honey. (A combination of 1 cup fish stock and 1 cup mushroom broth, made previously and kept in the refrigerator, may be used instead of fish stock.)

Serve with cooked or baked fish.

Anchovy Sauce

SOUS IZ ANCHOUSOV ILI SARDINOK

¾ cup fish or chicken stock
2 tablespoons light roux
4 anchovies
salt, pepper
lemon juice
2 tablespoons sour cream

Add hot stock to roux, cook for 2 minutes, and strain. Chop anchovies very finely and heat in the sauce. Bring to a boil. Season with salt, pepper, and lemon juice. Just before serving, fold in sour cream. Serve with fish dishes.

Squid Sauce

SOUS IZ KALMAROV

1 pound cleaned squid, well rinsed
1 cup sour cream
2–3 tablespoons prepared horseradish
salt, pepper
sugar
vinegar

Cover squid with cold water, bring rapidly to a boil, reduce heat, and simmer for 2–3 minutes. Rinse in cold water, drain, cool, and cut into noodle-shaped slices. Mix well with sour cream and horseradish. Season with salt, pepper, sugar, and vinegar and bring to a boil again. Serve with potatoes boiled in the skin or baked.

White Sauce for Fish I

BELY SOUS K RYBE I

1 cup butter, melted
juice of 1 lemon
1 bunch parsley, chopped
2 egg yolks
2 cups fish stock
2 tablespoons light roux
10 boiled crayfish, chopped
¼ pound mushrooms, sliced
salt

Mix butter with lemon juice and parsley. Stir in egg yolks. Add hot stock to roux and boil for 2 minutes. Place in the top of a simmering double boiler. Gradually stir the butter–egg yolk mixture into the sauce. Briefly sauté crayfish in butter. Heat mushrooms in sauce and season with lemon juice and salt. Serve crayfish and sauce with fish.

White Sauce for Fish II

BELY SOUS K RYBE II

2–3 medium onions, chopped
1/2 cup flour
2 tablespoons oil
3 cups fish stock
lemon juice or vinegar
gooseberry juice or apple juice
2–4 teaspoons sugar or honey

Sauté onions and flour lightly in oil. Do not allow flour to brown. Add hot fish stock. Boil for several minutes and season with lemon juice (or vinegar), gooseberry juice (or apple juice), and sugar (or honey) for a sweet-and-sour flavor. Strain the sauce. Serve with poached fish.

Crayfish Sauce

RAKOVY SOUS

salt
1/2 cup chopped dill
1/2 cup chopped parsley
10 crayfish
2 cups fish stock
4 tablespoons butter
1/2 cup flour
1/2 cup heavy cream
2 egg yolks
1/4–1/2 cup crayfish butter (see recipe below)
pepper
juice of 1/2 lemon

Bring 2 quarts water, salt, dill, and parsley to a boil and immerse well-rinsed crayfish. After 5 minutes, reduce heat and let the crayfish simmer 10 minutes longer.

Shell crayfish and use shells to prepare crayfish butter. Reserve cooking liquid.

Melt butter, add flour. Stir in cream and cook 2 minutes. Add hot crayfish stock and simmer 2 minutes more over low heat. Strain through a fine sieve. Mix egg yolks with crayfish butter and stir gradually into the strained sauce. Heat slowly and season with salt, pepper, and lemon juice. Heat crayfish in sauce. Serve with fish dishes.

Crayfish Butter

RAKOVOYE MASLO

shells of 10 boiled crayfish
4–8 tablespoons butter

Pound crayfish shells in a mortar as small as possible or pulverize in a food processer and brown in hot butter, stirring constantly. Strain through a fine sieve and cool. The finer the shells are pounded, the more beautiful the color will be.

White Marinade

BELY MARINAD

1 carrot, chopped
1 parsley root, peeled and chopped
1 medium onion, quartered
salt
peppercorns
pinch of sugar
pinch of cinnamon
pinch of ground cloves
2 bay leaves
2 cups fish stock or water acidified with fruit
vinegar

Boil vegetables, salt, and spices in the fish stock or water plus vinegar for approximately 10 minutes and strain. Serve hot with fish dishes or chilled with appetizers.

Tomato Marinade

TOMATNY MARINAD

5 medium carrots, julienned
2 medium onions, minced
$^1/_2$ pound parsley root, peeled and julienned
2 tablespoons oil
1 cup tomato paste
$1^1/_4$ cups vinegar
$^1/_2$ cup fish stock or water
1–2 tablespoons sugar
salt
peppercorns
$^1/_4$ teaspoon ground cloves
2 bay leaves

Sauté vegetables and onion in oil.

Stir in tomato paste and stew for 7–10 minutes. Add vinegar, fish stock (or water), sugar, and spices. Stir well and simmer for another 15 minutes. Serve hot or cold.

This marinade goes well with fish dishes.

Cold Sauce

KHOLODNYE SOUS

1 cup sour cream (or crème fraîche)
3 hard-boiled egg yolks, mashed
sugar
$^1/_4$ cup vinegar
salt
dill, chopped for garnish

Thoroughly blend sour cream, egg yolks, sugar, and vinegar. Season with salt and more vinegar.

Pour over salad or vegetables and sprinkle with dill.

Sauce Provençale

SOUS PROVENSAL

2 egg yolks
1 tablespoon prepared mustard
$1^1/_4$ cups olive oil
salt, pepper
sugar
1 tablespoon lemon juice or vinegar
$^1/_4$ cup heavy cream

Mix egg yolks with mustard and slowly add olive oil, stirring constantly. Beat until sauce is thick and creamy. Season with salt, pepper, sugar, and lemon juice (or vinegar), and fold in cream.

Serve with cold meat, venison, fowl, fish, or fried dishes.

Cream Dressing

ZAPRAVKA IZ SMETANY

$^1/_2$ cup half-and-half	sugar
3 egg yolks (cooked)	juice of 1 lemon
salt	

Mix cream well with egg yolks in blender. Season well with salt, sugar, and lemon juice.

Tomato Sauce for Fish

TOMATNY SOUS

3 tablespoons olive oil
1/2 cup chopped onions
6 tablespoons tomato paste
1 cup fish stock
2 bay leaves
2–3 cloves garlic, crushed
salt
sugar
1 teaspoon prepared mustard

Heat oil and sauté onions for 3 minutes until translucent. Add tomato paste, hot fish stock, and bay leaves. Stir and simmer, covered, over low heat for 15–20 minutes. Season with garlic, salt, and sugar. Stir in mustard and remove bay leaves before serving.

Pour over fish, bake, and serve.

Mustard Sauce

GORCHICHNY SOUS

2 tablespoons Dijon-style mustard
1/4 cup sugar
salt
1/4 cup olive oil
1/4 cup fruit vinegar

Blend mustard, sugar, and a little salt slowly with oil. Stir until sugar and salt are well integrated. Finally, beat vinegar into the sauce. Serve with herring and salad.

Garlic Sauce

CHESNOCHNY SOUS

6–8 cloves garlic, minced
salt
3/4 cup water or defatted stock
1 teaspoon vinegar
pinch of ground coriander

Mix garlic with a small amount of salt. Stir well with boiling water or stock. Season with vinegar and a pinch of coriander. Serve with cold dishes or with boiled or roasted poultry, fish, or lamb.

Garlic Sauce with Walnuts

CHESNOCHNY SOUS S OREKHAMI

2–3 cloves garlic, minced
1/4 pound shelled walnuts, chopped
1 chili pepper, seeded and finely chopped
salt
1 teaspoon saffron
1/2 teaspoon ground coriander
1 small bunch cilantro, finely chopped
3/4 cup water, boiled and cooled
6 tablespoons pomegranate juice (available in health food stores)

Mix garlic, walnuts, chili pepper, and salt in a mortar. Mix with saffron, a pinch of ground coriander, and cilantro. Stir well with water and pomegranate juice. (If pomegranate juice is not available, use slightly diluted wine vinegar to acidify the sauce.) Serve with cold roasts, boiled poultry, lamb, or fish.

Mushroom Sauce

GRIBNOY SOUS

3/4 pound mushrooms
salt
1 medium onion, finely chopped
1 apple, peeled and grated
1 1/2 cups sour cream
1 teaspoon vinegar
1 teaspoon mustard
1 tablespoon sugar
1 teaspoon chopped dill
1 tablespoon chopped scallions

Boil mushrooms in lightly salted water for 10 minutes. Strain, cool, and chop. Mix with onion and apple. Season sour cream with vinegar, mustard, salt, and sugar. Mix well with the mushroom mixture and sprinkle with dill and scallions.

Serve with appetizers, cold meat, or hot potatoes boiled in the skin.

Mushroom Sauce with Horseradish

GRIBNOY SOUS S KHRENOM

---

³/₄ pound mushrooms
salt
3–4 tablespoons grated fresh horseradish or 2
   tablespoons prepared horseradish
1 cup sour cream
sugar
1 teaspoon vinegar
1 tablespoon chopped scallions
1 teaspoon chopped dill
1–2 hard-boiled eggs, sliced

Cover mushrooms with lightly salted water and simmer for 10 minutes. Strain, cool, and chop. Mix with horseradish. Season sour cream with salt, sugar, and vinegar. Add to mushrooms. Sprinkle sauce with scallions and dill and garnish with thin slices of egg.

Serve with cold meat or hot potatoes boiled in the skin.

Currant Sauce

SOUS IZ KRASNOY SMORODINY

---

3 tablespoons red currant jelly
1 tablespoon prepared mustard
1 tablespoon oil
1 tablespoon lemon juice

Mix all ingredients thoroughly and stir until thick. This sauce goes well with game.

Tartar Sauce

SOUS TARTAR

---

2 egg yolks
1 teaspoon prepared mustard
1 cup olive oil
salt, pepper
sugar
juice of 1 lemon
¹/₂ cup heavy cream
¹/₃–²/₃ cup cornichons, chopped
1 bunch parsley, chopped

Mix egg yolks with mustard and stir until smooth. Add oil drop by drop. Stir (always in the same direction) until it is thick and creamy. Season with salt, pepper, sugar, and lemon juice. Stir in cream and finally add cornichons and parsley. Serve with cold meat, fish, venison, poultry, or fried dishes.

Vegetables

BLYUDA IZ OVOSHCHEY

Long ago our ancestors knew that cabbage and root vegetables taste good and are nutritious. In Russia to this day cabbage and turnips are our most important vegetables. Turnips, rutabagas, sugar beets, horseradish, and other radishes, black and white—these roots, naturally replete with healing agents, are grown all over the country.

Cabbage, either fresh or in the form of sauerkraut, is basic to Russian cuisine—especially during strict fast seasons, which total two hundred days of the year. On fast days, of course, no animal products are eaten. Red vegetables are also banned because they are a reminder of the blood of Christ.

The potato is another important element in Russian vegetable cuisine. Rumor has it that we have 999 dishes prepared with potatoes! At one time farmers were afraid of the "devil's apple," and Tsar Peter I had to issue a decree forcing the people to grow potatoes.

Pumpkins and beets are popular everywhere. Thanks to the unique construction of Russian stoves, whole big pumpkins fit easily into a Russian oven. In former times, red beets symbolized quarrels and strife, but this is now considered a quaint superstition. Isn't our famous borscht, for example, a true ambassador of peace and goodwill?

Beans, peas, lentils, tomatoes, and bell peppers are grown primarily in southern Russia, whereas wild mushrooms abound throughout this vast land. Formerly, all Russia went mushroom hunting every fall, a peaceable hunt, in keeping with the good-natured character of the Russian people.

Stuffed Potatoes
FARSHIROVANNY KARTOFEL

1–2 large potatoes per person, peeled
salt
softened butter or sour cream
bread crumbs
grated cheese

Potatoes should be as uniform in size as possible. If necessary, cut a small slice from the bottom so that they will not fall over while browning in the oven. Boil in salted water until half done, about 10 minutes. Hollow out, using a teaspoon. Mash the scooped out part of the potatoes. Mix with the following "stuffings" and fill the potatoes with the mixture. Place in an ovenproof dish, pour melted butter or sour cream over the top, sprinkle with bread crumbs and grated cheese, and bake in a 350°F oven for 15–20 minutes.

STUFFINGS

The following stuffings accommodate 4 large potatoes. Chop ingredients very fine and mix well with the flesh of the potatoes. Season to taste.

2 herring fillets
2 medium onions
1 hard-boiled egg
1 teaspoon oil
salt, pepper

12 sprats or anchovies
6 cooked morels or other mushrooms
2 hard-boiled eggs
1–2 teaspoons oil
1–2 tablespoons bread crumbs
salt, pepper

3 eggs
1½ cups heavy cream
1 cup bread crumbs
salt, pepper
nutmeg

11 ounces minced mushrooms browned in
   butter
1 medium onion, chopped and browned in
   butter
1 carrot, chopped and browned in butter
¼ cup cooked rice
1 egg
salt, pepper

¾ pound cooked meat (chopped or run through
   meat grinder)
1 egg
2 tablespoons tomato paste
2 medium onions, chopped and browned in
   butter
salt, pepper
dill

Potatoes with Pickled Cucumbers

KARTOFEL S SOUSOM IZ
SOLYONIKH OGURTSOV

Serves 4

5–6 medium potatoes, whole
2 tablespoons dried mushrooms
4 pickled cucumbers
1 tablespoon butter
1 tablespoon flour
1 medium onion, chopped
1 small bunch parsley, finely chopped
1 small bunch dill, finely chopped
salt, pepper

Shepherd's Pie

Boil unpeeled potatoes about 12 minutes until they are not quite soft. Peel and cut into medium slices. Place mushrooms in a bowl, cover with boiling water, and let steep 1 hour. Rinse thoroughly, cover with 3 cups of water, and cook 10–15 minutes until soft. Drain and save stock. Chop mushrooms.

Peel pickled cucumbers and cut lengthwise into strips. Prepare a roux using butter and flour. Add hot mushroom stock, pickled cucumbers, onion, herbs, and mushrooms. Stir well. Season with salt and pepper. Simmer until the cucumbers are soft. Add potatoes, heat in the sauce, and serve.

Shepherd's Pie

MYASNAYA-ZAPEKANKA S KARTOFELEM
Serves 8

2 pounds sirloin
6 medium potatoes
3–4 medium onions
$\frac{1}{2}$ cup butter
salt, pepper
ground cloves
3 slices day-old white bread
$1\frac{1}{2}$ cups milk
3 eggs
3 tablespoons bread crumbs
2 tablespoons grated cheddar cheese

Slice sirloin into very thin pieces and pound flat.

Boil peeled potatoes in salted water, drain, and press through a ricer. Mix with ¾ cup hot milk and 4 tablespoons butter. Cut onions into thin rings.

Layer these ingredients in a well-buttered casserole dish (meat, onion rings, then potatoes). Season meat layer with salt, pepper, and ground cloves. Dot the potato layer with butter.

Soak white bread in remaining milk, squeeze, and mix well with eggs and salt. (This can be done in the food processor.) Cover the pie with this mixture and sprinkle the top with bread crumbs and grated cheese. Dot with butter and bake in a 375°F oven for approximately 1 hour. (If the surface browns too quickly, cover with aluminum foil.)

Serve with salad.

Stuffed Mashed Potato Dumplings

FARSHIROVANNIYE KARTOFELNIYE KOTLETY

Serves 6

1 pound lean pork
salt, pepper
1 teaspoon sugar
2 tablespoons butter
9–10 medium potatoes, peeled
1 cup milk
1 cup sour cream
3 eggs
3 tablespoons flour
⅔ cup bread crumbs

Cut pork into 1-inch cubes. Season with salt, pepper, and sugar and sauté in butter 30 minutes, until almost done. Remove from pan and let cool.

Boil peeled potatoes in salted water, drain, and press through a ricer. Mix well with hot milk, 1 tablespoon sour cream, 1 egg, and flour. Season with salt. Shape warm potato mixture into dumplings approximately 2½ inches in diameter and stuff with a piece of sautéed pork.

Dip dumplings into 2 beaten eggs, coat with bread crumbs, and place on a carefully greased baking sheet. Bake until brown in a 450°F oven

for 5–10 minutes. Cover with remaining sour cream and return to the oven for 5 minutes more.

Serve with mushroom or tomato sauce and salad.

Baked Mashed Potatoes with Innards

KARTOFELNAYA ZAPEKANKA

Serves 4

½ **pound beef lungs**
½ **pound beef hearts**
salt
1 bunch soup greens
4 eggs
2 medium onions, chopped
4 tablespoons butter
pepper
6 medium potatoes, peeled
½–1 cup milk
2 tablespoons bread crumbs

Rinse lungs and hearts and boil in salted water with the soup greens 45 minutes, until tender. Drain. Cool and run through meat grinder or food processor. Hard-boil and chop two eggs. Sauté onions in 3 tablespoons butter. Add onions and eggs to meats and stir. Season with salt and pepper. Boil potatoes and push through ricer or purée in processor. Stir in hot milk, 1 egg, and 1 tablespoon butter. Season with salt.

Fill a buttered dish with half of the mashed potatoes, spread with the ground meats, and cover with the rest of the potatoes.

Brush top with a beaten egg, sprinkle with bread crumbs, and bake in a 400°F oven for 15–20 minutes. Serve with onion sauce.

You can also make a roulade using the same ingredients: Stir 1½ tablespoons potato flour into the mashed potatoes to make a dough. Roll out to the thickness of a finger on a dampened linen napkin. Spread the dough with meat and use the napkin to roll it up like a jelly roll. Place the roulade on a greased baking sheet, brush with beaten egg, and sprinkle with bread crumbs. Bake 15–20 minutes and serve with onion sauce.

Potato Croquettes

KARTOFELNIYE KOTLETY

Serves 4

6–8 medium potatoes, peeled
2 tablespoons potato flour
⅓ cup oil
salt, pepper
bread crumbs or flour
butter or oil for frying

Boil potatoes. Drain. Press potatoes through a ricer. Blend riced potatoes, potato flour, and oil into a smooth dough. Season with salt and pepper. (The dough may be enriched with 2–3 egg yolks.) Shape croquettes, coat with bread crumbs or flour, and sauté in butter or oil until golden brown.

Serve with mushroom sauce.

Vegetable Pudding with Herring

OVOSHCHNOY PUDING S SELYODKOY

Serves 4–6

1 pound white cabbage, sliced thinly
3 tablespoons butter
3 medium potatoes, peeled
½ pound white bread
1 cup milk
2 medium onions, chopped
¾ pound salted herring or sprats
½ cup sour cream
5 eggs, separated
salt, pepper
2½ tablespoons bread crumbs
½ cup grated cheese

Sauté cabbage in a little butter over low heat. Cook potatoes, drain, and press through a ricer. Soak white bread in milk and squeeze well. Mix onions and herring (or sprats) with cabbage, potatoes, and white bread. Stir in sour cream and egg yolks and season with salt and pepper. Beat egg whites until stiff and fold into vegetable mix-ture. Transfer to a buttered ovenproof dish and sprinkle with bread crumbs and cheese. Pour melted butter over pudding and bake in a 400°F oven 30–40 minutes until golden brown. Serve with sour cream.

Stuffed Eggplant

FARSHIROVANNIYE BAKLAZHANY

Serves 4

2 medium eggplants (about 1 pound each), halved
salt, pepper
1 carrot, chopped
1 parsley root, peeled and chopped
1 slice celeriac, peeled and chopped
1 small head white cabbage, shredded
½ cup butter
bread crumbs
low-fat sour cream
2 cloves garlic, minced

Scoop out the eggplant meat with a teaspoon. Salt the eggplant halves and let sit for 30 minutes. Blanch 2 minutes in boiling water, drain, and cool.

To prepare stuffing, chop eggplant meat, combine with vegetables, and sauté in butter. Cover and braise 5–7 minutes. Season with salt and pepper and fill the eggplant shells.

Place in an ovenproof dish and sprinkle with

bread crumbs and hot butter. Bake 15–20 minutes in a 375°F oven.

Season sour cream with salt and garlic. Stir well and serve with the hot eggplant. Stuffed eggplant can also be cooked in tomato sauce.

TOMATO SAUCE

1/2 **bunch scallions, finely chopped**
2–3 **cloves garlic, crushed**
butter or oil
2 **tablespoons tomato paste**
1 **cup water**
salt

Sauté scallions and garlic briefly in butter or oil, add tomato paste and water, bring to a boil, stirring well, and season with salt.

Stuffings for Eggplant

The following stuffings accomodate 3–4 medium eggplants, prepared as above.

GROUND MEAT

1 onion, chopped	1 egg
1 tablespoon butter	2–3 cloves garlic,
4 slices white bread	chopped
1 pound ground veal	salt, pepper

Sauté onion in butter. Soak bread in milk, squeeze, and mix well with the other ingredients.

MUSHROOMS AND RICE

1 **pound mushrooms, chopped,**
   or 1/4 **cup dried wild mushrooms**
2 **tablespoons butter**
1/2–3/4 **cup cooked rice**
1/2 **cup sour cream**
eggplant meat, chopped
3–4 **cloves garlic, chopped**
salt, pepper
parsley, chopped
dill, chopped

Sauté mushrooms briefly in butter. (If they are dried, soak 1 hour, drain, cook, and chop.) Mix well with the other ingredients.

MUSHROOMS AND MILLET

1/4 **cup dried mushrooms**
2/3 **cup millet**
2 **medium onions, minced**
2 **tablespoons butter**
eggplant meat, chopped
1 **egg**
salt, pepper
parsley, chopped

Soak dried mushrooms in boiling water for 1 hour. Strain, reserve liquid, and chop. Steep millet in hot mushroom stock. Sauté onions in butter. Mix all ingredients with chopped eggplant, add egg, and season well. Garnish with parsley.

RICE AND EGGS

1/2 **cup uncooked rice**
2 **medium onions, chopped**
2 **tablespoons butter**
eggplant meat, chopped
2 **hard-boiled eggs, chopped**
1/2 **cup bread crumbs**
salt, pepper

Cook rice. Sauté onions in butter and add eggplant meat. Combine rice, onion mixture, eggs, and bread crumbs. Season with salt and pepper.

NUTS

1 **cup shelled walnuts**
4–6 **tablespoons butter, softened**
cilantro, chopped
1 **bunch parsley, chopped**
1/2 **cup celery leaves, chopped**
2–3 **cloves garlic, crushed**
salt
chili pepper
eggplant meat, chopped

Coarsely grind nuts. Mix with butter, herbs, and garlic. Season with salt and chili pepper. Combine with eggplant meat.

Stuffed Eggplant ▷

Stuffed Cabbage

CONDIMENT SERVED WITH
STUFFED EGGPLANT

4 hard-boiled eggs, chopped
1 cup grated Swiss or Parmesan cheese
3 tablespoons clarified butter, softened
2 cups nonfat yogurt
3 cloves garlic, chopped

Blend eggs with cheese and clarified butter. Season yogurt with garlic and stir in egg mixture.
    Serve with eggplant.

Stuffed Cabbage

FARSHIROVANNAYA KAPUSTA
Serves 4

1 medium head cabbage, white or red
salt
melted butter
bread crumbs

Rinse and core the cabbage. Blanch for 10 minutes in boiling salted water, let cool, and drain. Use a knife and spoon to hollow out the cabbage. The remaining outer layer of leaves should be 1–1½ inches thick.

    Finely chop the inner leaves. Alternate layers of chopped cabbage and choice of stuffing inside the head of cabbage. Place the stuffed cabbage in a roasting pan, pour melted butter over it, and sprinkle with bread crumbs. Bake 25 minutes in a 375°F oven. (Cooking time depends on the type of stuffing used.) Serve with tomato, béchamel, sour cream, or sour cream–tomato sauce.

STUFFINGS
SAUSAGE, HAM, AND POULTRY
4–6 ounces smoked sausage
4–6 ounces cooked ham
4–6 ounces cooked pheasant, pigeon, or
  chicken
salt, pepper
nutmeg
5 medium carrots, chopped
butter
meat stock
³/₄ cup rice, cooked

Grind sausage, ham, and poultry in a meat grinder and season with spices.

Braise carrots briefly in butter and add a small amount of stock; cook 10 minutes or until soft. Drain, puree, and season. Layer meat, carrot puree, chopped cabbage, and rice.

GROUND MEAT
4 slices white bread (or ¹/₄ cup rice cooked until
  half done)
milk
1 medium onion, minced
butter
1 pound ground meat (turkey, chicken, or beef)
salt, pepper

Soak white bread in milk and squeeze. Sauté onion in butter and mix with bread and ground meat. Season to taste.

CARROT
3 carrots, sliced
4 tablespoons butter
¹/₂ cup rice, cooked
¹/₂ cup milk
chopped herbs (thyme, tarragon, parsley)
salt

Sauté carrots in butter. Add rice and milk and simmer over low heat about 15 minutes or until done. Season with herbs and salt.

QUARK
Quark is a curd cheese popular in Russia. See note, page 178. One could substitute cottage cheese, ricotta, or farmer cheese.

¹/₄ cup rice, cooked
1¹/₂ cups quark
1 egg
4 tablespoons butter, softened
chopped herbs (parsley, thyme)
salt, pepper

Mix rice, quark, egg, butter, and herbs and stir well. Season to taste.

Braised Cabbage Lithuanian-Style
TUSHONAYA KAPUSTA PO LITOVSKY
Serves 4

³/₄ pound bacon, diced
³/₄ pound roast beef, diced
2 tablespoons butter or oil
3 medium onions, sliced
1³/₄ pounds white cabbage, shredded, or
  sauerkraut
salt, pepper
1¹/₂ cups meat stock
8 small tart apples, peeled, cored, and diced
  (optional)

Cook bacon and beef in very hot butter or oil. Add onions and cabbage. Cook briefly, season with salt and pepper, and add stock. Cover and braise over low heat until done, a good 30 minutes. (Cabbage should be light brown.)

If using fresh cabbage, apples should be added for the final 10 minutes of cooking time. The cabbage may also be garnished with smoked sausages.

If using sauerkraut instead of cabbage, rinse well and squeeze dry before cooking.

Wild Mushroom Fritters

BELIYE GRIBY V KLYARE

dried white mushrooms, as many as required
  (about 6–8 per person)
bay leaf
salt, pepper
batter (see basic recipe, page 206)
oil

Cover mushrooms with boiling water and let steep 1 hour. Drain. Simmer with bay leaf and pepper in ½ cup lightly salted water until soft. Drain and pat dry carefully.

Dip mushrooms one by one into batter and fry in plentiful oil in a frying pan or deep-fat fryer. Drain on paper towels. Season with salt and pepper and serve.

Stuffed Mushrooms

FARSHIROVANNIYE GRIBY
Serves 4

8–12 large wild mushrooms or white mushroom
  caps
salt, pepper
¼ pound whole white mushrooms
2 slices bread
½ cup heavy cream
1 bunch parsley
1 egg
½ cup grated cheddar cheese
bread crumbs
butter

Clean wild mushrooms (or white mushroom caps) with a fine cloth or paper and remove stems. Salt and pepper the caps. Soak bread in cream and squeeze. Run mushroom stems, white mushrooms, parsley, and bread through a meat grinder or food processor. Mix with egg and ¼ cup cheese and season with salt and pepper.

Stuff mushroom caps with the mixture, sprinkle with bread crumbs and remaining cheese, and put in a well-buttered dish. Bake in a 400°F oven for approximately 15 minutes.

Stuffed Mushrooms ▷

Wild Mushrooms au Gratin

ZHARENNIYE BELIYE GRIBY
Serves 4

1/4 pound dried wild mushrooms
1 quart milk
1 bunch soup greens
1 medium onion, chopped
2 tablespoons oil
salt, pepper
3 egg yolks
bread crumbs
1/2 cup sour cream
scallop shells

Rinse mushrooms and soak overnight in milk. Drain well and cook with soup greens in water to cover for 5 minutes until soft. Drain again, reserving broth, and cut into small pieces. Sauté mushrooms and onions in oil. Season with salt and pepper. Remove from heat. Stir in egg yolks, bread crumbs, sour cream, and a small amount of mushroom stock, if necessary, to make a smooth dough. Pile mixture into scallop shells or a buttered au gratin dish, sprinkle with bread crumbs, and bake in a 400°F oven for 15 minutes.

Wild Mushrooms in Sour Cream

BELIYE GRIBY V SMETANNOM SOUS
Serves 4

1 1/2 pounds fresh wild mushrooms, sliced
1 medium onion, chopped
3–4 tablespoons butter
1 tablespoon flour
1/4 cup water
1 1/3 cups sour cream
salt, pepper
1 bunch parsley, chopped

Heat mushrooms in a skillet until they release their juices. If the liquid is bitter tasting, drain the mushrooms and substitute water for the mushroom stock. Braise mushrooms in their own (or substitute) liquid until all moisture has evaporated. Remove mushrooms and use skillet to sauté onions in a small amount of butter. Add braised mushrooms and brown lightly.

Melt 1 tablespoon butter and add flour. Stir in water, mix with mushrooms, and stir in sour cream. Season with salt and pepper and garnish with parsley.

Mushroom Pudding

PUDING IZ GRIBOV
Serves 4

1/4 pound dried mushrooms
1/2 pound white bread
1 cup milk
1 cup chopped onions
2–3 tablespoons butter
6 eggs, separated
salt, pepper
1/2 cup bread crumbs

Boil rinsed, dried mushrooms in water for 10–15 minutes until soft and drain. Soak white bread in milk and squeeze. Braise onions in butter until they are transparent. Run onions, mushrooms, and white bread through meat grinder or food processor. Mix thoroughly with egg yolks, season to taste, and fold in stiffly beaten egg whites.

Butter an 8–12-inch pudding or soufflé mold and coat with bread crumbs. Fill half full with mushroom mixture.

Place mold in a roasting pan with a couple of inches of water and bake for 1 hour in a 375°F oven.

Serve with mushroom sauce (see recipe, page 156).

Stuffed Beets ▷

Stuffed Beets

FARSHIROVANNAYA KRASNAYA SVYOKLA

Serves 2–4

---

4 medium beets
1 carrot, chopped
1 parsley root, peeled and chopped
1 small turnip, peeled and chopped
1 medium onion, chopped
2 tablespoons butter
1 hard-boiled egg, chopped
1 apple, cored and diced
1 bunch dill, chopped
salt
1 tablespoon bread crumbs
1 tablespoon grated cheddar cheese
butter or sour cream for braising

Rinse beets. Boil unpeeled (or bake in the oven) until half done, about 40 minutes. Cool, peel, and hollow out.

Sauté vegetables in butter and cool briefly. Mix with egg, diced apple, and chopped dill. Season with salt. Stuff beets with this mixture, sprinkle with bread crumbs, grated cheese, and butter or sour cream. Bake in a 350°F oven for 15–20 minutes.

This stuffing can be varied using salted herring, boiled meat, sautéed mushrooms, or cooked rice.

Beets with Prunes

KRASNAYA SVYOKLA S CHERNOSLIVOM

Serves 4

---

3 medium beets
3 tablespoons olive oil
½ pound prunes, pitted and chopped
2 tablespoons sugar
salt

Bake washed, unpeeled beets in a 375°F oven for 45 minutes. (Use a toothpick to test for doneness.) Let cool slightly, peel, slice into strips, and cover with olive oil.

In the meantime, rinse prunes, cover with water, add sugar, and simmer 10–15 minutes until soft. Drain and mix with beets. If necessary, add a small amount of prune stock and salt to taste. Serve as a side dish with roasted meat or venison or as an appetizer.

Baked Pumpkin

ZHARENNAYA TYKVA
Serves 4

---

approximately 2¹/₂ pounds pumpkin meat
4 tablespoons butter
1 tablespoon flour
5–6 eggs
2 cups milk
salt, pepper

Cut pumpkin meat into pieces the thickness and length of a finger. Melt butter in a large ovenproof dish or pan, add pumpkin, and sprinkle lightly with flour. Bake in a 375°F oven until the top is light brown. Carefully turn the pieces of pumpkin. Beat eggs and milk and pour over pumpkin. Bake until golden brown and season with salt and pepper.

Stuffed Artichokes

FARSHIROVANNIYE ARTISHOKI
Serves 4

---

16 small artichokes
1 lemon
salt
20 boiled crayfish
¹/₂ pound roasted veal
2 eggs
1 tablespoon sour cream
pepper
¹/₂ teaspoon nutmeg

SAUCE

1 tablespoon butter
1¹/₂ teaspoons flour
1 cup stock
1 cup heavy cream

Remove chokes from artichokes and cut off stems and tough outer leaves. Sprinkle artichokes with lemon juice. Boil in lightly salted water for about 30 minutes and drain.

Chop crayfish and veal, mix well with eggs and sour cream, and season with salt, pepper, and nutmeg. Force this mixture between the artichoke leaves. Place stuffed artichokes in an ovenproof dish.

To prepare sauce, make light roux using butter and flour, add stock and cream, and bring to a boil. Pour sauce over artichokes, and bake for 5 minutes in a 350°F oven.

Stuffed Pumpkin

FARSHIROVANNAYA TYKVA
Serves 4–6

1¹/₂ cups rice
salt
¹/₂ cup raisins
1 medium pumpkin
6 tablespoons butter

Cook rice and season with salt. In the meantime, soak raisins in warm water 30 minutes. Drain.

Cut a lid from the pumpkin. Scoop out seeds with a spoon and, if necessary, take out enough pumpkin meat for the stuffing to fit.

Mix cooked rice with butter and drained raisins and stuff the pumpkin. Cover with the lid. Bake in a 375°F oven until the pumpkin is soft, about 1 hour. (Use a toothpick to test for doneness.) Cut crosswise into slices with a large knife and serve.

Stuffed (Russian) Pumpkin ▷

Groats, Pasta, and Quark Dishes

KASHI, MUCHNIYE, BLYUDA

I BLYUDA IZ TROROGA

Groats and cooked wheat have a long history in Russian cuisine and are considered national dishes. It was once the custom during armistice talks, for example, for the opposing sides to fix porridge and eat it while signing the peace treaty. Hence the Russian proverb, "You can't cook porridge with him," meaning, "You can't come to an agreement with him."

Among migrant harvesters and in the Cossack territories, eating porridge together was a ritual that enabled people to get to know each other. These communities became known as "porridges." And groats and porridge were traditionally served at christenings, weddings, and funerals. In the fourteenth century the word for groats was synonymous for "princely hospitality." All varieties of grains grow in Russia, and all are used for groats and porridge. Buckwheat, however, is the most popular. Peter the Great was an exception; he preferred barley.

From the fourteenth century on, the Tartars and their neighbors in other countries adjacent to Siberia significantly influenced Russian cuisine. To them we owe the recipe for noodle dough—luckily, because today it is hard to imagine Russian cuisine without pasta. Nearly every family has its own house recipe for *pelmeni*, *vareniki*, *kolduny*, and *galushki*. There are as many ways of serving pasta (as side dishes, in soup, or as a main course) as there are of preparing it.

Quark is also very popular. Available in gourmet shops and health food stores, it is a curd cheese with the consistency of sour cream but more tart in flavor, and it has a higher fat content than cottage cheese. It can be combined with fruit, vegetables, or fish; used in sauces, stuffings, pasta, and cakes; and served spiced or sweet. The jewel of our quark dishes is *paskha*, our celebrated, traditional Easter cake, about which I write extensively in the chapter on desserts and paska.

◁ *St. Petersburg*

Buckwheat Groats

KASHA GRECHNEVAYA
Serves 8

¼ **cup dried mushrooms**
2½ **cups buckwheat groats**
3–4 **tablespoons butter**
salt
¾ **pound beef marrow, sliced**

Cover dried mushrooms with boiling water and steep for 1 hour, until soft. Strain, reserving stock, and save mushrooms for another meal.

Add buckwheat groats to the mushroom stock and cook until it is a thick porridge. Add a little water as needed. Add 2–3 tablespoons butter and season with salt.

Layer groats and marrow slices alternately in a buttered casserole, ending with marrow. Bake covered in a 375°F oven for 30 minutes.

Buckwheat Groats "Krupenik"

KASHA GRECHNEVAYA "KRUPENIK"
Serves 4

7½ **cups buckwheat groats**
2 **cups quark or farmer cheese**
1 **cup sour cream**
1 **egg**
3 **tablespoons butter**
¼ **cup sugar**
salt

Cook buckwheat covered with twice the quantity of water about 20 minutes, until it becomes a grainy porridge, and let cool briefly. Beat in quark, ¾ cup sour cream, egg, 2 tablespoons butter, sugar, and a pinch of salt.

Spread the mixture in a large buttered dish (or on a buttered baking sheet), cover with the remainder of the sour cream, and bake about 20 minutes in a 375°F oven until golden brown.

Serve with butter or sour cream.

Gretchnevyk

GRETCHNEVYK

Serves 3–4

---

1 cup buckwheat groats
3 cups water
1 egg, beaten slightly
4 tablespoons butter or vegetable fat
salt

Gretchnevyk is a popular Russian snack often sold by street vendors. Boil buckwheat in water until it is a thick porridge. Cool and stir in beaten egg. Spread mixture on a greased baking sheet. Cool. Cut into 2 × 2-inch squares and fry in butter or vegetable fat on both sides until golden brown.

Stuffed Rice Balls

RISOVIYE ZRAZY

Serves 4

---

2 cups rice
1 medium onion, whole
1 small bunch parsley, chopped
salt, pepper
1/2 teaspoon nutmeg
6 cloves
3–4 eggs
1/2 cup bread crumbs
oil

STUFFING

1/4 cup dried mushrooms
1/2 onion, chopped
1 tablespoon butter

Boil rinsed rice with onion, parsley, salt, pepper, nutmeg, and cloves in 4 cups of water, until soft and dry. Remove the onion and mix cooled rice with 2–3 eggs. Shape little balls, push a small amount of mushroom stuffing into the middle, dip into fourth beaten egg, and coat with bread crumbs. Fry in oil until golden brown.

To prepare the stuffing, cover the mushrooms

with boiling water, steep until soft, drain, chop, and sauté with onion in butter.

Serve with green peas, chicken, or duck.

Oatmeal

OVSYANNAYA KASHA

Serves 4

---

1 1/4 cups rolled oats
1/2 cup flour
2 tablespoons cocoa
1 quart milk
2 tablespoons butter
2 tablespoons raisins
1/4 cup sugar
2 teaspoons vanilla extract
1/2 cup nuts or pumpkin seeds

Sift 1 cup rolled oats in a sieve with flour and cocoa. Pour into hot milk and simmer, stirring constantly, until thick.

Roast remaining 1/4 cup oats in butter and stir into porridge along with raisins. Simmer for 5 minutes. Season with sugar and vanilla, let cool, and serve sprinkled with nuts or pumpkin seeds.

Serve with cold milk.

Grainy Buckwheat Groats

KASHA GRECHNEVAYA RASSYPCHATAYA
S GRIBAMI

Serves 2–3

---

3 cups water
20 dried wild mushrooms
1 cup buckwheat groats
salt
3–4 tablespoons sunflower oil
2 medium onions, chopped
2 hard-boiled eggs, diced

Cover mushrooms with 1 cup boiling water and steep 1 hour. Drain. Pour 2 cups water over buckwheat groats and add soaked mushrooms, salt

Buckwheat Groats ▷

lightly, cover, and bring to a boil. Stir in 2 tablespoons oil and simmer over low heat until soft. Liquid should be completely absorbed. If not, uncover the pot and let liquid evaporate. Meanwhile, sauté onions in oil. Add onions and eggs to pot and let steep a little longer.

Wheat Porridge

KUTYA

Serves 4

---

2 cups wheat berries
1 cup sugar
¹/₃ cup honey

Blanch wheat berries in boiling water, drain, and cover with fresh cold water. Bake covered in a 300°F oven for approximately 4 hours. When done, mix the soft wheat berries with sugar and honey.

Wheat berries prepared this way can also be served in other combinations:

2 cups wheat berries
2 cups ground poppy seeds
1 cup shelled walnuts
¹/₂ cup raisins
¹/₄ cup honey
1¹/₂ cups sugar

2 cups wheat berries
2 cups chopped onions, sautéed
1 cup shelled walnuts
¹/₂ cup sugar
several pinches of salt

Filled Dumplings

PELMENI, VARENIKI, KOLDUNY

Pelmeni, vareniki, and kolduny are very popular in Russia. They are pockets of dough (similar to ravioli) with spicy or sweet fillings. Poached in salted water, they are served topped with melted butter, fried bread crumbs, peppered vinegar, sour cream, heavy cream, or sugar. In Siberia pelmeni are frozen in the open air and stored in cloth sacks. This is more than just a practical way to store them; preserved in this manner pelmeni seem to acquire a particularly delicious flavor. Fortunately, in the West we don't have to wait for a Siberian cold spell: the little pockets can be stored in the freezer. With this in mind, it is worth preparing large quantities.

The pockets themselves may be shaped in various ways. Always roll the dough thin (to about ¹/₁₆ inch). Cut out rounds with a glass (about 2¹/₂ inches in diameter), cover with a small amount of filling, brush the edges with egg white, and fold over to form a half-moon. Pinch the edges well so that the filling cannot leak out during the cooking process.

Alternatively, pile small amounts of filling on rolled-out dough, brush the spaces in between with egg white, cover with another sheet of dough, and cut out half-moons.

Or, cut squares of dough, top with filling, brush the edges with egg white, and fold over to make triangles. Pinch edges well.

These variations are known as vareniki and kolduny. Vareniki can be a little larger than 2¹/₂ inches in diameter. Pelmeni are shaped into little "ears" by pressing the two corners together and twisting them once between thumb and index finger.

Basic Recipe

Serves 4

---

3 cups flour
4 eggs
¹/₂–³/₄ cup water
¹/₂ teaspoon salt

Mix flour with eggs and enough water to form a smooth, elastic dough (like noodle dough). Season with salt and roll out on a floured surface to a thickness of approximately ¹/₁₆ of an inch. Cut out squares or circles. Fill with any of the following, shape into little pockets, and simmer in salted water over low heat for 10–15 minutes.

Remove with a slotted spoon, drain, and transfer to a heated bowl.

Siberian Pelmeni I ▷

In the following recipes only the filling is described, since the instructions for preparing the dough, putting the pocket together, and cooking remain the same.

Siberian Pelmeni I
ZNAMENITIYE SIBIRSKIYE PELMENI I

½ pound beef
½ pound pork
1 medium onion, quartered
5 cloves garlic, minced
3 tablespoons beef stock or water
salt, pepper

Run meats, onion, and garlic through meat grinder or food processor, stir in stock or water until smooth, and season with salt and pepper. Fill pockets of dough and proceed as above. Serve with melted butter, sour cream, or pepper vinegar.

Siberian Pelmeni II
ZNAMENITIYE SIBIRSKIYE PELMENI II

1 pound beef
6 tablespoons kidney fat or butter
2 medium onions, quartered
salt, pepper

Run all ingredients through meat grinder or food processor, mix well, and season to taste. Fill pockets of dough and proceed as above.

Siberian Pelmeni III
ZNAMENITIYE SIBIRSKIYE PELMENI III

½ pound ham
½ pound game or beef
1 medium onion, quartered
2 ice cubes, crushed
salt, black and white pepper
¼ tablespoon ground cloves

Run ham, meat, and onion through meat grinder or food processor and stir in enough ice to make mixture elastic. Season with salt, pepper, and cloves. Fill pockets of dough and proceed as above.

Pelmeni with Wild Mushrooms
PELMENI S GRIBAMI

¼ pound dried wild mushrooms
1 medium onion, chopped
1 tablespoon butter
salt, pepper
1–2 hard-boiled eggs, chopped

Cover mushrooms with water and simmer 20 minutes until soft. Drain and chop. Sauté onion in butter, add mushrooms, and brown briefly. Season with salt and pepper. Let cool and stir in eggs. Fill pockets of dough and proceed as above.

Pelmeni with Mushrooms and Ham
PELMENI S GRIBAMI I VECHINOY

¼ pound dried mushrooms
1 medium onion, chopped
1 tablespoon butter
1 pound boiled ham, diced
salt, pepper

Cover mushrooms with water and simmer 20 minutes until soft. Drain and chop. Sauté onion in butter, add mushrooms, brown briefly, and add diced ham. Mix well and season. (Optional: Stir 1 diced hard-boiled egg into the mixture.) Fill pockets of dough and proceed as above.

Pelmeni with Wild Mushrooms and Groats

PELMENI S GRIBAMI I KASHEY

2 tablespoons dried wild mushrooms
2 tablespoons sunflower oil
1 medium onion, chopped
1 cup prepared buckwheat groats (or ½ cup cooked rice)
1 hard-boiled egg, diced
salt

Cover mushrooms with water and simmer 20 minutes until soft. Drain, reserving stock, and chop very fine. Sauté in oil with onion and mix with grainy buckwheat groat porridge (see basic recipe, page 179) and egg, or substitute cooked rice for the groats. Stir well and season with salt. Fill pockets of dough and proceed as above.

Pelmeni with Fish

PELMENY S RYBOY

1 pound fish fillet
3 medium onions, quartered
½ cup butter, softened
salt, pepper

Run fish and onions through meat grinder twice. Add butter and stir until mixture is elastic. Season with salt and pepper. Fill pockets of dough and proceed as above.

Pelmeni with Cabbage

PELMENI S KAPUSTOY

¾ pound pork
2 medium onions, quartered
½ medium white cabbage, chopped
salt, pepper
1–2 tablespoons water

Run meat, onions, and cabbage through meat grinder or food processor. Season with salt and pepper. Add water and stir until elastic. Fill pockets of dough and proceed as above.

Kolduny with Veal and Herring

KOLDUNY S TELYATINOY I SELYODKOY

1 salted herring
1 pound veal
1 medium onion, chopped
1 tablespoon butter
2 hard-boiled eggs, chopped
6 each black and white peppercorns, crushed
½ teaspoon nutmeg
½ cup bread crumbs

Fillet herring and run through meat grinder or food processor with veal. Sauté onion in 1 tablespoon butter, add to meat mixture, and cool. Stir in eggs. Season with peppercorns and nutmeg. Fill pockets of dough and proceed as above. Serve with bread crumbs sautéed in butter.

Vareniki with Apples

VARENIKI S YABLOKAMI

2 pounds apples (soft, if possible)
½ cup sugar

Pare apples, core, and dice or grate. Mix with sugar and let steep for 15 minutes. Drain before using. Fill pockets of dough and proceed as above.

Vareniki with Potatoes

VARENIKI S KARTOFELEM

5–6 medium potatoes, peeled
3 medium onions, chopped
2 tablespoons butter or oil
salt, pepper

Boil potatoes, drain, and put through ricer. Sauté onions in butter and combine with potatoes. Season with salt and pepper. Thinly sliced and sautéed mushrooms may also be added to the potato mixture. Fill pockets of dough and proceed as above.

Vareniki with Sour Cherries
VARENIKI S VISHNEY

2 pounds sour cherries
1¼ cups sugar

Remove pits from cherries. Mix with sugar and put in the sun (or other warm place) for 3–4 hours.

Pound 5–6 cherry pits in a mortar and boil with the remainder of the stones in approximately ½ cup water. Strain stock through very fine sieve or filter. Drain cherries and fill the pockets of dough, sealing sides with wet fingers. Proceed to poach the varenikis as above. Drain. Bring cherry juice and filtered stock from cherry pits to a boil, add sugar, and cook until syrupy. Let cool and serve with sour cream and sugar.

Vareniki may also be filled with pitted plums, strawberries, or poppy seeds mixed with sugar.

Vareniki with Quark
VARENIKI S TVOROGOM

2 heaping cups quark, cottage cheese, or
**   farmer cheese**
2 eggs
2–3 tablespoons sugar
4 tablespoons butter, melted

Press quark through a sieve or drain in damp cheesecloth. Add eggs and sugar and stir until smooth. Fill varenikis and cook as above. Drain. Serve with sugar and melted butter.

Vareniki with Quark ▷

Vareniki with Liver and Bacon

VARENIKI S PECHONKOY I SALOM

1 pound calf's liver, skin removed and trimmed
1 pound bacon, cooked
3 medium onions, chopped
2 tablespoons butter
salt, pepper
olive oil

Cook liver covered in water until soft, about 5–8 minutes. Run liver and bacon through meat grinder. Sauté onions in butter. Stir into liver and bacon mixture. Season with salt and pepper. Fill varenikis and cook as above. Drain. Sprinkle with olive oil before serving.

Vareniki with Beans and Mushrooms

VARENIKI S FASOLIYU I GRIBAMI

2 cups cooked white beans
2 medium onions, chopped
1 tablespoon butter
1/4 pound dried mushrooms
salt
cayenne

Puree beans in food processor. Sauté onions in butter. Cover mushrooms with boiling water and steep 20 minutes. Drain. Slice thinly. Add beans and mushrooms to onions. Cook 5 minutes. Fill varenikis and cook as above. Drain.

Season with salt and cayenne.

Vareniki with Meat

VARENIKI S MYASOM

2 slices bread
1 pound boiled or roasted beef or pork
2 medium onions, chopped
1 tablespoon butter
salt, pepper

Soak bread in water, squeeze, and run with meat through meat grinder or food processor. Sauté onions in butter. Add meat and season with salt and pepper. Fill varenikis and cook as above.

Cabbage may be substituted for some of the meat. Boil, drain, squeeze well, and grind with bread and remaining meat as above. Serve varenikis with sautéed bread crumbs in butter.

Vareniki with Sauerkraut or Cabbage

VARENIKI S KAPUSTOY

2 pounds sauerkraut or fresh cabbage
2 tablespoons sunflower oil
1½ tablespoons tomato paste
1 cup stock or water
2–3 medium onions, chopped
1 carrot, chopped
1 bunch parsley, chopped
salt, pepper

Rinse and squeeze sauerkraut and cut into small pieces. (Slice fresh cabbage very fine.) Braise briefly in 1 tablespoon oil. Add tomato paste and stock or water, cover, and continue to braise until tender. Sauté onions, carrot, and parsley lightly in the remaining oil. Mix with sauerkraut or cabbage and season to taste. Continue to simmer, uncovered, until all the liquid has evaporated. Fill varenikis and cook as above.

Serve with onions sautéed in butter.

Sweet Quark Dumplings

SYRNIKI
Serves 4

2 cups quark, cottage cheese, or farmer cheese
4 tablespoons flour
1 egg
3 tablespoons sugar
1/4 cup confectioners' sugar
butter
1 cup sour cream

Combine first four ingredients well and roll out on a floured surface to a thickness of 3/4 inch. Cut out round or square little dumplings and sauté in hot butter on both sides until golden brown. Dust with confectioners' sugar and serve with sour cream.

Galushki

GALUSHKI

Galushki is a typical everyday Ukrainian dish that can be made with wheat or buckwheat flour, semolina, potatoes, or quark. Shape the dough in a 3/4-inch roll and cut off 3/4-inch-long pieces. Or the dough can be rolled out to a thickness of 3/4 inch and cut into small squares or strips. Boil galushki in salted water, milk, or stock until they rise to the surface. Remove with a slotted spoon, drain well, and serve with butter, oil, sour cream, rendered bacon, or sautéed onions.

Quark Galushki

GALUSHKI IZ TVOROGA

Serves 4

2 cups quark, cottage cheese, or farmer cheese
2 tablespoons butter, softened
1/2 cup flour
2 tablespoons sugar
4 egg whites, stiffly beaten
sour cream

Press quark through a ricer and stir well with butter, flour, and sugar. Fold in egg whites. Make dough squares. Cook as above. Drain. Serve with sour cream.

Small Quark Dumplings

SYRNIKI

Serves 4

3 medium potatoes	1 egg
1 2/3 cups quark, cottage	salt
cheese, or farmer cheese	butter
4–5 tablespoons flour	sour cream

Boil potatoes, peel, and push through ricer. Stir well with quark, egg, and flour. Add salt. Shape dough into rolls the length and thickness of a finger and sauté in hot butter until brown. Serve with sour cream.

Simple Galushki

PROSTIYE GALUSHKI

Serves 4

4 cups flour
approximately 1/3 cup water
2 eggs
salt
1/2 cup butter
1 cup sour cream
salt

Sift flour into a bowl. Add water, eggs, salt, and 8 tablespoons butter, and beat until dough is smooth. It should be stiffer than the dough for vareniki. Cook as described above.

Coat galushki with remaining butter and serve with sour cream.

Potato Galushki

GALUSHKI IZ KARTOFELYA

Serves 4

5 boiled medium potatoes
2 tablespoons grated raw potato
2 tablespoons flour
2 eggs
1 medium onion, chopped
1 tablespoon sunflower oil
salt, pepper
2–3 tablespoons butter, melted

Mash boiled potatoes and add raw potatoes, flour, and eggs. Work into a dough. Boil onion, drain, and sauté in oil. Mix into the dough and season with salt and pepper. Cook as above. Drain. Serve with melted butter or in soup.

Russian Pancakes
and
Filled Crepes

BLINY I BLINCHIKI

The Russian writer Alexander Kuprin (1870–1938) wrote of our celebrated Russian pancakes: "Bliny are round and hot and beautiful like a glorious sun. Bliny evoke sacrificial offerings to the gods. Bliny symbolize the sun, clear days, a good harvest, a happy marriage, healthy children . . ."

Bliny are baked year-round, but traditionally they are associated with *Maslenitsa*, Butterweek, a boisterous celebration to drive out the long, cold winter and welcome spring. People wrap themselves in animal skins and paint their faces with soot, making fearful noises to chase away evil spirits. If the heat of battle leads to actual blows, that too is good, for blood brings rain and is important for a good harvest.

No meat is allowed during *Maslenitsa*. Therefore, we prepare delicious pancakes of buckwheat, rye, or wheat flour. They are served with hot butter, sour cream, herring, salmon, and, of course, caviar; they are also served with honey, marmalade, and marinated fruits. Toward the end of Butterweek the ingredients and trimmings are skimpier and more humble; we grieve for the festivities as we prepare for the seven weeks of Lent that follow.

There are many bliny variations as well as many toppings for bliny, as you will see in the following recipes. What follows are the basic steps for making any bliny recipe.

BASIC RECIPE

In a large mixing bowl, dissolve yeast in ¼ cup lukewarm milk with a pinch of sugar. When mixture becomes thick or a little foamy, gradually stir in flour and milk. Cover and let rise for 1 hour. Deflate by punching with a wooden spoon and add remaining ingredients. Stir, cover again, and let rise for an additional 1½ hours. Just before making the bliny—as you would crepes or pancakes—fold the stiffly beaten egg whites into the batter. Your bliny batter is now ready for cooking. In a heavy skillet or nonstick pan, melt ½ teaspoon butter over medium heat. Tilt skillet so it is well coated with the melted butter and pour a small ladleful of bliny batter for each bliny—you may be able to fit two, three, or four bliny per skillet (depending on the size you use). As with pancakes, when you see little air bubbles on the surface of the batter, flip the bliny over, adding a little butter to lubricate the skillet again. Cook for a minute. Transfer bliny to an ovenproof pan, cover, and keep warm in the oven until ready to serve. In a small saucepan, melt additional butter—do not brown it. Serve the bliny. On each bliny pour a little melted butter and top with caviar or salmon and sour cream.

Buckwheat Bliny

BLINY GRECHNEVIYE

Serves 8–10

4 cups buckwheat flour
4 cups milk
2 tablespoons yeast, dissolved in ¼ cup
    lukewarm milk with a pinch of sugar
salt
1 teaspoon sugar
1 tablespoon butter, softened
2 egg yolks
2 stiffly beaten egg whites (optional)

To prepare batter, add buckwheat flour and 3 cups milk to yeast. Cover and let rise 1 hour. Punch down with a wooden spoon. Bring remainder of the milk, salt, and sugar to a boil and stir into batter along with butter and egg yolks. Let rise again. (Optional: Fold stiffly beaten egg whites into the dough.) Proceed with basic bliny recipe.

Buckwheat and Wheat Bliny I

BLINY PROSTIYE I

Serves 10–12

3 cups wheat flour
2 tablespoons yeast, dissolved in ¼ cup
    lukewarm milk with a pinch of sugar
2 cups water
3 cups buckwheat flour
3 cups milk
¾ cup butter
5 eggs, separated
2 teaspoons salt
2 teaspoons sugar

Prepare a batter using wheat flour, yeast, and warm water. Let rise 1½–2 hours. Punch down with a wooden spoon. Beat in buckwheat flour and warm milk and let rise again. Blend butter, egg yolks, salt, and sugar and work into the batter. Let rise 1 hour more. Fold in stiffly beaten egg whites. Proceed with basic bliny recipe.

Buckwheat and Wheat Bliny II

BLINY PROSTIYE II
Serves 10–12

1 cup wheat flour
4 cups buckwheat flour
2 tablespoons yeast, dissolved in ¼ cup
   lukewarm water with a pinch of sugar
2 cups water
2 cups milk
4 tablespoons butter, melted
3 eggs
1 teaspoon salt
1 teaspoon sugar

Prepare a batter using wheat flour, 2 cups buckwheat flour, yeast, and warm water. Let rise. Bring milk to a boil and pour milk over rest of buckwheat flour, let cool, and add to yeast mixture. Stir. Cover and let rise for 1 hour. Punch down with a wooden spoon. Stir in butter, eggs, salt, and sugar and let rise 1 hour more. Proceed with basic bliny recipe.

Wheat Flour Bliny

BLINY PSHENICHNIYE
Serves 8–10

5 cups wheat flour
2 cups water
2 cups milk
2 tablespoons yeast, dissolved in ¼ cup
   lukewarm water with a pinch of sugar
¾ cup butter
5 eggs, separated
1 teaspoon salt
1 teaspoon sugar

Add wheat flour, water, and milk to yeast. Cover and let rise for 1 hour. Punch down with a wooden spoon. In a bowl, beat butter, egg yolks, salt, and sugar until foamy. Stir into batter and let rise 1 hour more. Just before cooking, fold in stiffly beaten egg whites. Proceed with basic bliny recipe.

Wheat Bliny with Whipped Cream

BLINY PSHENICHNIYE SO SLIVKAMI

2 tablespoons yeast, dissolved in ¼ cup
   lukewarm water and a pinch of sugar
4 cups wheat flour
3½ cups milk
1 cup butter
2 eggs, separated
1 teaspoon salt
1 teaspoon sugar
½ cup heavy cream, whipped

Prepare batter as in previous recipe, but fold in whipped cream with the stiffly beaten egg whites. Proceed with basic bliny recipe.

Tsar-Style Buckwheat and Wheat Bliny

BLINY TSARSKIYE
Serves 12–14

5 cups buckwheat flour
3 tablespoons yeast, dissolved in ¼ cup
   lukewarm water with a pinch of sugar
6 cups milk
5 cups wheat flour
¾ cup butter
10 eggs, separated
½ cup sour cream
2 cups heavy cream
1 tablespoon salt
1 tablespoon sugar

Prepare a batter using buckwheat flour, yeast, and 2 cups milk. Let rise 1 hour. Punch down with a wooden spoon. Work in remainder of milk and wheat flour and let rise again. Blend butter, egg yolks, sour cream, heavy cream, salt, and sugar and stir into the batter. Let rise another 1½–2 hours. Fold in stiffly beaten egg whites. Proceed with basic bliny recipe.

Lenten Bliny

BLINY POSTNIYE

Serves 10–12

2 cups buckwheat flour
3 cups wheat flour
2 tablespoons yeast, dissolved in ¼ cup
   lukewarm water with a pinch of sugar
approximately 1 quart water
1 teaspoon salt
1 teaspoon sugar

Prepare a batter using buckwheat flour, 1½ cups wheat flour, yeast, and approximately 2 cups water. Let rise for 24 hours. Punch down with a wooden spoon. Work in remainder of flour, salt, sugar, and enough water to reach the correct consistency. Let rise another hour. Proceed with basic bliny recipe.

Lenten bliny are prepared without milk or eggs and are cooked in vegetable fat.

Tsar-Style Bliny

TSARSKIYE BLINY SLADKIYE

Serves 4–6

1 cup butter
6 egg yolks
1 cup sugar
1 cup flour
1½ cups heavy cream
1½ teaspoons orange liqueur
lemon juice
2 tablespoons jam or jelly

Heat ½ cup butter, strain through a cloth, and let cool. Beat with egg yolks and sugar until foamy.

Refrigerate. Stir flour with 1 cup cream until smooth. Heat and slowly bring to a boil, stirring constantly until thick (the same consistency as bliny batter).

Let cool and blend thoroughly with butter mixture. Flavor with liqueur. Whip remaining cream until stiff and fold into the batter. Cook at once in remaining butter. Sprinkle bliny with sugar, drizzle with lemon juice, and pile on top of each other. Decorate with a little jam or jelly.

Quick Bliny

BLINY SKORIYE

Serves 10–12

8 eggs, separated
1 cup butter, softened
7 cups wheat flour
buttermilk

Stir egg yolks and butter into flour until smooth. Add buttermilk until the batter reaches desired smooth, thick, but liquid consistency. Fold in stiffly beaten egg whites. Proceed with basic bliny recipe.

Blinchiki

BLINCHIKI

Blinchiki are wafer-thin crepes best cooked in a nonstick pan. The batter must be thin so that it flows easily over the bottom of the pan. Blinchiki are cooked in butter. The pan must be regreased when the blinchiki are flipped.

Basic Batter Recipe

Serves 10–12

2 eggs, separated
1½ teaspoons butter, softened
½ teaspoon salt
½ teaspoon sugar
3 cups milk
2 cups flour

Beat egg yolks with butter, salt, and sugar until foamy. Add milk and, stirring constantly, gradually add flour to make a smooth batter. Beat egg whites until stiff and fold carefully into batter.

Coat pan with butter (see above) and cook wafer-thin crepes.

Blinchiki with Quark

BLINCHIKI S TVOROGOM

QUARK FILLING

1 cup quark, cottage cheese, or farmer cheese
1½ teaspoons butter, softened
2 egg yolks
2 tablespoons sugar
pinch of salt
1–2 ounces raisins (optional)

Prepare batter following the basic recipe. Prepare filling by blending quark with the other ingredients. Cook blinchiki on one side only. Spread some of the filling on the cooked side of the blinchiki and fold up like an envelope. Brown on both sides in butter.

Blinchiki with Apples

BLINCHIKI S YABLOKAMI

APPLE MIXTURE

2½ pounds apples, peeled, cored, and sliced
½ cup sugar
1 teaspoon cinnamon
½ teaspoon ground cloves
½ cup butter

Prepare batter according to basic recipe. Cook blinchiki on both sides.

Mix apples with sugar, cinnamon, and cloves.

Layer blinchiki and apples in a buttered casserole, ending with a layer of apples. Dot each layer of apples with butter. Bake in a 375°F oven for about 1 hour until golden brown. Serve with sugar.

Blinchiki with Cream

BLINCHIKI S KREMOM

CREAM MIXTURE

5 egg yolks
½ cup sugar
½ cup sour cream
bread crumbs

Prepare batter according to basic recipe. Cook blinchiki on both sides. Beat 4 egg yolks and sugar until foamy. Stir in sour cream. Grease a casserole and sprinkle with bread crumbs. Alternately layer blinchiki and cream. Brush the top layer of blinchiki with the remaining egg yolk and bake approximately 20 minutes in a 375°F oven.

Blinchiki with Liver

BLINCHIKI S PECHONKOY

LIVER FILLING

½ calf's lung, well rinsed
½ calf's liver
1 carrot, sliced
1 bunch parsley, chopped
salt, pepper
1 medium onion, chopped
1½ tablespoons butter
4–5 hard-boiled eggs, diced
1 teaspoon nutmeg

Prepare batter according to basic recipe. Cook blinchiki on both sides. Cover lung, liver, carrot, and parsley with salted water and cook until soft. Drain. Run through meat grinder or food processer. Sauté onion in butter, add ground meat, and cook briefly. Mix with eggs, season with nutmeg, salt, and pepper, and let cool.

Layer blinchiki alternately with filling in a greased casserole dish and bake in a 375°F oven for about 1 hour.

Serve with a spicy, dark sauce.

Blinchiki ▷

Pirozhki Made with Blinchiki

PIROSHKI IZ BLINCHIKOV

Cook blinchiki on one side only, turn over, and let cool briefly.

Spread a thin layer of filling over the cooked side. Fold opposite sides in and carefully roll up from a third side. Brush the fourth side with a small amount of egg whites and press together so that the rolls will not unravel. Sauté in hot butter or in a deep-fat fryer until they are golden all over. Drain on absorbent paper.

Serve with fresh or fried parsley or garnish with sour cream.

Crayfish Filling

NACHINKA IZ RAKOV

4 eggs, beaten
½ bunch parsley, finely chopped
1 tablespoon butter
meat of 30 crayfish, cooked and chopped
¼ cup bread crumbs
2–3 tablespoons heavy cream
salt
1 teaspoon nutmeg

Mix eggs and parsley and scramble in butter. Mix with crayfish, bread crumbs, and cream. Season with salt and nutmeg. Proceed as described above.

Beef Filling

MYASNAYA NACHINKA

1 pound cooked beef
1 medium onion, chopped
1 tablespoon butter
2–3 hard-boiled eggs, diced
½ cup parsley, finely chopped
½ cup dill, finely chopped
salt, pepper

◁ *Piroshki Made with Blinchiki*

Run beef through meat grinder or food processor. Sauté onion in butter. Add beef, eggs, and herbs. Season with salt and pepper. Proceed as described above.

Layered Stuffed Blinchiki

BLINCHIKI SLOYONIYE

MEAT FILLING

1 pound cooked beef
1 medium onion, chopped
1½ teaspoons butter
1–2 hard-boiled eggs, diced
salt, pepper

Run beef through meat grinder or food processor. Sauté onion in butter. Combine sautéed onion, meat, eggs, salt, and pepper.

QUARK FILLING

1 cup quark, cottage cheese, or farmer cheese
1 egg
1–2 tablespoons sour cream
1½ teaspoons butter

Thoroughly mix all ingredients.

SEMOLINA FILLING

½ cup milk
1 tablespoon butter
1 egg
⅓ cup semolina flour
salt

Bring milk and butter to a boil. Beat egg into semolina, add hot milk and salt, and stir constantly until it reaches a grainy consistency.

Prepare blinchiki batter according to basic recipe, page 195. Cook blinchiki on both sides. Place alternate layers of meat, quark, and semolina filling with blinchiki in between in a greased casserole dish. Bake in a 375°F oven for 20 minutes or so until the top is golden brown.

Pirogi Made with Bliny

BLINCHATIYE PIROGHI

A famous, traditional preparation.

Prepare bliny using wheat or buckwheat flour and layer the bottom and sides of a springform pan with them. They should overlap on the sides of the pan enough to form a high edge. Alternately layer filling and bliny in the form. Turn down the high edge so that the filling is completely covered. Pour heavy or sour cream and egg yolk or hot butter over the top, sprinkle with bread crumbs, and bake in a 375°F oven for 20–30 minutes until crisp and golden brown. Cut as you would a pie or cake.

Serve with broth, as an appetizer, or for breakfast.

FILLINGS

Chopped hard-boiled eggs with chopped parsley, dill, salt, and hot butter
Quark with chopped hard-boiled eggs and salt
Quark with buckwheat groats
Meat or innards (see Fillings for Pirogi), page 209)
Grated cheese
Braised fruit
Jam, etc.

Bliny can also be filled individually, rolled up, placed in an ovenproof dish, covered with béchamel sauce and grated cheese, and baked 20 minutes until top turns brown.

Cover sweet bliny with a mixture of sour cream, egg yolks, and sugar and bake for 15–20 minutes in a 375°F oven.

Northern Russia ▷

Pirogi and Pâtés

PIROGI I PASCHTETI

This chapter would seem an appropriate place to tell you about Russian stoves. In former times, the stove was the focus of the house, around which everything revolved. The Russian stove had many functions other than serving as an oven for baking bread, pirogi, and cakes and a convenient place to cook meat, fish, soup, and groats. Old people and children slept on top of it. It was large enough to be an ideal sauna. Onions, garlic, hops, and herbs were dried around the stove, as well as wet clothes and shoes. People even grew barley on top of it, taking advantage of the warmth to brew beer.

Chimneys were unknown in former times, so the whole house was covered in soot. Even that had certain advantages in that the smoke acted as a disinfectant and the evenly distributed heat assured a healthy room temperature.

There are many legends about our stoves, including this one about Ivan Philippov. The legend goes that Ivan was so famous for his wonderful bread, the tsar insisted that the bread baked by his own baker be as good as Ivan's. In vain did the royal cooks try to bake bread of equal quality. Philippov knew that they could never succeed, because the water of the Neva was not good enough. Philippov used flour from his own mills for his bread and cakes and he bought his wheat in Tambov, the little village in which I grew up.

Pirogi is another national dish of Russia. Fillings vary regionally: fish in Siberia, vegetables and eggs in the south, and mushrooms in the west.

Pâtés were introduced to Russia by French chefs and have been adapted and refined to taste and to availability of local ingredients.

The first pâté restaurants in Russia were opened in the middle of the nineteenth century. The most famous belonged to Afanasyev in St. Petersburg. Guests could choose among 20 varieties of pâtés served with hot and cold sauces.

Pirogi, Pirozhki, Vatrushki
PIROGHI, PIROSHKI, VATRUSHKI

These celebrated Russian specialties are prepared with yeast dough, short pastry, or puff pastry; stuffed with sweet or spicy fillings; and baked until golden brown. They differ only in size and shape.

PIROGI

Pirogi are large and usually round. Thinly rolled pastry is spread with filling, covered with another sheet of pastry, and decorated with pastry trimmings. The edges are brushed with egg and pressed together; the surface is pierced several times with a fork and brushed with egg yolk. They are baked in a 375°F oven for 30–60 minutes, depending on the filling.

PIROZHKI

Pirozhki are small pirogi. The pastry is also rolled thin and cut into 3–5-inch circles. Pirozhki are topped with a spoonful of filling. The edges are brushed with egg and the circles and filling are then covered with another pastry circle and baked in the oven. (Or the filling may be put on the circle and the edge pulled up around it and pressed firmly together.) Savory pirozhki are served with plenty of oil or butter or deep-fat fried with whole parsley.

VATRUSHKI

Vatrushki are open-faced, baked pirozhki. Circles of pastry are covered with filling and the edges of the dough are pulled up to form a little bowl. For savory fillings, yeast dough or short pastry is best. For sweet fillings, puff pastry is most suitable.

Russian Yeast Dough

RUSSKOYE DROZHZHIVOYE TESTO

Serves 6–8

4 cups flour
2 tablespoons yeast
1 cup water
3 egg yolks
³/₄ cup butter
pinch of salt
pinch of sugar
¹/₂ cup milk

It is very important to have all the ingredients for yeast pastry at room temperature. Sift half the flour into a bowl. Dissolve yeast in lukewarm water and add to sifted flour. Stir everything well with a wooden spoon, cover the bowl with a cloth, and let dough rise in a warm spot for ³/₄–1 hour. The dough should have expanded to 1¹/₂–2 times its size and have the consistency of sour cream.

Beat egg yolks with butter until foamy, add salt and sugar, and stir into the dough. Add milk and work into a smooth dough. Sift in the rest of the flour, stir well, and place on a floured board. Knead until the dough no longer sticks to the board or to your hands. (If it is too stiff, add a little milk or water. If too soft, add a little flour.)

Cover the dough and let rise in a warm place for 1–2 hours.

Punch down, knead a few times, and roll as per master pirogi recipe on page 204.

Lenten Pastry Dough

TESTO DLYA POSTA

Serves 6–8

4 cups flour
2 tablespoons yeast
¹/₂–1¹/₂ cups water
2 tablespoons sunflower oil
pinch of salt
pinch of sugar

Lenten yeast pastry is made exclusively of vegetable products. It is prepared like Russian yeast dough (see above), but oil is used instead of egg yolks and butter. If you are filling the pastry, seal the edges with beer or kvass instead of egg (see recipes, pages 263–266). This pastry is used to make a kind of cracker.

Yeast Puff Pastry

SLOYONOE DROZHZHIVOYE TESTO

The same ingredients as Russian yeast dough
³/₄ cup butter

Prepare Russian yeast dough and let rise. Deflate. Divide dough into four pieces, roll each out to a thickness of 1¹/₂–2 inches. Let sit for 10 minutes and roll even thinner (approximately ³/₄ inch). Place a piece of butter equal to about 2 tablespoons in the center of each of three pieces of rolled-out pastry, place on top of each other, cover with the fourth piece, and press the edges firmly together. Roll the dough again to a thickness of approximately 1 inch, dot with 3 tablespoons butter, and fold in half. Dot with 3 tablespoons butter once more, fold over, roll out lightly, and refrigerate for ¹/₂ hour. Yeast puff pastry is used to make sweet pirogi or delicate sweet rolls filled with marzipan, marmalade, poppy seed, or cinnamon.

Short Pastry with Sour Cream

TESTO RUBLENNOYE SO SMETANOY

Serves 6–8

4 cups flour
3 egg yolks
¹/₃ cup sour cream
1 cup butter
pinch of salt

Sift flour on a board and make a well in the middle. Add salt. Beat egg yolks with sour cream and pour into the well. Use a flat knife to blend in the flour. Add dots of cold butter and continue to chop with the knife until all ingredients are well blended. With cold hands, quickly knead into a smooth, stiff dough, cover with kitchen parchment or aluminum foil, and refrigerate for 20 minutes.

Short pastry must be prepared quickly, with cold ingredients. If it crumbles, carefully add a small amount of water. If the pastry is too stiff, add 1 tablespoon sour cream.

Short pastry is suitable for pirogi, pâtés, and vatrushki.

Simple Short Pastry

PROSTOYE RUBLENNOYE TESTO

Serves 6–8

---

4 cups flour
1/2 cup water
1 cup butter
1 tablespoon rum
pinch of salt

Prepare like short pastry with sour cream.

Russian Fritter Batter

RUSSKY KLYAR

Serves 4

3/4 cup water
1 cup flour
1 teaspoon butter
1 tablespoon olive oil
pinch of salt
2–3 egg whites, stiffly beaten

Stir hot water into flour and beat until smooth. Mix well with butter, oil, and salt, and fold in egg whites.

Or:
1 cup beer   flour
1 tablespoon olive oil   pinch of salt

Blend beer and oil and add enough flour to make a thick batter. Add salt.

Brioche Pastry

TESTO BRIOSHNOYE

Serves 6–8

---

3 cups flour   1/2 cup milk
2 tablespoons yeast   3/4 cup butter, softened
1 cup water   pinch of salt
pinch of sugar
3 egg yolks

Sift a third of the flour into a bowl with salt and make a well in the center. Dissolve yeast in warm water with sugar and pour into well. Start with a broad knife, then use your hands to knead dough until smooth. Shape into a ball and make four incisions from the outer edge to the center. Place for 10–15 minutes in a pot filled with warm water. (It will float to the top.)

In the meantime, sift remaining flour on a board and make a well in the center. Combine the egg yolks and lukewarm milk, pour into well, then work into the flour.

Remove risen dough from water with a slotted spoon, drain, and work with butter into the other dough. Knead until the dough no longer sticks to your hands or the board. Cover, put in a warm place, and let rise for 1 1/2–2 hours.

Brioche pastry is less acidic than Russian yeast pastry, because it rises faster.

Noodle Dough I

LAPSHOVOYE TESTO I

Serves 6–8

---

3 cups flour
4 egg yolks
1 cup water
1 tablespoon butter
salt

Make a well in the flour. Place eggs, water, and butter in it. Using a knife first, then cold hands, work all ingredients into a smooth dough. Knead. Roll out thin and cut strips.

Noodle Dough II

LAPSHOVOYE TESTO II

Serves 6–8

4 cups flour
2 egg yolks
approximately ³/₄ cup water
4 tablespoons butter
1 teaspoon lemon juice
1 tablespoon sugar
pinch of baking soda
salt

Proceed as in previous recipe. Work all ingredients quickly into a smooth, stiff dough. Roll out and cut strips.

Pâté Pastry I

PASHTETNOYE TESTO I

¹/₂ cup boiling water
2 tablespoons butter, chicken fat, or lard, melted
1¹/₂ cups rye flour
1¹/₂ cups wheat flour (or use wheat flour only)
pinch of salt
2 eggs

Pour boiling water and butter, fat, or lard over flour. Add salt, stir well, and let stand for several minutes. Mix in eggs and knead into a firm dough.

Pâté Pastry II

PASHTETNOYE TESTO II

4 cups flour
1¹/₂ cups cold butter, cut in pieces
1 cup sour cream
1 tablespoon rum or cognac
1 egg
pinch of salt
pinch of sugar
2 eggs, beaten with water, optional

Mix flour with cold butter, sour cream, rum or cognac, egg, salt, and sugar, and knead dough until smooth. Put in a cool place.

This pastry is especially delicate if it is allowed to sit overnight in the refrigerator and then treated like a puff pastry. Divide into four pieces, roll out, and brush with egg beaten with a little water. Place the four pieces on top of each other, roll out, brush again with egg, fold over, etc.

Wedding Pirog

KURNIK

Serves 6

1 oven-ready chicken
salt
¹/₂ cup flour
1 cup butter
1¹/₂ cups chicken stock
¹/₂ cup heavy cream
1 bunch parsley, chopped
pepper
1 cup rice
¹/₂ pound mushrooms
5 hard-boiled eggs, chopped
1 bunch dill, chopped
1 egg, beaten
short pastry made with 4 cups flour (see recipe, page 206)

Boil rinsed chicken in salted water until tender, about 40 minutes. Let cool, carve, remove skin and bones, and slice. Prepare a light roux using flour and 4 tablespoons butter. Add stock, bring

Wedding Pirog

to a boil, and stir in cream and parsley. Season the sauce with salt and pepper.

Cook rice in water until it is al dente, about 15 minutes. Drain.

Cut mushrooms into thin slices and sauté in butter. Melt remaining butter and mix with eggs and dill. Add some sauce to chicken slices and stir. Add some sauce to mushrooms and stir.

Roll one fourth of the dough into a circle the thickness of half a finger. Place on a floured baking sheet. Cover with cooked rice, egg mixture, chicken slices, and mushrooms. Repeat in the same order until all ingredients have been used up. Make the layers smaller toward the top, so that they form a dome.

Roll out remaining pastry to a large circle and cover the filling with it. Cut off excess dough and press edges together. Decorate with dough trimmings and cut a small hole (a chimney) in the top for steam to escape.

Brush with egg and bake in a preheated oven at 375°F approximately 40 minutes.

Serve with a sauce of your choice or as a side dish with soup.

Baked bliny (see basic recipe, page 192) may also be layered between the other ingredients.

Fillings for Pirogi and Pirozhki

NACHINKA DLYA PIROGOV I PIROZHKOV

MEAT FILLING

1¾ pounds beef or lean pork, finely ground
½ cup butter
3 medium onions, minced
1–2 cups meat stock or water
3 hard-boiled eggs, finely chopped
salt, pepper

Sauté meat in butter with the onions for about 10 minutes over medium heat. Add stock or water, cover, and braise until tender. When liquid has evaporated, mix with eggs. Season with salt and pepper and add 1–2 tablespoons stock if the mixture is too dry.

Soaked (squeezed) white bread or a few chopped anchovies can be added to this filling.

BRAIN FILLING

1 beef brain
salt
6 peppercorns
bay leaf
vinegar
1 medium onion, minced
4 tablespoons butter
1½ teaspoons flour
½ cup sour cream
lemon juice
½ teaspoon nutmeg

Soak brain and boil in a small amount of water with salt, peppercorns, bay leaf, and a dash of vinegar for 10 minutes. Let cool, drain, and cut into small pieces. Sauté onion in butter, briefly brown flour with the onion, and add sour cream. Stir well and bring to a boil. Add brain, season with lemon juice, nutmeg, salt, and pepper and let steep for a few more minutes.

KIDNEY FILLING

1 calf's kidney
2 tablespoons vinegar
6 strips bacon, diced
1 medium onion, minced
1 bay leaf
½ teaspoon nutmeg
4 slices white bread
milk
dill, chopped
parsley, chopped
½ cup rum
⅓ cup Madeira
salt, pepper

Soak kidney in water and vinegar. Rinse and dry. Place in a kettle with the bacon, onion, and spices and cook until well done. Soak bread in milk and squeeze. Combine onion, bacon, and bread with meat and run through a meat grinder. Stir in herbs, rum, Madeira, salt, and pepper.

CHICKEN FILLING

1 oven-ready chicken
salt
1 bunch soup greens
1 cup buckwheat groats
5 hard-boiled eggs, diced
1 cup butter, softened
pepper
dill, chopped

Cook chicken in salted water with soup greens for about 40–45 minutes. Drain and remove meat from bones. Chop finely. Cook buckwheat groats until grainy. Mix well with chicken, eggs, and butter. Season with salt, pepper, and dill.

FISH FILLING I

½ pound pike or perch
4 tablespoons butter
½ pound salmon, cut in pieces
parsley, chopped
salt, pepper
nutmeg

Remove bones from pike or perch. Chop fish or run through meat grinder or food processor. Sauté in butter. Carefully combine with pieces of salmon, continue cooking 10 minutes, and season with parsley, salt, pepper, and nutmeg.

CRAYFISH FILLING

1 tablespoon flour
4 tablespoons crayfish butter (see recipe, page 154)
2 tablespoons sour cream
salt
nutmeg
20 crayfish, cooked, shelled, and chopped
2 egg yolks, beaten

Brown flour lightly in crayfish butter, stir in sour cream, simmer 2 minutes, and season to taste with salt and nutmeg. Add crayfish and heat in sauce for several minutes. Thicken with egg yolks.

FRESH MUSHROOM FILLING

1 pound fresh mushrooms, thinly sliced
1/2 cup butter
1 small bunch parsley, chopped
1 small bunch dill, chopped
4 scallions, chopped
5 hard-boiled eggs, diced
1/2 cup sour cream
salt, pepper

Sauté mushrooms in butter, mix with herbs, scallions, and eggs, stir in sour cream, and season with salt and pepper.

SAUERKRAUT FILLING

2 pounds sauerkraut, rinsed and squeezed dry
3–4 tablespoons butter
2–3 medium onions, minced
salt, pepper

Cut sauerkraut into small pieces and braise until tender in a small amount of butter and a little water. In a separate skillet sauté onions in butter. Combine sauerkraut with onions and season with salt and pepper.

SAUERKRAUT AND FISH FILLING

1 medium onion, minced
1/2 cup vegetable fat (or oil)
1 pound sauerkraut, rinsed and squeezed dry
salt, pepper
1 1/4 pounds smoked salmon or sturgeon, etc.

Sauté onion in 1/4 cup fat. Add sauerkraut and a small amount of water or stock, season with salt and pepper, and braise until tender. Remove bones from fish, cut fish into pieces, and sauté in remaining fat. Layer the sautéed fish with the sauerkraut mixture.

FRESH CUCUMBER FILLING

2–3 cucumbers (approximately 2 1/2 pounds), peeled and diced
3–4 hard-boiled eggs, peeled
4 tablespoons butter, softened
dill, chopped
salt

Combine cucumber, eggs, butter, dill, and salt.
It is advisable to put a layer of baked bliny between layers of this filling.

CARROT FILLING

5 carrots, diced
4 tablespoons butter
salt
sugar
2–3 hard-boiled eggs, diced

Cook carrots in butter with salt and sugar until tender. Chop or mash the mixture and add eggs. Season to taste.

RICE FILLING

2/3 cup rice, cooked
3 hard-boiled eggs, diced
4 tablespoons butter, softened
1 bunch parsley, chopped
salt, pepper

Combine rice, eggs, butter, and parsley. Season with salt and pepper.

APPLE FILLING

4–5 tart apples (approximately 2 pounds)
1 cup sugar
cinnamon
raisins or crystallized fruit (optional)

Peel and core apples, cut into thin slices, combine with sugar and cinnamon, and let stand 15–20 minutes. Add raisins and crystallized fruit (optional).

QUARK FILLING

1²/₃ cups quark, cottage cheese, or farmer cheese
¼ cup sugar
1 egg
4 tablespoons butter
pinch of salt
raisins, crystallized fruit, vanilla sugar (optional)

Apple Pirog

Stir quark well with sugar, egg, butter, and salt. Add raisins, crystallized fruits, or vanilla sugar (optional).

FRUIT FILLING

1³/₄ pounds blueberries or sour cherries
1–1¹/₂ cups sugar

Mix berries or pitted cherries with sugar and let stand 15–20 minutes. Drain.

Pirog with White Cabbage
PIROG S KAPUSTOY
Serves 4

1 medium white cabbage
salt
1–2 medium onions, minced
¹/₄–¹/₂ cup butter
3–4 hard-boiled eggs
pepper
short pastry made with 4 cups flour (see basic recipe, page 206)
1–2 egg yolks

Shred cabbage into thin strips. Salt and let sit for about 10 minutes. Squeeze.

Braise cabbage and onions in butter until tender, stirring often to keep from burning. Cool.

Chop hard-boiled eggs and mix with cooled cabbage. Season with salt and pepper.

Roll out short pastry to half the thickness of a finger on a board dusted with flour. Divide into two rectangular pieces, one of which should be slightly larger than the other. Place the smaller piece on a baking sheet dusted with flour and pile cabbage mixture on top. Cover with the second rectangle of pastry and press the edges down.

Decorate the pirog with dough trimmings, brush with egg yolk mixed with 1 tablespoon water, and pierce several times with a fork. Bake in a preheated 375°F oven for about 30 minutes.

Pirog with White Cabbage ▷

Kulebyaka

KULEBYAKA
Serves 4

1½ pounds perch
1 medium onion, minced
¾ cup mushrooms, thinly sliced
4 tablespoons butter
salt, pepper
⅓ cup semolina
yeast puff pastry made with 4 cups flour (see recipe, page 205)
4–6 bliny (see recipe, page 192)
5 hard-boiled eggs, sliced
dill, chopped
parsley
1 egg, beaten with water

Kulebyaka is a typical Moscow specialty. Preparation is similar to pirogi, but the pastry is longer and higher. It may also be stuffed with meat instead of fish.

Remove skin and bones from fish and make a stock with the bones and scraps. Chop the fish.

Sauté onion in 2 tablespoons butter. Braise mushrooms in 1 tablespoon butter and fish stock, add fish and onion, season with salt and pepper, and continue to braise until done.

Combine 1 cup water, 1 tablespoon butter, and a little salt and bring to a boil. Add semolina and simmer until thick and grainy.

Sprinkle flour on a cloth and roll out puff pastry to approximately 12 × 15 inches. Cover with half the baked bliny. Trim edges. Spread semolina flour down the center to a width of approximately 3½ inches. Arrange half the egg slices on top, add fish-mushroom mixture, and cover with the remaining egg slices, semolina, and bliny. Sprinkle dill between the layers.

Using a cloth, fold the sides of the pastry over the top, pinch the edges well, and place the pastry on a moistened baking sheet, seam side down. Decorate with pastry trimmings in a grid pattern and brush with egg and water. Make small incisions with a sharp knife and bake in a preheated 300°F oven for approximately 40 minutes. Garnish with parsley.

Kulebyaka ▷

Duck Pâté

PASHTET IZ UTKI

Serves 8–12

1 oven-ready duck
salt, pepper
1 carrot, chopped
1 medium onion, chopped
1 parsley root, peeled and chopped
1 leek, chopped
1 slice of celeriac, peeled and chopped
4–5 cloves
1 cup chicken stock
pâté filling of calf's liver and veal (see recipe, page 219)
pâté pastry (see recipes, page 207)
2 tablespoons butter
1 egg, beaten
1 tablespoon flour
½ peeled lemon, diced
2 tablespoons sherry

Rinse and dry duck, carve into serving pieces, and rub with salt and pepper. Place in a pot with vegetables and cloves. Add chicken stock, cover pot, and braise over low heat until tender, about 1 hour. Reserve the stock.

In the meantime, prepare a filling of calf's liver and veal. Remove bones from duck and cut meat into slices.

Layer filling and duck slices in a buttered pâté mold (beginning and ending with filling). Cover with pastry, press the edges down, and make several incisions in the pastry. Decorate with dough trimmings.

Combine 1 tablespoon melted butter with egg and brush on the pâté. Bake for approximately 1 hour in a preheated 350°F oven. (If the pastry is browning too quickly, cover with aluminum foil.)

Strain duck stock, add flour, and stir until smooth. Add lemon and sherry and bring to a boil. Season.

Serve hot duck pâté with sauce.

◁ *Duck Pâté*

Rastegai Moscow-Style

RASTEGAY MOSCOVSKY

Serves 4

¼ pound salmon or sturgeon spine
½ pound salmon head with cartilage
1 bunch soup greens
½ cup minced onion
½ cup butter
½ cup rice
yeast puff pastry made with 4 cups flour (see
    recipe, page 205)
½ pound salmon fillet
¼ cup milk or heavy cream
salt

Boil spine and salmon head with soup greens in water for 2½ hours until completely soft. Strain broth.

Sauté onion in 2 tablespoons of butter. Cook rice and mix with the remaining butter.

Roll out thin circles of yeast pastry, 3–4 inches in diameter. Layer with onion and small pieces of salmon fillet. Salt each layer carefully, pull up the sides of the pastry, and squeeze together to make a little boat. Leave a small opening in the middle and place a piece of butter in the opening. Brush with hot milk or cream and bake approximately 20 minutes until golden brown in a 375°F oven. Pour a little of the hot fish broth into the opening of the rastegai.

Goose Liver Pâté

PASHTET IZ GUSINOY PECHONKI

Serves 8–12

4–5 duck or goose livers
2 cups milk
½ pound fatback
2–3 anchovies
½ cup olive oil
juice of 1 lemon
2 chicken breasts
¼ pound boiled ham
½ cup mushrooms
2 shallots, quartered
5 eggs
4 tablespoons butter
2 tablespoons chicken broth
salt, pepper
1 teaspoon nutmeg
yeast puff pastry or Russian yeast dough (see
    recipes, page 205)
1 cup sour cream
2 tablespoons grated Parmesan
1 pound smoked bacon, sliced

Soak rinsed livers in milk for 2–3 hours. Pat dry. Lard liver with thin strips of fatback and anchovies. Heat olive oil, add lemon juice, and pour over larded livers. Marinate for 2 hours.

Combine chicken, remaining fatback, ham, mushrooms, and shallots and run through a meat grinder or a food processor. Mix well.

Prepare scrambled eggs using 2 eggs and 2 egg yolks (save 1 whole egg for egg wash) in butter. Shred scrambled eggs and combine with the chicken mixture and broth. Season with salt, pepper, and nutmeg. Place the pastry dough in a pâté or soufflé mold. Brush the sides with sour cream and dust with Parmesan.

Fill with half the chicken mixture. Add livers, marinade, and remaining sour cream. Cover with the rest of the chicken mixture.

Place bacon on top. Cover with the rest of the pâté dough and pinch edges together tightly.

Make small incisions in the top crust for steam to escape. In a small bowl make the egg wash by beating together 1 egg and 3 tablespoons water.

Brush pâté with egg wash and bake in a 350°F oven for approximately 45 minutes. Turn heat off and leave the pâté in the oven another 15 minutes.

Carefully lift top crust, remove bacon slices, and replace crust.

Serve hot with anchovy sauce (see recipe, page 153).

Pâté Fillings

PASHTETNIYE FARSHI

CALF'S LIVER AND VEAL PÂTÉ FILLING

Serves 4–6

½ pound calf's liver
½ pound fatback, diced
1 carrot, chopped
1 medium onion, chopped
1 slice celeriac, peeled and chopped
1 leek, chopped
5–10 peppercorns
1 bay leaf
½ pound veal
2 slices white bread
1 cup milk
4–5 eggs
3–4 tablespoons meat broth
salt

Cut liver in pieces and sauté with fatback. Add vegetables, peppercorns, and bay leaf and cook until done. Run through meat grinder or food processor.

Grind veal and combine with the liver mixture. Soak bread in milk and squeeze. Add with eggs to the liver mixture and stir in carefully. Add broth by the spoonful until the filling is elastic. Season with salt.

PÂTÉ FILLING WITH CALF'S LIVER AND BÉCHAMEL

Serves 4–6

½ calf's liver
fatback (⅓–½ the weight of the calf's liver), diced
1 medium onion, chopped
thyme
marjoram
bay leaf
1 tablespoon béchamel sauce (see recipe, page 147)
¼–½ cup Madeira
2 tablespoons grated Parmesan
salt, pepper

Soak liver in cold water, changing water repeatedly until it is clear. Dry liver and cut into pieces.

Sauté fatback; add onion, liver, and seasonings and cook until done. Cool briefly and run everything together through a meat grinder. Add béchamel, Madeira, and cheese to the mixture, stirring until it is elastic. Season with salt and pepper to taste.

CHICKEN FILLING FOR PÂTÉ I

Serves 4–6

1 chicken or ½ turkey
1 cup bread crumbs
1 cup milk
2 eggs, beaten
4 tablespoons butter or crayfish butter (see recipe, page 154)
2–3 tablespoons heavy cream
salt, pepper
½ teaspoon nutmeg

Rinse and dry chicken or turkey and remove skin and bones. Run meat through meat grinder twice (or puree in food processor). Soak bread crumbs in milk. Blend eggs, bread crumbs, butter, and cream with chicken mixture and season with salt, pepper, and nutmeg.

CHICKEN FILLING FOR PÂTÉ II

Serves 4–6

1 chicken or ¹/₂ turkey
1 cup heavy cream
salt, pepper

Rinse and dry chicken or turkey. Remove skin and bones. Run meat through fine blade of meat grinder twice or puree in food processor.

Place the mixture in a bowl resting on ice cubes or in ice water. Gradually stir in cream and season with salt and pepper.

Test for consistency: Shape a small dumpling and drop into boiling water. If it hardens, stir more cream into the mixture. If it falls apart, add a small amount of light roux.

This pâté filling can also be used by itself to make dumplings for soup.

FISH FILLING FOR PÂTÉ

Serves 4–6

1¹/₄ pounds fish fillets (pike, perch, trout)
1 medium onion, chopped
3 tablespoons butter
2 slices white bread
¹/₂ cup milk
¹/₂ cup heavy cream
1 cup chopped parsley
1 cup chopped dill
3–5 tablespoons meat stock
salt, pepper
¹/₂ teaspoon nutmeg

Cut fish fillets into small pieces. Sauté onion in 1 tablespoon butter. Add fish and continue to sauté. Soak bread in milk and squeeze well. Run fish, onion, and bread through fine blade of meat grinder or puree in food processor.

Blend cream, remaining butter, and herbs into chicken mixture and stir in stock by the spoonful until it is elastic. Season with salt, pepper, and nutmeg.

Salmon Pâté

PASHTET IZ OSETRINY
Serves 6

1³/₄ pounds salmon fillets
salt
1 medium onion, chopped
3 tablespoons butter
¹/₂ cup white wine
2 tablespoons cider vinegar
5 peppercorns
2 bay leaves
pâté pastry II (see recipe, page 207)
fish filling (see previous recipe)
2–3 tablespoons olive oil

Rinse, dry, and slice salmon. Season with salt. Sauté onion in butter. Cook salmon in the same pan. Add wine, vinegar, and a small amount of water. Season with peppercorns and bay leaves. Cover and braise over low heat until done, about 10 minutes.

Remove salmon and let cool. Strain the liquid and reserve.

Put pastry into a pâté mold and cover with layers of fish filling and salmon slices. (Begin and end with fish filling.) Add a small amount of fish stock, cover with pastry, pinch the edges tightly,

and make several incisions in the top crust. Bake in a preheated 300°F oven for approximately 1 hour.

Beat olive oil into the remainder of fish stock until it turns creamy and serve with the pâté.

Rabbit Pâté

PASHTET IZ ZAYTSA

Serves 8–12

---

1 oven-ready rabbit
vinegar or beer
¼ pound fatback
salt, pepper
4 tablespoons butter
½ cup sour cream
6 eggs
½ cup grated Parmesan cheese
nutmeg
pâté pastry I or II (see recipes, page 207)
1 cup chicken stock
½ peeled lemon, sliced
3–4 tablespoons Madeira

Rinse rabbit carefully and marinate for 24 hours in vinegar water (two parts water to one part vinegar) or beer.

Dry rabbit well, lard with thin strips of fatback, and rub with salt and pepper. Sauté on all sides in 1 tablespoon butter and roast in a 375°F oven until done, about 40–50 minutes. Baste frequently with pan juices. Add water by the spoonful as necessary.

Spread sour cream over the rabbit 10 minutes before the end of cooking time.

Cool and remove bones. Cut the best pieces into thin slices. Put the rest of the meat through a meat grinder for the filling.

Prepare an omelet using 5 eggs. Cool and shred the omelet. Combine with cheese, remaining butter, and ground meat. Season with salt, pepper, and nutmeg and blend well.

Place pastry dough into a pâté mold and cover with layers of filling and rabbit slices. (Begin and end with filling.) Cover the top with pastry, pinch the edges tightly together, make several incisions in the top crust, and brush with beaten egg. Bake in a preheated 350°F oven for approximately 45 minutes.

In the meantime, prepare the sauce: Roast chopped rabbit bones in the oven. Add chicken stock and simmer on top of the stove for 10 minutes. Strain. Discard bones. Add lemon slices and Madeira, stir, and bring to a boil. Season to taste and serve with pâté.

The Banks of a River in Central Russia ▷

221

Desserts and Paska

DESERT I PASKHI

The final enjoyment of a Russian meal, the dessert, has two purposes: that of sweetly concluding it, as is traditional the world over, but more important, to enhance conviviality. For a long time in Russia, dessert consisted of tea and jam, cookies, fresh cucumbers with honey, baked apples, crystallized fruit, *kisel* (fruit compote), or fruit gelatins. (Our "Muscovite" gelatin is world famous.) Over the years, a wider variety of more substantial desserts made their appearance, such as custards, puddings, and soufflés.

The celebration of Easter is one of Russia's most important festivities. Paska occupies a special place in the Russian kitchen. Specifically prepared for Easter, paska is a delicious, creamy architecture made with almonds and cream. As our traditional Easter dessert, this celestial quark dish is a symbol of resurrection, redemption, the awakening of nature, and the beginning of spring. We celebrate Easter with so many family members and good friends that my shopping list for the paski alone calls for 33 pounds of quark, 100 eggs, and 10 quarts of heavy cream.

While paska is being prepared—a ritual requiring considerable time and patience—everything else that is needed for Easter is made ready. We bake *kulich* and ham in bread dough, prepare fish pâtés, dye Easter eggs, and set the traditional Easter table. Candles are lighted everywhere. It is difficult to describe the singular mood of long-awaited Easter eve: wistful, full of joyous anticipation, love, friendship, and hope. The feast of the Resurrection begins at sunrise, and paska is the culinary crown.

Slavic Dessert

SLAVYANSKY DESERT
Serves 4

½ **pound dry rye bread**
¼ **pound chopped nuts**
grated peel of 1 lemon
scant ½ cup sugar
½ **cup heavy cream**
2 scant tablespoons lemon juice

Make bread crumbs with the rye bread and mix with nuts, lemon peel, and ¼ cup sugar (easy to do in the food processor). Whip cream with remaining sugar until stiff. In a glass bowl, alternately layer bread crumb mixture and cream, and drizzle each layer with lemon juice. Chill well and serve with jam and cold milk.

Compote Made with Apples, Cherries, Plums, Currants, or Raspberries

KISEL FRUKTOVY
Serves 4

1–1¼ **pounds fruit**
½ **cup sugar**
juice of 1 lemon
1 tablespoon potato flour

Peel, core, and dice apples and pit cherries or plums. Cover fruit with water, simmer until soft (about 10 minutes), strain, purée in food processor, and season with sugar and lemon juice. Stir potato flour into a small amount of cold water until smooth. Add to fruit in a saucepan, bring to a boil, turn off, and chill. Serve with cream or milk.

Gooseberry Compote

KISEL IZ KRIZHOVNIKA

Serves 8

3 pounds gooseberries, stems and leaves
   removed
sugar to taste
1 vanilla bean
2 tablespoons potato flour
2 cups heavy cream or almond milk

Cover berries with water, and simmer with sugar
and vanilla bean until the berries fall apart. Stir
potato flour in a small amount of cold water until
smooth, add to berries, mix well, and bring to a
boil. Remove from stove. Place in a bowl, chill,
and serve with heavy cream or almond milk.

Almond Kisel

KISEL IZ MINDALYA

Serves 4

1 cup sweet almonds, peeled
1/2 cup bitter almonds, peeled
1 scant cup sugar
1 tablespoon potato flour

Puree peeled almonds with a small amount of
water in food processor and cook for several minutes in 1 quart water. Strain through a cloth and
squeeze almonds well. Reserve liquid. Add sugar
to the liquid. Stir potato flour in cold water, add to
almond liquid, stir well again, and bring to a boil.
Remove from heat. Place in a bowl, chill, and
serve with fruit syrup. It should have a pudding-
like consistency.

If bitter almonds are unavailable, use 1 1/2 cups
regular almonds.

Oat Kisel

OVSYANY KISEL

Serves 4

oats   water

A classic and wholesome dish.
   Place oats in a pottery dish, cover with warm
water, and let stand in a warm place for 2–3 days.
Do not skim the foam that forms, but stir it in.
   Strain soaked oats and squeeze well. The liquid
will be cloudy and mealy. (Discard the oatmeal.)
Boil the liquid, stirring constantly, until thick.
(Do not season!) Serve with jam, cold milk, or
onions sautéed in oil.

Rye Bread Kisel

KISEL IZ CHORNOVO KHLEBA

Serves 4

3/4 pound dark rye bread, sliced
1 quart water
2 tablespoons potato flour
1/2 pound dried fruit
1 scant cup sugar
1 tablespoon grated orange peel

Toast bread slices in oven, cover with hot water,
cook for 5 minutes, and press through a sieve.
Mix potato flour with 2 tablespoons cold water.
Return pressed bread to saucepan. Add potato
flour mixture. Bring to boil and cook 1 minute
until it thickens. Soak dried fruit until soft,
strain, and stir into bread mixture. Season with
sugar, return to a boil again, and chill. Sprinkle
with orange peel and serve with cold milk.

Apricot Cream

ABRIKOSOVY KREM

Serves 4

1 pound ripe apricots
1 scant cup sugar
6 tablespoons unflavored gelatin
1/2 cup heavy cream, whipped

Blanch apricots in boiling water, peel, remove
pits, and cut into pieces. Simmer with sugar until
tender and puree in a food processor. Dissolve
gelatin in 1/2 cup water, bring to a boil, and add
pureed fruit. Stir in whipped cream. Pour into a
mold and chill for several hours.

Apple Cream

YABLOCHNY KREM
Serves 4

5–6 apples
2 egg whites, beaten stiff
$1/2$–1 cup sugar
juice of 1 lemon
grated peel of 1 lemon
$1/2$ cup maraschino liqueur
6 tablespoons unflavored gelatin, dissolved

Peel and core apples and bake 30 minutes in a 375°F oven. Puree in food processor. Mix with egg whites and sugar and chill. Mix lemon juice, maraschino liqueur, and grated lemon peel. Stir in gelatin and bring to a boil. Turn off heat. Stir in apple mixture. Place in a mold and refrigerate for at least 4 hours. (One cup lightly sweetened whipped cream may be folded into the mixture before it sets.) To unmold, place mold in lukewarm water, run a knife around the sides, and invert on to a serving platter.

Rice Cream

RISOVY KREM
Serves 4

1 cup rice pudding
$1/2$ cup sugar
grated peel of 1 lemon
1 teaspoon vanilla
3–4 egg yolks
$1/2$ cup milk
4 tablespoons unflavored gelatin
$1/4$ cup crystallized fruit, chopped
$1/4$ cup cognac
$1^1/2$ cups heavy cream, whipped

Prepare rice pudding according to a basic recipe to make 1 cup and season with 2 tablespoons sugar, lemon peel, and vanilla. Beat 6 tablespoons sugar with egg yolks until foamy. Mix in $1/2$ cup milk and dissolve gelatin, bring to a boil, and turn off heat. Drizzle crystallized fruit with cognac. Stir gelatin mixture and fruit into pudding and fold in whipped cream. Refrigerate for several hours.

Wine Cream

KREM IZ VINA
Serves 4

4 egg yolks
1 scant cup sugar
1 cup heavy wine such as Malaga, port, or marsala
4 tablespoons unflavored gelatin, dissolved in $1/2$ cup water
$1^1/2$ cups heavy cream, whipped

Beat egg yolks with 6 tablespoons sugar until foamy. Add wine and beat in a double boiler until the mixture is thick and creamy. Remove from heat. Bring gelatin to a boil. Turn off heat. Add to egg-wine mixture and pour through a fine-meshed sieve.

Chill mixture, stirring several times. Just before it sets, add cream, whipped and sweetened with remaining sugar, and chill well.

Apple and Prune Compote

KOMPOT IZ YABLOK I CHERNOSLIVA
Serves 4

1 pound apples, peeled and cored
10 cloves
1 stick cinnamon
1 cup sugar
1 cup prunes, pits removed

Cut apples into quarters or eighths, spike with cloves, and simmer in a small amount of water with the cinnamon stick and $1/2$ cup sugar for 15 minutes. Strain, reserve juice, and place apples in a bowl.

Soak prunes, simmer in a small amount of water 10 minutes until tender, strain, and make a layer on top of the apples.

Boil apple juice and the remaining sugar until syrupy and pour over the compote. Chill well.

The apples may also be cooked with grated orange or lemon peel.

Prunes with Quark Filling

CHERNOSLIV FARSHIROVANNY
TVOROGOM

Serves 4

¾ **pound prunes**
¼ **cup sugar**
1 **egg yolk**
¾ **cup quark, cottage cheese, or farmer cheese**
½ **cup sour cream**
2 **tablespoons butter, melted**

Wash prunes, blanch in boiling water, cover, let steep, strain, and remove pits. Stir sugar and egg yolk into quark and stuff the prunes with this mixture. Place in a flat baking dish, cover with sour cream, and bake at 375°F until golden yellow. Drizzle with a small amount of melted butter and serve with additional sour cream.

Cherry and Pear Compote

KOMPOT IZ VISHNI I GRUSH

Serves 4

---

1 **pound cherries**
6–8 **pears, peeled, halved, and cored**
3½ **cups sugar**

Pit the cherries. Prepare a syrup using 2½ cups sugar, 2 cups water, and several cracked cherry pits. Remove pits. Add cherries and bring to a boil. Strain, refrigerate the cherries, and boil the syrup until it thickens. Let cool and pour over cherries.

Simmer pear halves in approximately 2 cups water sweetened with 1 cup sugar. When they are soft, remove them with a slotted spoon and place them on top of the cherries. Strain the liquid through a fine sieve, reduce by half, and pour over the pears.

"Muscovite" Jello

ZHELE "MOSKVICH"

Serves 4

---

juice of 4 oranges and 2 lemons
2 cups water
1 cup sugar
6 tablespoons unflavored gelatin

Fresh orange and lemon juice are used in this very famous Russian dessert. Boil juice with water and sugar until syrupy. Dissolve gelatin in cold water in a saucepan and bring to a boil. Turn off. Stir in fruit juice. Fill coronet-shaped molds with gelatin, refrigerate, and allow to set. Turn occasionally.

To serve, place mold in warm water, top with a platter, invert, and unmold.

Red Beet Jello

ZHELE IZ SOKA KRASNOY SVYOKLY

Serves 4

---

3 **cups beet juice (available in health food stores)**
1 **scant cup sugar**
pulp of one vanilla bean
9 **tablespoons unflavored gelatin**
1 **cup heavy cream, whipped**

Boil beet juice with sugar and vanilla bean, remove from heat, dissolve gelatin in hot juice, and pour into a bowl or individual serving molds. Let set, unmold, and serve with cream.

Beet gelatin can also be seasoned with salt, pepper, and lemon. Unmold, top with a spoonful of mayonnaise, and serve as an appetizer.

Fruit Jello

FRUKTOVOYE ZHELE

Fruit gelatin is very popular in Russian cuisine. It comes in one or many colors and is prepared with the juices of lemons, oranges, melons, pineapple, apples, cherries, mirabelle plums, currants, cranberries, and raspberries; and also with tea, coffee, wine, milk, or cream. Boil the juice with sugar until syrupy. Then add gelatin according to package directions. Place in the refrigerator and allow to set.

In multicolored gelatin desserts as this one, each layer has to set before the next is added.

Hot gelatin can be poured into rinsed molds, bowls, or individual molds. To unmold, dip briefly in hot water.

Only natural food coloring is used in the Russian kitchen:

For *green*, boil ³/₄ pound spinach with 2¹/₂ cups water, strain through a fine sieve, add 3 cups sugar, lemon juice, and a glass of white wine. Bring to a boil.

For *blue* coloring, blanch ¹/₄ pound cornflowers in 1¹/₂ cups water, strain, add 1³/₄ cups sugar, and bring to a boil. (If cornflowers are not available, substitute two drops of blue food coloring.)

For *light green*, blanch green pistachio nuts.

For *white*, use heavy cream, milk, or almond milk.

For *spicy flavoring*, boil 1¹/₂ cups white or red wine with cinnamon, cloves, cardamom, mint, and lemon peel. Strain.

◁ *Fruit Jello*

"Mosaic" Gelatin

ZHELE "MOZAIK"

To make this pretty and famous dessert, prepare as many differently colored gelatins as possible in different bowls, refrigerate, let set, and dice. Mix the colors, place in individual serving molds. Cover with one layer of clear lemon gelatin. Refrigerate and let set. Unmold and serve.

Layered Apple Charlotte Made with Rye Bread

SHARLOTKA IZ CHORNOVO KHLEBA S YABLOKAMI
Serves 4–6

1 pound dry rye bread, made into bread crumbs
1 cup unsalted butter
1 cup sugar
$\frac{1}{2}$ cup port wine
1 tablespoon candied orange peel, chopped
grated peel of 1 lemon
1 teaspoon cinnamon
$\frac{1}{2}$ teaspoon ground cloves
1 pound apples, peeled, cored, and sliced
2 tablespoons apricot jam
confectioners' sugar
1 cup heavy cream or 1 cup ice cream

Sauté bread crumbs in $\frac{3}{4}$ cup butter, stirring constantly. Let cool and add sugar, port wine, candied orange peel, lemon peel, cinnamon, and cloves.

Butter a tall soufflé mold and sprinkle with sugar. Cover the bottom with kitchen parchment (optional).

Layer bread crumbs, apples, and jam and finish with a layer of bread crumbs. Press down lightly and drizzle with melted butter. Bake in a 350°F oven for approximately 1 hour. Unmold, cover with confectioners' sugar, and serve with whipped or unwhipped cream or ice cream.

Apple Charlotte

SHARLOTKA S YABLOKAMI
Serves 4–6

1 pound apples, peeled and cored
1 cup unsalted butter
$\frac{1}{2}$ cup sugar
rum
8–10 slices of white bread, 1 day old
$\frac{1}{2}$ cup milk
2 egg yolks, beaten

Cut apples into strips and cook in 4 tablespoons butter with sugar and a dash of rum until tender. Cut half of the bread into strips. Moisten both slices and strips with milk. Butter a deep baking dish and cover the bottom with kitchen parchment (optional). Dip the bread strips into egg yolks so they will stick together. Layer the bottom of the dish with half the remaining bread slices and prop the strips upright along the sides.

Dice leftover bits of bread and sauté in 2 tablespoons butter. Let cool, mix with apples, and fill the baking dish. Cover completely with the last of the bread slices. Melt remaining butter and drizzle on the top layer. Bake in a 325°F oven for approximately 1 hour. Unmold and serve hot or cold with fruit syrup or vanilla sauce.

Watermelon with Champagne

ARBUZ S SHAMPANSKIM
Serves 4–6

1 ripe watermelon, medium size
1–2 bottles sparkling white wine or champagne

Cut off the upper third of the melon horizontally and use a melon baller to remove the fruit. Carefully discard seeds. Return melon balls to the hollowed fruit and fill with chilled sparkling white wine or champagne. (Crimean sparkling wine, of course, is best.) Chill well before serving this refreshing dessert.

Watermelon with Champagne ▷

Sour Cherry Pudding
PUDING IZ VISHNI
Serves 4

5 eggs, separated
4 tablespoons unsalted butter
2¹/₂ cups sugar
1¹/₂ slices dried black bread, ground into
    crumbs
¹/₂ cup ground almonds
6 tablespoons flour
cinnamon
³/₄ pound sour cherries, pits removed

SAUCE

cherry pits
¹/₂ cup red wine
sugar
1 teaspoon potato flour

Beat egg yolks with butter and sugar until foamy and mix well with bread crumbs, almonds, flour, and cinnamon. Whip egg whites until stiff and fold into the yolk mixture.

Place a thin layer of the mixture in a buttered soufflé mold and bake in a 400°F oven for 15 minutes, until firm. Cover with some of the sour cherries, add a few spoonfuls of batter as the second layer, and bake in the oven for 15 minutes. Cover second cooked layer with cherries. Repeat this process until all ingredients have been used up. (The final layer must be batter.)

To prepare sauce, crush several cherry pits using a hammer and boil with ¹/₂ cup water for 20 minutes. Strain, add wine and sugar, and return to a boil. Stir potato flour into ¹/₄ cup cold water, add to the hot liquid, and stir until it boils again. Serve pudding with warm sauce.

Carrot Soufflé
SUFLE IZ MORKOVI
Serves 4

4 carrots, sliced
2 tablespoons butter
¹/₂ cup raisins
8 ounces zwieback, softened in milk
4 eggs, separated
¹/₂ cup sugar
¹/₂ cup sour cream or 4 tablespoons butter,
    melted

Sauté carrots in butter until tender, about 15 minutes. Purée in food processor and mix with raisins and zwieback. Beat egg yolks with sugar until foamy, stir into carrot mixture, and fold in stiffly beaten egg whites. Pour into a buttered soufflé mold and bake in a 400°F oven for 30–40 minutes. Serve with sour cream or melted butter.

Pumpkin Pudding
PUDING IZ TYKVY
Serves 4

1 pound pumpkin meat
1 tablespoon zwieback crumbs
¹/₂ cup sugar
1 teaspoon cinnamon
5 eggs, separated
1¹/₂ tablespoons butter
1 cup heavy cream

Dice pumpkin meat and simmer with zwieback crumbs in a small amount of water until soft. Purée in food processor. Let cool and add sugar and cinnamon. Beat egg yolks with butter until foamy and stir into pumpkin mixture. Fold in stiffly beaten egg whites and pour into a buttered pudding mold or bake in a buttered soufflé mold in a 375°F oven for 30 minutes. Serve with sugar and cream.

Spinach Pudding

PUDING IZ SHPINATA

Serves 4

---

¹/₂ pound day-old white bread
1¹/₄ cups milk or heavy cream
1 tablespoon salt
approximately ¹/₂ pound spinach
6 eggs, separated
¹/₂ cup sugar
1¹/₂ teaspoons nutmeg
4 tablespoons butter
¹/₄ cup bread crumbs

Remove crust from bread, cover bread with boiling milk or cream, and let steep for ¹/₂ hour. Puree in food processor. Cook spinach in a small amount of salted water, drain, and press through a sieve. (The amount of spinach determines how green the pudding will be.)

Beat egg yolks and sugar until foamy, mix thoroughly with spinach and bread, and season with nutmeg. Fold in stiffly beaten egg whites. Butter a pudding or soufflé mold and sprinkle with bread crumbs. Fill no more than three-quarters full with pudding. Bake in 375°F oven for 30 minutes.

Transfer to a serving dish and serve with sweet egg sauce. (See recipe below.)

Sweet Egg Sauce

SLADKY YAICHNY SOUS

Serves 4

---

3 egg yolks
2 whole eggs
¹/₂ cup sugar
grated peel and juice of 1 lemon
¹/₂ cup Madeira

Blend egg yolks, eggs, and sugar well. Beat egg mixture in a double boiler until creamy. (The water should never boil. Stir in only one direction.) Add lemon peel and juice. Gradually add Madeira. Beat until the mixture is foamy and coats the back of a spoon. Serve warm with puddings, charlottes, or sweet vegetables (such as pumpkin).

Paska

PASKHA

Paska is the traditional Russian Easter dish made with quark (cottage cheese, farmer cheese, or ricotta cheese). It is prepared in a pyramid-shaped wooden mold, the narrow part of which is flattened and has one or more holes to allow liquid to run out. A new, clean flowerpot lined with rinsed, damp cheesecloth or thick cotton is an excellent substitute for a paska mold. The cloth must be larger than the mold, so that it covers the filling, and the flowerpot must have a hole in the bottom.

In old Russia, quark was prepared at home with milk or sweet or sour cream. It should be as fresh and as dry as possible.

Quark must be drained and then pressed. Wrap in cloth and let it sit overnight between 2 wooden boards, weighed down with a stone or a pot filled with water. Blend with the ingredients listed in any of the following recipes, place in a mold, and refrigerate for 24 hours. Top it again with a weight and place the mold in a dish to catch any more liquid that is squeezed out.

The paska is then unmolded on a serving dish and decorated with candied fruit, colored sugar, etc., depicting religious subjects.

In the following recipes only the ingredients and preparation of the quark mixture will be given, since the pretreatment, drying, and art of the serving are always the same.

Paska of the Tsars

PASKHA TSARSKAYA
Serves 6–12

1½ quarts heavy cream
2 cups butter
4 cups confectioners' sugar
pulp of 1–2 vanilla beans
6 egg yolks
1¼ pounds prepared quark
½ cup crystallized honeydew or watermelon, diced
½ cup crystallized cherries, diced
1½ cups whipped heavy cream

Pour 1½ quarts heavy cream in a wide ovenproof pot or skillet and place in a 350°F oven. A thick, light brown film will form on the surface. Skim and put it in a bowl. Repeat this process until all the cream has been transformed into browned "cream skin."

Beat butter, confectioners' sugar, and vanilla until smooth. Gradually add egg yolks. Add quark and the cooled "cream skin," blending well. Mix with crystallized fruit and fold in whipped cream. Transfer the mixture to a mold.

Simple Paska

PROSTAYA PASKHA
Serves 6–12

3½ pounds prepared quark
1 cup sour cream
1 cup unsalted butter
3½ cups sugar
1 cup chopped almonds or 1 cup raisins
pulp of 2 vanilla beans or 1½ tablespoons vanilla extract or grated peel of 1½ lemons
2 tablespoons salt

Thoroughly mix quark with all other ingredients and transfer to a mold. Proceed as before.

Paska with Whipped Cream I

PASKHA SYRAYA I
Serves 6–12

2 cups unsalted butter, softened
2–3 egg yolks
3½ cups sugar
pulp of 1 vanilla bean or grated peel of 1 lemon
3½ pounds prepared quark
1½ cups whipped heavy cream

Beat butter with egg yolks, sugar, and vanilla or lemon peel until foamy. Stir carefully into quark. Fold in whipped cream and transfer to a mold. Refrigerate overnight.

Paska with Whipped Cream II

PASKHA SYRAYA II
Serves 6–12

2 cups unsalted butter
2 egg yolks
1½ cups heavy cream
1¾ cups sugar
pulp of 1 vanilla bean or 1 tablespoon vanilla extract
½ cup chopped almonds (optional)
1¾ pounds prepared quark

Beat butter until smooth. Blend egg yolks with ½ cup cream. Carefully stir butter, egg mixture, sugar, vanilla, and almonds into quark. Whip 1 cup cream and fold in. Transfer to a mold.

Red Baked Paska

PASKHA KRASNAYA
Serves 10–12

¹/₂ cup unsalted butter
2¹/₂ cups sugar
6 egg yolks
¹/₃ cup sour cream
2¹/₂ pounds prepared quark
¹/₄ pound candied orange or lemon peel
¹/₂ cup raisins
1 cup chopped almonds
pulp of 1 vanilla bean or 1 tablespoon vanilla
 extract

Beat butter, sugar, egg yolks, and sour cream until smooth. Blend into quark with candied orange or lemon peel, raisins, almonds, and vanilla. Stir well.

Line a large cake, soufflé, or pudding mold with cheesecloth or a cotton cloth and fill with quark mixture. Do not fill more than three-quarters full. Cover with aluminum foil and bake in a 325°F oven for 3–4 hours.

This paska should be browned ("red") all the way through.

Allow to cool before removing mold.

Paska with Hard-boiled Egg Yolks I

PASKHA S VARYONYMI YAYTSAMI I
Serves 6–12

2 cups unsalted butter
6 cups sugar
pulp of 1 vanilla bean or 1 tablespoon vanilla
 extract
12 hard-boiled egg yolks, mashed
1¹/₂ cups thick sour cream
3¹/₂ pounds prepared quark
¹/₂ pound crystallized fruit, chopped
¹/₂ pound raisins

Beat butter with sugar and vanilla until smooth. Press egg yolks through a sieve, combine with sour cream, and beat into the butter. Gradually add quark, crystallized fruit, and raisins. Stir well and spoon into a mold.

Paska with Hard-boiled Egg Yolks II

PASKHA S VARYONYMI YAYTSAMI II
Serves 6–12

2 cups unsalted butter
3¹/₂ cups sugar
pulp of 1 vanilla bean or 1 tablespoon vanilla
 extract
6 hard-boiled egg yolks, mashed
1³/₄ pounds prepared quark
¹/₂ pound crystallized fruit, chopped
1¹/₂ cups whipped heavy cream

Beat butter, sugar, and vanilla until smooth. Press egg yolks through a sieve and mix thoroughly with butter mixture. Gradually add quark and crystallized fruit. Stir to mix, fold in whipped cream, and spoon into a mold.

Heated Paska I

PASKHA VARYONAYA I
Serves 6–12

2¹/₂ pounds prepared quark
1³/₄ cups butter
1¹/₂ cups sour cream
6 cups sugar
5 egg yolks
1 cup finely chopped almonds
1 tablespoon vanilla or orange extract

Carefully mix quark with butter, sour cream, sugar, egg yolks, and almonds. Stirring constantly, place mixture over low heat until it almost begins to simmer. (Do not allow to boil, or it will separate and be runny. At most, heat until small bubbles form.) Remove pot from heat, add vanilla or orange extract, stir, cool, and transfer to a mold.

Festive Table ▷

Heated Paska II

PASKHA VARYONAYA II

Serves 6–12

2 cups butter
1½ cups heavy cream
4 egg yolks
1¾ cups sugar
1¾ pounds prepared quark
pulp of one vanilla bean or 1 tablespoon vanilla
  extract

Beat butter and cream until foamy, add egg yolks mixed with sugar and quark, and mix thoroughly. Beating constantly, heat over low heat, remove from heat, and season with vanilla. Cool and transfer to a mold.

Heated Paska III

PASKHA VARYONAYA III

Serves 10–12

10 egg yolks
3½ cups sugar
1½ cups milk
1 tablespoon vanilla extract or 1 tablespoon
  grated lemon peel
2 cups butter, cut into small pieces
3½ pounds prepared quark

Beat egg yolks and sugar until foamy and dilute with milk. Add vanilla or grated lemon peel. Heat, stirring constantly. (Do not let boil.) Remove from heat and beat pieces of butter into the hot mixture. Let cool and mix thoroughly with quark. Transfer to a mold.

Heated Paska IV

PASKHA VARYONAYA IV

Serves 6–12

8–12 egg yolks
approximately 3½ cups sugar
2 cups heavy cream
pulp of 1 vanilla bean or 1 tablespoon vanilla
  extract
2 cups butter
3½ pounds prepared quark
½–1 pound crystallized fruit, chopped
1 cup raisins

Over low heat, beat egg yolks, sugar, cream, and vanilla until creamy. (Do not let boil—see Recipe #1.) Remove pot from heat and stir dots of butter into the hot mixture. Blend in quark, chopped crystallized fruit, and raisins, and heat the mixture once more stirring constantly. Cool and transfer to a mold.

Chocolate Paska

PASKHA SHOKOLADNAYA

Serves 10–12

6 egg yolks
3¹/₂ cups sugar
3 cups unsweetened cocoa powder
¹/₂ cup heavy cream
pulp of 1 vanilla bean or 1 tablespoon vanilla
    extract
2 cups butter
1³/₄ pounds prepared quark

Beat egg yolks with sugar until fluffy. Add cocoa powder, cream, and vanilla. Heat, stirring constantly. (Do not let boil.) Remove pan from heat. Beat butter until foamy and add with quark to the chocolate mixture. Cool and transfer to a mold.

Almond Paska

PASKHA MINDALNAYA

Serves 6–12

2¹/₂ pounds prepared quark
6 cups heavy cream, whipped
¹/₂ pound almonds, finely chopped
2–3 bitter almonds, finely chopped
1³/₄ cups sugar

Stir quark and cream until smooth. Blend in almonds and sugar and pour into a mold.

Paska with Apricots, Raspberries, or Strawberries

PASKHA ABRIKOSAMI, MALINOY ILI
KLUBNIKOY

Serves 10–12

1 pound apricots, raspberries, or strawberries
    pureed in the blender
3¹/₂ cups sugar
6 egg yolks
1³/₄ pounds prepared quark
¹/₂ cup raisins
¹/₂ pound crystallized fruit, chopped
2 cups butter
grated peel of 1 lemon

Beat fruit puree, sugar, and egg yolks over low heat until mixture is thick and creamy. (Do not boil, or the egg yolks will curdle.)

Cool slightly and mix in quark, raisins, and crystallized fruit. Reheat, stirring constantly. Remove pan from heat, beat dots of butter into the hot mixture, and season with lemon peel. Cool and transfer to a mold.

Novgorod ▷

239

Cakes, Cookies, and Pastries

KULICHI, KRENDELI,

PECHENYA I TORTY

As a matter of tradition, homemade cakes and cookies are always served at tea time. Cookies are also displayed on the "sweet table" with which the bride and her parents traditionally regale their guests on the third day after a wedding.

The influence of French, Italian, and German chefs and pastry cooks is evident in many recipes, and many have retained the original foreign names—*ekler* (eclair), *bise* (baiser), *merengi* (meringue), *savaren* (savarin), *briosh* (brioche), etc.

Of course, we also have typically Russian cakes: sweet pirogi, for example, with quark or jam fillings (*vatrushki*); our famous, heavily spiced gingerbread (*tula*) with its unique designs; delicious, rich cakes such as baba and *karavay*; and, above all, *kulich*, the traditional Easter cake baked only once a year.

After seven weeks of Lenten fast, the senses of smell and taste are particularly receptive to the aromas permeating a house while kulich is being prepared. Baking and decorating the cake is almost a ceremonial rite. And the entire family waits impatiently for Easter Sunday, for not until then can the cake be eaten.

Easter Cake

SHAFRANOVY KULICH
Serves 10–12

4 tablespoons yeast
2 cups milk (or heavy cream)
10 cups flour
15 egg yolks
1³/₄ cups sugar
1¹/₂ cups butter
¹/₂ cup raisins
¹/₂ cup almonds, ground
¹/₂ teaspoon saffron
1 teaspoon nutmeg
15 cardamom seeds
pinch of salt
bread crumbs
¹/₂ cup candied lemon peel or crystallized fruit

Dissolve yeast in lukewarm milk (or cream) and stir in half the flour. Put in a warm place and let rise until double. Add remainder of ingredients (except bread crumbs and candied or crystallized fruit) and knead until the dough forms air bubbles. Let rise again for 1¹/₂–2 hours. Butter a deep, round baking dish and sprinkle with bread crumbs. Two large, clean coffee cans may also be used, with a wide aluminum foil collar wrapped around the top to make taller. Fill half the mold with dough and let rise. (After the dough rises, the mold should be three-quarters full.) Punch down and bake in a 375°F oven for at least 1¹/₄ hours.

The cake may be iced and decorated with crystallized fruit.

It is advisable to bake this amount in two baking forms.

Chocolate Kulich

SHOKOLADNY KULICH
Serves 10–12

2 tablespoons yeast
2 cups flour
16 egg yolks
1¹/₄ cups sugar
2 cups almonds, ground
¹/₂ cup cocoa powder
¹/₂ cup rum
¹/₂ cup red wine
¹/₂ cup water
¹/₄ cup chopped candied orange peel
1 teaspoon cinnamon
¹/₂ teaspoon ground cloves
juice of 1 lemon
12 egg whites, stiffly beaten
¹/₂ cup rye bread crumbs

Dissolve yeast in lukewarm water. Allow the mixture to foam. Mix with flour, cover, and let rise. Beat egg yolks with sugar until smooth and stir with remaining ingredients (except egg whites and bread crumbs) into the yeast dough. Knead well and let rise for 1¹/₂–2 hours.

Fold in egg whites. Grease a deep, round baking dish and sprinkle with bread crumbs. (See recipe for Easter cake for alternative container.)

Easter Table ▷

Cake may be decorated with a cross made of dough. Brush with egg yolk and bake in a 350°F oven for 1–1½ hours.

Cover with chocolate icing (see quark cake recipe, page 252).

Simple Kulich

PROSTOY KULICH

Serves 10–12

1 cup milk
½ cup butter
5 cups flour
pinch of salt
2 tablespoons yeast
1 teaspoon saffron
½ cup rum or cognac
¾ cup sugar
2–3 eggs
½ cup chopped almonds
10 cardamom seeds
bread crumbs

Bring milk to a boil and stir in 1 teaspoon butter and 2 cups flour. Add salt and let cool. Stir in yeast previously dissolved in a small amount of lukewarm water and let rise for 1½–2 hours.

Dissolve saffron in rum or cognac and stir with all remaining ingredients (except bread crumbs) into the dough. Knead well until dough is elastic. Let rise another 1–1½ hours. Grease a high, round baking form and sprinkle with bread crumbs. Fill with dough and bake approximately 1¼ hours in a 375°F oven.

Fine Homemade Bread

KARAVAY VKUSNY KHLEB
PO-DOMASHNY

4 tablespoons yeast
10 cups flour
3 cups milk (or water), lukewarm
½ teaspoon saffron
pinch of salt
9 egg yolks
1½ cups butter
1 egg yolk for glaze, beaten

Dissolve yeast in ¼ cup warm water. Mix in flour, milk, saffron, salt, and egg yolks and knead to form a ball. Let rise for 1½ hours. Punch down. Shape into a ball again. Knead in the butter and let rise another 20–30 minutes, brush with egg yolk, and bake in a preheated 400°F oven for approximately 1 hour.

This dough can also be baked in a round, high form that should be no more than three-quarters full.

Festive Karavay

PRAZDNICHNY KARAVAY

Serves 8–10

4 tablespoons yeast
3 cups milk
7 cups flour
6 egg yolks
3½ cups sugar
1 tablespoon vanilla extract
½ cup melted butter
1 teaspoon salt

Dissolve yeast in a small amount of warm milk. Bring the remainder of the milk to a boil. In another bowl, pour boiling milk over 2 cups flour. Stir, let cool, and mix with the yeast. Let rise in a warm place for 1½–2 hours. Beat egg yolks and sugar until foamy, add vanilla, butter, and salt, and mix into the yeast dough. Gradually add the remainder of the flour, knead well, and let rise another 1–1½ hours. Place in greased baking form and bake in a 375°F oven for 1–1½ hours.

Millet Karavay

PSHONNY KARAVAY

Serves 10–12

4–6 cups milk
1⅓ cups millet
2 tablespoons yeast
6 eggs, separated
¾ cup butter, melted
2 cups flour
salt

Prepare a thick porridge with milk and millet and strain through a sieve. Discard liquid. Dissolve yeast in a small amount of lukewarm water. When porridge has cooled, add to yeast with egg yolks, butter, and flour. Let rise in a warm place for 1½ hours. Punch down. Beat egg whites and a pinch of salt until stiff and fold into dough. Bake in a round, high form in a 375°F oven for 40 minutes. Unmold and serve hot.

This millet dough can also be used to prepare pirogi filled with meat.

Saffron Baba

SHAFRANOVAYA BABA
Serves 10–12

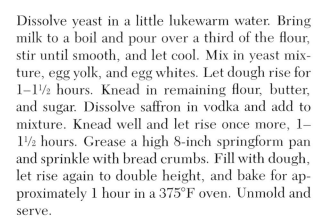

2 tablespoons yeast
½ cup milk
3⅓ cups flour
1 egg yolk, beaten
2 egg whites, stiffly beaten
¾ cup sugar
½ teaspoon saffron
½ cup vodka
4 tablespoons butter
bread crumbs

Dissolve yeast in a little lukewarm water. Bring milk to a boil and pour over a third of the flour, stir until smooth, and let cool. Mix in yeast mixture, egg yolk, and egg whites. Let dough rise for 1–1½ hours. Knead in remaining flour, butter, and sugar. Dissolve saffron in vodka and add to mixture. Knead well and let rise once more, 1–1½ hours. Grease a high 8-inch springform pan and sprinkle with bread crumbs. Fill with dough, let rise again to double height, and bake for approximately 1 hour in a 375°F oven. Unmold and serve.

Almond Baba

MINDALNAYA BABA
Serves 10–12

4 cups sweet almonds
1 cup bitter almonds
24 eggs, separated
3½ cups sugar
salt
2 cups potato flour or cornstarch
bread crumbs

Blanch almonds in boiling water, peel, and grind. Stir in 1 egg white. Beat egg yolks with sugar until foamy and blend into almonds. (Stir in only one direction.) Beat remaining egg whites with salt until stiff and fold into the yolk-almond mixture. Add sifted potato flour or cornstarch and fold together carefully but thoroughly. Grease a high baking form and sprinkle with bread crumbs. Fill three-quarters full with dough and bake in a 375°F oven for approximately 1 hour. Allow to cool in the pan before serving.

Lemon Baba

LIMONNAYA BABA
Serves 10–12

3 whole lemons, unpeeled
1¼ cups sugar cubes
15 eggs, separated
1½ cups flour
1½ cups potato flour or cornstarch
pinch of salt

Peel the lemons and cover with water. Cook until soft. Remove seeds and puree in food processor.

Rub sugar cubes with the lemon peel. Integrate cubes into lemon puree. Add egg yolks. Sift flour and potato flour over lemon mixture and blend into a smooth dough. Beat egg whites with salt until stiff and fold into the dough. Grease a baking form, sprinkle with flour, and add dough. Bake in a 375°F oven for 1 hour.

Famous Pastries

Famous Russian Small Pastries

ZNAMENITAYA "KARTOSHKA"

Serves 8–10

6 eggs
6 tablespoons sugar
4 tablespoons flour
1 tablespoon potato flour or cornstarch

BUTTER CREAM

³/₄ cup butter
6 tablespoons confectioners' sugar
2 tablespoons cognac or rum
cocoa powder or chocolate icing

In a double boiler, beat eggs and sugar with a wire whisk until creamy. Cool briefly and carefully stir in flour and potato flour. Place in a greased baking form 8–10 inches high and bake in a 400°F oven for 30–40 minutes. Remove from oven. Let cool on rack.

In the meantime, prepare butter cream. Stir butter, confectioners' sugar, and cognac or rum together.

Run the cooled sponge cake through food processor (or mash with forks), stir thoroughly with the butter cream (save 1 tablespoon for decoration), and shape mixture into 10 "potatoes." Refrigerate for 20–30 minutes, roll in cocoa powder, or cover with chocolate icing. Dot with remaining butter cream to imitate eyes on a potato.

Apple Pirog

YABLOCHNY PIROG
Serves 8–10

1 pound apples, peeled, cored, and sliced
4 tablespoons butter
1 tablespoon rum
³/₄ cup sugar
¹/₂ cup sweet almonds, ground
2–3 bitter almonds, ground
short pastry, made with 2 cups flour (see recipe, page 206)
2 tablespoons raisins
1 egg yolk, beaten

Cook apples in butter with rum, sugar, and ¹/₂ cup water until soft. Mix in almonds. Let cool. Roll out three-quarters of the pastry, place in a buttered 8 × 8-inch pan, and pull up the sides. Fill with cooled apples and top with the rest of the pastry in a grid pattern. Fill the spaces between the pastry grid with raisins. Brush with egg yolk and bake in a 350°F oven for 25–35 minutes. Cool. Cut in small squares and serve.

Apples St. Petersburg-Style

YABLOKI PO PETERBURGSKY
Serves 4

4 large apples, peeled and cored
lemon juice
¹/₂ cup sugar mixed with 4 teaspoons vanilla extract
³/₄ pound frozen puff pastry (see recipe, page 205)
2 egg yolks, beaten

Rub apples with lemon juice and fill with vanilla sugar. Thaw puff pastry, cut into strips 1 inch wide, and brush one side with egg yolks. Wrap the pastry strips around the apples, overlapping the dough. Brush with remainder of egg yolks and

bake in a 400°F oven for 10 minutes, then at 375°F for 25 minutes until golden brown.

Quark Snails

TVOROZHNIYE BULOCHKI

1 pound quark, cottage cheese, or farmer cheese
1 cup butter, softened
2¹/₂ cups sugar
4 cups flour
2 teaspoons baking powder
1 tablespoon cinnamon
1–2 egg yolks, beaten

Mix quark well with butter, sugar (reserving 1 tablespoon for later), flour, and baking powder. Roll out dough on a floured board to a thickness of ¹/₁₆ inch. Mix 1 tablespoon sugar with cinnamon and sprinkle over the dough. Roll dough loosely and cut into slices 1 inch thick. Push up the center of each "snail." Place on a greased baking sheet, brush with egg yolks, and bake in a 350°F oven for 30 minutes until golden brown.

Saffron Krendel

SHAFRANOVIYE KRENDELI
ILI KALACHI

4 tablespoons yeast
1¹/₂ cups heavy cream
7 cups flour
8 egg yolks
1³/₄ cups sugar
¹/₂ teaspoon saffron
1¹/₂ cups butter, melted
1 cup almonds, ground
¹/₂ cup raisins
¹/₂ cup candied lemon peel, chopped
1 egg, beaten
slivered almonds

Dissolve yeast in ¹/₄ cup lukewarm water. Wait until it thickens a little. Mix with 1 cup cream and combine with 4 cups flour. Put in a warm place and let rise. Beat egg yolks and sugar until creamy and pale yellow. Dissolve saffron in a little water to cover, and combine with melted butter in yolk-sugar mixture. Add to yeast dough, knead in remaining flour, almonds, raisins, lemon peel, and the rest of the cream. Shape thin rolls, twist into pretzels, and place on a greased baking sheet. Let rise briefly, brush with egg, and sprinkle with almond slivers. Bake in a 375°F oven for approximately 30 minutes.

Krendel Moscow-Style
MOSKOVSKIYE KALACHI

4 tablespoons butter
4 egg yolks
3 tablespoons sugar
2 tablespoons yeast
4 cups flour
3 tablespoons sour cream
pinch of salt
$^1/_2$ cup confectioners' sugar

Melt butter and beat in 3 egg yolks (one at a time) and 2 tablespoons sugar. Mix yeast with remaining sugar; add $^1/_4$ cup lukewarm water and let thicken. Add flour, sour cream, and salt and stir into the butter mixture. Work into a stiff dough and put in a warm place. Cover and let rise.

Shape small circles, place on a greased baking sheet, and brush with the remaining egg yolk mixed with $^1/_3$ cup water. Sprinkle with confectioners' sugar and bake in a 375°F oven for approximately 30 minutes. Cool on rack.

Siberian Rolls
"SHANEZHKI"—SIBIRSKIYE BULOCHKI
Serves 8–10

3 tablespoons yeast
7 cups whole wheat flour
1$^1/_2$ cups milk
6 egg yolks, beaten
1 cup butter, softened
$^3/_4$ cup sugar
salt

GLAZE

2 tablespoons sour cream
1 tablespoon butter, softened
2 tablespoons flour

Dissolve yeast in $^1/_4$ cup lukewarm water and allow to become foamy and thick. Prepare a batter with yeast, half the flour, and milk. Let rise. Add egg yolks, butter, sugar, salt, and the remaining flour and knead dough until smooth. Let rise 1$^1/_2$–2 hours. Shape into round, flat rolls, place 1 inch apart on a greased baking sheet, and let rise until almost double. For the glaze, beat sour cream with butter and flour and brush on the rolls. Bake in a 375°F oven for 20–30 minutes.

Centennial Cookies
STOLETNEYE PECHENYE

$^1/_2$ cup butter, cut up in pieces
1$^3/_4$ cups sugar
6 eggs
2 cups potato flour
grated peel of 1 lemon

Beat butter and sugar until creamy and pale yellow and gradually stir in eggs. Mix in flour and lemon peel and drop walnut-sized cookies 1 inch apart on a greased baking sheet. Bake in a 375°F oven until golden brown, approximately 20 minutes.

Oatmeal Cookies

OVSYANIYE PECHENYA

½ cup butter, cut up in pieces
1 tablespoon sugar
1 egg
2 tablespoons milk or sour cream
1½ cups coarse oatmeal
2 cups flour, sifted
several pinches of baking soda dissolved in ½
    tablespoon vinegar

Mix butter, sugar, egg, and milk or sour cream. Add oatmeal, flour, and baking soda in vinegar and run the dough through the food processor. Using two spoons, place small, flat piles 1 inch apart on a greased baking sheet and bake in a preheated oven at 300°F for approximately 15 minutes or until edges begin to brown.

Royal Cake

KOROLEVSKY TORT

2 cups butter
3½ cups sugar
10 eggs, separated
4 cups potato flour
1 cup sweet almonds, ground
½ cup bitter almonds, ground
grated peel of 1 lemon
1 tablespoon bread crumbs

ICING

1½ cups confectioners' sugar
⅓ cup heavy cream
crystallized fruits

Beat butter, sugar, and egg yolks until they are creamy and pale yellow. Mix in potato flour, almonds, and lemon peel. Whip egg whites until stiff and fold into the dough. Butter a springform pan, sprinkle with bread crumbs, and fill with dough.

Bake in a 375°F oven for 60–70 minutes. Mix confectioners' sugar and cream to make icing, frost cake, and decorate with crystallized fruits.

Almond Cake

MINDALNY TORT
Serves 10–12

3½ cups sugar
10 eggs
2 cups almonds, ground

FILLING

1 cup heavy cream
1¾ cups sugar
pulp of 1 vanilla bean or 1 tablespoon vanilla
    extract
whole almonds for decoration

Beat sugar and eggs until creamy and pale yellow. Stir in almonds. Divide dough and bake two layers, one after the other, in a buttered and floured springform pan in a 375°F oven for 15–20 minutes each. Let cool.

To prepare filling, boil cream with sugar and vanilla pulp or vanilla extract until it thickens and turns light brown. Let cool.

Cover one cake layer with part of the filling, top with second layer, and spread remaining filling all over the cake. Decorate with whole almonds.

Baumkuchen Cake

"BAUMKUKHEN" TORT

½ cup butter, softened
½ cup sugar
slightly less than ⅔ cup flour
6 egg whites
pinch of salt

Place bowl on ice and beat butter until fluffy. Stir in sugar and flour. Beat egg whites and salt until stiff and fold into the butter-flour mixture.

Pour a thin layer of dough into a buttered springform pan and bake in a 375°F oven approximately 20 minutes until it is light brown. Add another thin layer of dough onto the first layer

and bake. Repeat until all the dough is used up.
(The more layers, the better the cake.)

Cover the cake with an icing of your choice.

Napoleon Cake

TORT "NAPOLEON"

4 tablespoons butter
1 tablespoon sugar
2 egg whites, stiffly beaten
1 cup sour cream or crème fraîche
1 tablespoon vodka or cognac
pinch of salt
approximately 3 cups flour

FILLING

10 egg yolks
1 egg white
3½ cups sugar
6 tablespoons flour
6 cups milk
1 tablespoon vanilla extract
1 cup butter
slivers of chocolate and walnuts for decoration

Beat butter and sugar until creamy and pale yellow. Fold in egg white, sour cream (or crème fraîche), and vodka (or cognac). Add salt and fold in flour by the spoonful. The dough should be soft, like a thick batter.

Butter an 8-inch springform pan and dust with flour. Cover the bottom with a wafer-thin layer of batter and bake in a 375°F oven until golden brown, approximately 10 minutes. Proceed to bake 14 layers in this manner. Remove each layer when done and set aside to cool. If dough blisters while baking, puncture blisters with a fork.

To prepare filling, beat egg yolks, egg white, and sugar until creamy and mix well with flour. Pour slowly into heated milk and stir constantly until thick and creamy. Add vanilla and butter and let the creamed filling cool. Stir frequently while it is cooling. Spread 12 cake layers with creamed filling and cover with the 13th. Crumble the 14th over the top, decorate with chocolate slivers and walnuts. Refrigerate for 4–5 hours.

Napoleon Cake ▷

Quark Cake

TVOROZHNY TORT

Serves 10–12

1 cup butter, cut up in pieces
3½ cups sugar
10 egg yolks
2½ pounds fresh quark, cottage, or farmer cheese
1 tablespoon vanilla extract
2 tablespoons vanilla wafer crumbs
2 tablespoons raisins, chopped
¼ cup candied lemon peel, chopped
½ cup candied tangerine or orange peel, chopped
10 egg whites, stiffly beaten
1 cup bread crumbs

ICING

⅔ cup sour cream
3½ cups sugar
2 squares unsweetened chocolate (2 ounces)

Beat butter and sugar until creamy and stir in egg yolks one at a time. Add the cheese to butter-egg mixture. Add vanilla. Stir well and add vanilla wafer crumbs, raisins, lemon peel, and half the tangerine or orange peel. Fold in egg whites.

Butter a 12-inch cake pan and sprinkle with bread crumbs. Fill with cake dough and bake in a preheated 375°F oven for approximately 1 hour until tester comes out clean. If the top browns too quickly, cover with aluminum foil.

Let the cake cool in the pan, unmold, and place on a serving dish.

To prepare icing, bring sour cream and sugar to a boil and simmer for about 10 minutes until thick. Melt chocolate in a double boiler and add to cream and sugar. Cover the cake with icing and decorate with the remaining tangerine or orange peel.

Apple or Berry Cake

YABLOCHNO ILI YAGODNY TORT

6–9 apples (or 1 pound currants, gooseberries, or raspberries)
1½ teaspoons butter
½ cup sugar
dash of wine
¼ cup raisins
1 tablespoon cinnamon
grated peel of 1 lemon
yeast dough prepared with 4 cups flour (see recipe, page 205)
1 egg yolk, beaten

Peel, core, and cut apples into small pieces. Cook apples (or berries) with butter, sugar, wine, raisins, cinnamon, and lemon peel for 10 minutes. Do not allow fruit to become mushy. Let cool.

Roll out three-quarters of the yeast dough quite thin and place in a buttered 12-inch baking pan. Pull up the sides. Fill with the braised apples or the cooked berries. Make thin strips with the rest of the dough and place them latticelike on top of the apples. Brush with egg yolk and bake for 20–40 minutes in a 375°F oven.

Walnut Cake

OREKHOVY TORT

18 eggs, separated
3½ cups sugar
2½ cups walnuts, ground
3 tablespoons bread crumbs

FILLING

½ pound almond paste (marzipan)
1¾ cups sugar
4 tablespoons heavy cream
4 eggs

ICING

1½ cups confectioners' sugar
¼ cup heavy cream
halved walnuts for decoration

Beat egg yolks with sugar until creamy and pale yellow. Add nuts and bread crumbs. Beat egg whites until stiff and fold in.

Butter and flour two 8-inch springform pans, divide dough in half, and bake for approximately 20 minutes in a 375°F oven. (Do not open oven door during baking time or the cooking dough might collapse.)

Let layers cool and cut horizontally in two. You now have four layers.

To prepare filling, mix almond paste with sugar, cream, and eggs. Heat in a saucepan. (Do not allow to boil.) Let cool.

To make the icing, mix confectioners' sugar and cream.

Spread filling on cake layers, place them on top of one another, cover with icing, and decorate with walnut halves.

Siberian Cake

SIBIRSKY TORT

1 cup butter
1¾ cups sugar
4 cups flour
2 teaspoons baking powder

FILLING

1–1½ lemons
2½ cups sugar
½ pound cranberries
4 egg whites

Beat butter and sugar until creamy and stir in flour and baking powder. In a 375°F oven bake three layers in three 8-inch buttered springform pans for 15–20 minutes each. Let cool.

For the filling, peel lemons, remove seeds, and puree with 1¾ cups sugar and berries.

Beat egg whites, gradually adding remaining sugar until stiff.

Spread two cake layers thinly with beaten egg whites and half the berry mixture, place on top of each other, and cover with the third layer. Spread remaining beaten egg whites over the cake and decorate with berries. Refrigerate for 24 hours.

Icings

GLAZURI DLYA TORTA

Blend all ingredients well.

Sugar Icing

SAKHARNAYA GLAZUR

1 cup confectioners' sugar
juice and grated peel of 1 lemon

Orange Icing

APPELSINOVAYA GLAZUR

1 cup confectioners' sugar
juice and grated peel of 1 orange

Coffee Icing

KAFEYNAYA GLAZUR

1 cup confectioners' sugar
1–2 tablespoons strong, black coffee

Rum Icing

ROMOVAYA GLAZUR

1 cup confectioners' sugar
1–2 tablespoons rum
juice of ½ lemon

Pistachio Icing

FISTASHKOVAYA GLAZUR

⅓ cup peeled, green pistachios (pounded in mortar)
½ cup confectioners' sugar
peel of 1 lemon
1–2 tablespoons orange blossom water

Peter and Paul Fortress—St. Petersburg ▷

Pickled Vegetables and Jams

KVASHENNIYE OVOSHCHI

I VARENIYA

It is no exaggeration to say that a Russian could not survive without pickled cucumbers, sauerkraut, or pickled tomatoes. These ingredients are the basis for so many dishes that for us they are nearly as important as our daily bread. Throughout Russia at harvesttime, our beloved sour preserves are prepared for the winter. We are not limited to cucumbers, cabbage, and tomatoes. We use the same methods to pickle almost everything: peppers, onions, pumpkins, beets, eggplants, lemons, melons, plums. . . .

And still another fever rages at harvesttime throughout the land: putting up jams and preserves, particularly Russian *varenye*. No household would be without homemade varenye. Varenye is best translated as "sweet fluid" or "boiled sweetness." If prepared correctly from beginning to end, using the highest-quality ingredients, and if the syrup is thick and clear, then this delicacy is so good, so substantial, that one teaspoonful can sweeten a large cup of tea, says old Russian kitchen wisdom. We prepare it in special copper pots, wide and not too high, designed to distribute heat evenly. All kinds of fruit, nuts, rose hips, carrots, pumpkin, rose petals, and chrysanthemums are used to make varenye.

peppermint, and linden leaves. Fill with boiling water, let cool, and remove herbs and leaves. Then brush the bottom and sides of the barrel with honey. Finely shred cabbage and mix with carrots, apples, salt, and thyme. Place part of the mixture in the barrel and squeeze firmly with a wooden spoon. Pound and squeeze until the cabbage begins to release juice. Add the rest of the cabbage in several batches and pound and squeeze each batch until it is juicy. Cover with a clean cloth and weigh down with a stone. Let stand at room temperature for 3–4 days, then put in a cool place. Remove foam from top with a cloth. Sauerkraut is ready when it stops producing foam (3–4 weeks).

The barrel must be kept very clean. Wipe the rim once a week, wash the stone, and change the cloth.

For homemade sauerkraut, the cabbage must be fresh and mild, with tightly curled leaves. St.-John's-wort is an aromatic herb available in health food stores, as are linden leaves.

Sauerkraut

KAPUSTA KVASHENNAYA

Serves 6–8

chervil
St.-John's-wort
peppermint
linden leaves
honey
2 pounds white cabbage
2 tablespoons shredded carrots
1/4 cup shredded apples or 1 tablespoon
    cranberries
1–1 1/2 tablespoons salt
1 teaspoon thyme

Prepare sauerkraut in a clean wooden barrel (not fir or pine) lined with chervil, St. John's-wort,

Tomatoes in Brine

POMIDORY SOLYONIYE

15 pounds tomatoes
salt
1 bunch dill
2 tablespoons horseradish leaves
2 tablespoons celery leaves
2–3 chili peppers
1 handful fresh marjoram
1 handful coriander
1 handful bay leaves
1 handful cinnamon

Ripe, half-ripe, or small green tomatoes may be used. For ripe tomatoes, use 1/4 cup salt per 1 quart water; for half-ripe or green tomatoes, use 1/4 cup plus 1 tablespoon salt per 1 quart water.

Layer rinsed tomatoes with herbs and spices in a barrel. The first and last layers should be herbs. Add enough saltwater to cover tomatoes. Use a plate as a lid and cover. Let stand at room temperature for 24 hours, then move to a cool place.

Pickled Cucumbers Nezhin-Style

ZNAMENITIYE "NEZHINSKIYE" OGURCHIKI

220 pounds cucumbers
½ pound garlic, chopped
cherry, oak, and currant leaves
3 pounds fresh dill
¾ pound horseradish root, chopped
¾ pound horseradish leaves
¼ cup plus 1 tablespoon fresh chili peppers (or 2 tablespoons dried)
1 pound parsley
1 pound chervil
tarragon and celery leaves
1 pound salt per 10 quarts water
2–3 slices dark rye bread or several leaves of white cabbage

Use small cucumbers, no longer than 6 inches. Use either an earthenware crock or a wooden barrel (oak, beech, or linden wood), which must be washed thoroughly and rinsed with hot water before using. Rub bottom and sides with garlic or wild basil. Cover the bottom of the barrel with cherry, oak, and currant leaves and layer the cucumbers upright (so they keep their shape). Cover each layer with herbs and spices. Cover with a wooden disk and weigh down with a weight or stone. Pour in saltwater to 1½–2 inches above wooden disk. (Formerly, spring water was used. Nowadays, noncarbonized mineral water may be used.)

Cover the barrel with a cloth, let stand for a day or two at room temperature, and then move to a cool place.

Fermentation can be accelerated by adding 2–3 slices of dark rye bread or several leaves of white cabbage to the barrel.

Preserves

VARENYE

1 pound fruit
1 tablespoon rum or cognac
3½ cups sugar
1 cup water
2 teaspoons lemon juice

Sour cherries, strawberries, raspberries, red or black currants, quinces, grapes, water- or honeydew melon, or orange peel may be used.

Fruit should be dry. If possible, clean only by rubbing with a cloth. If it must be washed, dry thoroughly. Discard stems, remove cherrystones, and dice large fruits.

Drizzle fruit with rum or cognac and let steep for 2–3 hours.

Bring sugar and water to a boil and cook slowly, stirring constantly, until it forms a thick syrup. It is ready when bubbles no longer rise to the top and the surface resembles a "net."

Carefully add fruit and lemon juice, shake the pan, and return to a boil. Remove from heat, skim foam, and cool for 3–4 hours. Repeat this process three times, until the fruit has soaked up so much syrup that it sinks to the bottom of the pan. The fruit should not fall apart, however, so do not stir; simply shake the pan.

Sterilize cans or jars.

Fill cans or glass jars with preserves and seal three-quarters full. The rum or cognac is necessary to prevent mold from forming. Lemon juice will keep the colors bright.

Apple or Pear Preserves

VARENYE IZ YABLOK ILI GRUSH

These preserves are prepared the same way. If possible, use firm fruit, peeled, cored, and quartered. Drizzle immediately with lemon juice to prevent discoloring. Lemon slices without seeds or vanilla extract may be cooked with the fruit.

Pear and Carrot Preserves

VARENYE IZ GRUSH I MORKOVI

2 pounds pears
6 cups sugar
2 cups water
3 carrots, thinly sliced
3–4 bay leaves

Peel, core, and quarter pears, but leave a small piece of stem on each quarter. Make a thick syrup with the sugar and water. Cover pears with hot sugar syrup and let stand overnight.

The next day, boil for several minutes, shaking the pan. Let stand for another 24 hours.

Thread sliced carrots onto twine and add to the pears along with bay leaves. Boil another 10–20 minutes (shaking pan), remove carrot slices and bay leaves, pour fruit and syrup into jars, and seal.

Gooseberry Preserves

VARENYE IZ KRIZHOVNIKA

1 pound gooseberries
1 cup water
cherry leaves
80-proof vodka
3½ cups sugar
1 tablespoon rum
2 teaspoons lemon juice
vanilla pulp or lemon slices (optional)

Rub gooseberries with a cloth, discard stems, make an incision on the side, and remove seeds. Place in a flat dish, cover with ice water or ice cubes, and let stand for 10–15 minutes. Drain well and layer with cherry leaves in a copper pan. Cover with 80-proof vodka and bring to a boil two or three times. Drain, remove cherry leaves, and chill gooseberries for 3–4 minutes in ice water.

Mix sugar with 1 cup water and bring to a boil. Cook until it thickens and becomes a syrup. Add drained berries, rum, and lemon juice. Shake pan and return to a boil. Remove from heat. After several minutes, bring to a boil again. Repeat twice, adding optional vanilla pulp or seeded lemon slices the last time.

Pour into glass jars or cans and seal.
Gooseberries should be transparent and the syrup a pretty green.

Gooseberry preserves can be made even more special by stuffing the seeded berries with walnut pieces.

Pumpkin Preserves

VARENYE IZ TYKVY

4½ cups sugar
1½ cups water
1 pound pumpkin meat, shredded
juice of 1 lemon

Combine sugar and water to make syrup and add pumpkin and lemon juice. Shake pan and boil for 5–10 minutes. Skim foam and remove pumpkin with a slotted spoon. Reserve pumpkin meat. Let sit for 24 hours, reheat syrup, and add pumpkin and a small amount of lemon juice (optional). Boil for 10–15 minutes (shaking pan).

Pumpkin shreds should be transparent and the syrup very thick. Pour into glass jars or cans and seal.

Troika Ride near St. Petersburg ▷

259

Drinks

NAPITKI

A detailed treatise on Russian beverages lies outside the framework of this cookbook. But I do want to introduce our most important drinks as well as explain a little of their historic development.

In 1638, Russian Ambassador Starikov returned from a journey to Mongolia with a special present for Tsar Mikhail Fedorovich: 120 pounds of Chinese tea. At first the tsar and boyars were suspicious of this "dried Chinese grass," but they quickly discovered its stimulating effects, which kept them awake during long discussions (and church services). In 1679, Russia signed an agreement with China, providing for regular delivery of tea, after which nothing could stop its victorious advance. Tea became our national beverage—welcome everywhere, at all times, and at every opportunity. In Russia, business deals are often sealed over a cup of tea, family problems solved over tea, marriages arranged, intrigues plotted.

Russian writers have depicted tea ceremonies in novels, stories, and plays. A tea ceremony requires a samovar—a kettle of copper, brass, or silver in which water for tea is heated and kept warm. A ceramic pot is rinsed with hot water. Then boiling water is poured over the tea leaves and the pot is covered with a cloth and placed on the samovar to keep warm. For every $1/3$ ounce of tea, we use 1 cup water. The tea leaves release their flavor within five to ten minutes. A small amount of this concentrated strong tea is poured into cups, and then hot water is added in a ration of one to four. Honey and lemon slices are served and, occasionally, milk and cream are also served in warmed jugs.

Artistically decorated samovars and teapots painted with traditional scenes are among the most sought-after examples of Russian folk art and are on exhibit in museums all over the world. Long before tea was introduced, ceramic pots and samovars were used for the preparation of *sbiten*, Russian mulled wine. This popular hot honey drink, so suited to our cold winters, used to be sold by street vendors. They carried on their backs large vessels wrapped in layers of thick cloth to keep the wine hot as long as possible. In the recipes that follow you will find several for sbiten.

Kvass, arguably the best nonalcoholic drink in the world, must also be considered one of our national beverages. Kvass has been known for a very long time. It is extremely refreshing, quenches thirst, contains many vitamins, and maintains a sound balance of intestinal bacteria. In the past, kvass was prepared with malt and rye, wheat, or buckwheat flour—a method used now only in mass production. At home kvass is made with brewer's yeast nowadays. Kvass is more than a popular drink; it is also the basis for borscht and cold soup, etc. In the recipe section I share several typical kvass recipes with you.

Fruit and herbal teas and vegetable and fruit juices are also popular in Russia. In the recipe section there are several suggestions about their preparation.

Alcohol, too, is popular in Russia. We drink to acquaintances and friendship, to family and children. Often, the toasts at the beginning of every meal turn into long, strange stories.

One of these toasts, which I have heard all my life, is: "Raise your glasses. May you and your loved ones, your children and friends, have as many sorrows, as much bad luck and misfortune, as the number of drops you leave in your glass."

Like many other ethnic groups, the Russians originally made strong wine from honey. In the long run this proved to be expensive, since large amounts of honey yielded relatively little wine. In the sixteenth century, under Ivan the Terrible, wine production was stopped and was replaced by distilled spirits, our famous (or infamous) "little water," vodka. From the very beginning, the distilling of vodka was a government monopoly. The widespread distribution of vodka brought riches to the state and misery to the poor. *Kabaka*, inns with a license to sell vodka, proliferated like mushrooms. By 1847 there were 3,178 such inns in Moscow alone. But in moderation, before dinner or with appetizers, vodka is both a pleasure and an aid to digestion.

Russia is not good wine-growing country. In the seventeenth century, it is true, French grapes were planted in the North Caucasus, Astrakhan, and the Don Basin, because the tsar wanted to drink French wine. But the yield was so poor that there was only enough for the court. In 1783, the Crimean peninsula, a fertile wine area cultivated by the Greeks, became part of Russia. As early as 1804, the first Russian school of viniculture was opened in the Crimea, and soon not only wine but the famous Crimean champagne was produced there.

Prince Lev Galitzin was an important person for the wine-growing industry. He owned huge vineyards, and the name of his wineries—"Novysvet" or "Abrau-Durso"—stands to this day for famous Crimean wines and superior Crimean champagne.

Boyar Kvass

BOYARSKY KVAS

35 glasses

7 pounds rye bread
$^{1}/_{2}$ cup peppermint leaves
17 quarts water
$4^{1}/_{2}$ pounds brown sugar
4 tablespoons brewer's yeast
2 tablespoons flour
$^{1}/_{2}$ cup raisins

Slice and toast rye bread in the oven until brown. Place toasted bread in a large pot with peppermint leaves, add boiling water, and cover tightly. Let steep for 24 hours. Strain and use part of the liquid to combine with sugar, yeast, and flour.

Return to the pan with the rest of the liquid and allow to ferment in a warm place for 5 hours. Strain through a fine sieve into bottles, add raisins, and cork the bottles tightly. Let sit for 5 days.

Golden Kvass

ZOLOTOY KVAS

2 pounds carrots, grated
$3^{1}/_{2}$ cups sugar
juice of 1 lemon
2 tablespoons brewer's yeast
1 slice rye bread
5 cloves
2 quarts water

Combine all ingredients. Cover with boiling water. Place in a warm spot for 12 hours, strain through a fine sieve into bottles, cork, and let cool for 24 hours.

Apple Kvass

YABLOCHNY KVAS

3 pounds unripened apples, cored and sliced, unpeeled
$^{1}/_{2}$ cup raisins
3 cups sugar
2 tablespoons brewer's yeast
10 quarts water

Place apples, raisins, sugar, and yeast into an earthenware crock and add boiling water. Cover and let ferment for 1–2 days. Strain through a fine sieve into bottles, cork, and let stand at room temperature for 3–4 days.

Alcohol-free Drinks ▷

Apple-Rowanberry Kvass

YABLOCHNO-RYABINOVY KVAS

3 pounds tart apples, cored and sliced, unpeeled
1 cup cranberry or rowanberry juice
2½ cups sugar or 1½ cups honey
1 tablespoon brewer's yeast
cinnamon
1 grated lemon or orange peel
5 quarts water

The preparation is the same as that for apple kvass (see recipe, page 263).

Beet Kvass

SVYOKOLNY KVAS

6 medium beets, peeled and shredded
3–4 quarts water
3 cups sugar
2 tablespoons lemon juice
2 tablespoons brewer's yeast
1–2 slices rye bread
several pinches of salt

Cover beets with boiling water. Let steep for 1–2 hours, add the rest of the ingredients, and put in a warm place until foamy. Strain kvass through a fine sieve into bottles, cork, and let cool for 24 hours.

An elegant cocktail can be prepared with beet kvass. Mix 1 quart kvass with 1 tablespoon chopped dill and 1 fresh grated cucumber. Season with salt, sugar, and ground black pepper.

Lemon Kvass

LIMONNY KVAS

12 quarts water
6 ripe lemons, sliced, with seeds removed
2½ pounds brown sugar or honey
1 pound golden raisins
2 tablespoons brewer's yeast

Pour 2–3 quarts water over lemon slices and sugar or honey. Cover and let ferment for 24 hours. Add remaining ingredients and water, cover again, and keep in a warm place until the raisins and lemon slices float to the top. Strain through a fine sieve into bottles, cork tightly, and let sit for 5 days.

Old Moscow Kvass

KVAS PO "STARO-MOSKOVSKY"

4 pounds cranberries
4 quarts water
1 pound peppermint
1 teaspoon brewer's yeast
3½ cups sugar
1 teaspoon vanilla extract

Puree berries in food processor. Add to 3 quarts boiling water, cover, and leave in a warm place for 24 hours. Strain.

Cover peppermint with 1 quart boiling water and let steep for 7 hours. Strain. Reserve liquid.

Let berry liquid and brewer's yeast ferment for several hours. If it becomes very foamy, strain again. Stir in peppermint liquid, sugar, and vanilla, pour into bottles, and cork.

Spiced Honey Drink Moscow-Style

MOSKOVSKY SBITEN

1 cup water
3 tablespoons sugar
3 tablespoons honey
2 bay leaves
1 tablespoon whole cloves
1 tablespoon cinnamon
1 tablespoon ginger or cardamom

Bring all ingredients to a boil, skim, and let steep for 30 minutes. Strain and drink warm.

Slavic Spiced Honey Drink

SBITEN "SLAVYANKA"

1 cup water
4 tablespoons honey
1 tablespoon cinnamon
1 tablespoon whole cloves
2 tablespoons grated nutmeg

Boil all ingredients in water for 15 minutes, skim, strain, and serve hot.

Siberian Spiced Honey Drink

SIBIRSKY SBITEN

2 teaspoons tea leaves
1 cup water
4 tablespoons honey
1 tablespoon cinnamon
1 tablespoon whole cloves

Brew strong tea, strain, and add all other ingredients. Boil for 5 minutes. Let steep for 30 minutes, strain, and drink hot.

Popular Spiced Honey Drink

NARODNY SBITEN

1 quart water
1 cup honey
1 tablespoon hops
1 teaspoon cinnamon

Bring water to a boil with all other ingredients and simmer for 2–3 hours. Stir occasionally and skim foam. Strain and serve cold.

Pumpkin Juice with Pickled Cucumbers

TYKVENNY SOK S SOLYONYMI OGURTSAMI

2 pounds pumpkin meat
3 pickled cucumbers
1 cup pickle brine
salt, pepper
sugar

Extract juice from pumpkin by pressing pumpkin meat over a colander. Puree cucumbers and brine in food processor, mix with pumpkin juice, and season with salt, pepper, and sugar according to taste. Serve cold.

A Drink from the Volga

VOLZHSKY NAPITOK

2 cups pumpkin juice (extract by pressing
    2 pounds pumpkin meat over a colander)
2 tablespoons beet juice (available in health
    food stores)
2 tablespoons cranberry juice
sugar
ice cubes

Mix the juices, sweeten with sugar, and pour over ice cubes.

Tomato Juice with Pickled Cucumbers

TOMATNY SOK S SOLYONYMI OGURTSAMI

2 cups water
2 cups tomato juice
2 tablespoons lemon juice
2 pickled cucumbers, chopped
salt
sugar
chopped scallions

Mix water with tomato and lemon juice and add pickled cucumbers. Season with salt and sugar to taste and sprinkle with scallions. Serve iced.

"Wintertime" Drink

NAPITOK "ZIMA"

1 cup white cabbage juice (available in health food stores)
4 tablespoons carrot juice (available in health food stores)
4 tablespoons apple juice
sugar

Blend juices well and season with sugar. Serve hot or cold.

"Petersburg" Cider

MORS "PETERSBURG"

1 quart water
juice of 2 lemons
6 tablespoons sugar
1 tablespoon baking soda

Stir ingredients well, pour into bottles, cork tightly, and leave for at least 2 weeks in a cool place. Serve chilled.

Index